FROM THE
FOREIGN PRESS

VOLUME 2 1876-PRESENT

from the
foreign
press

two centuries
of american history

ROBERT E. KRIEGER PUBLISHING COMPANY
HUNTINGTON, NEW YORK 1979

The pagination is continuous from Volume 1 to Volume 2.

First edition 1979 (2 Vols.)
Based upon the title
AS OTHER SEE US: American History in the Foreign Press

Printed and Published by
ROBERT E. KRIEGER PUBLISHING COMPANY, INC.
645 New York Avenue
Huntington, N.Y. 11743

Original book and contents
Copyright © 1972 by
Holt, Rinehart and Winston, Inc.
Transferred to Ralph E. Weber, 1976
Reprinted by arrangement

Copyright © 1979 new material by
Robert E. Krieger Publishing Company, Inc.

Printed in the United States of America

Library of Congress Cataloging in Publication Data

Weber, Ralph Edward.
  From the foreign press.

  Edition for 1972 published under title: As other see us.
  Includes index.
  1. United States—Foreign opinion—History—Sources.
  2. United States—History—Sources.   I.   Title.
E173.W375   1979   973   79-887
ISBN 0-88275-893-4 (v. 1)
ISBN 0-88275-974-4 (v. 2)

For my wife, Rosemarie, and our children,
Mary, Elizabeth, Ralph, Anne, Catherine,
Neil, Therese, Thomas, and Andrew

The editor wishes to acknowledge with gratitude
the following newspapers and news sources:

Allgemeinen Zeitung (Augsburg)
Asahi Shimbun (Tokyo)
The British Colonist (Victoria)
Central Daily News (Taipei)
China Mail (Hong Kong)
Chung-hua Hsín-pao (Shanghai)
The Courier (London)
Deutsche Allgemeine Zeitung (Berlin)
Diario Oficial del Gobierno Mexicano (Mexico City)
Étoile (Paris)
European Magazine and London Review (London)
Excelsior (Mexico City)
Frankfurter Zeitung (Frankfurt)
Gazette de Lisbonne (Lisbon)
The Guardian (Capetown)
La Ilustracion Espanola y Americana (Madrid)
El Imparcial (Mexico City)
Izvestia (Moscow)
The Japan Times (Tokyo)
The Japan Times & Advertiser (Tokyo)
The Japan Times & Mail (Tokyo)
Jen-min Jih-pao (Peking)
The Jerusalem Post (Jerusalem)
Journal des Débats (Paris)
Journal de l'Empire (Paris)
The Korea Times (Seoul)
El Liberal (Caracas)
The London Gazette (London)

El Mercurio (Valparaiso)
Millard's Review (Shanghai)
Le Monde (Paris)
El Monitor (Mexico City)
The Montreal Gazette (Montreal)
Neue Frei Presse (Vienna)
Neue Preussische Zeitung (Berlin)
The Nippon Times (Tokyo)
North China Herald (Shanghai)
North China Herald and Supreme Court Consular Gazette (Shanghai)
North China News Agency (Peking)
The Observer (London)
L'Osservatore Romano (Vatican City)
Le Point du Jour (Paris)
Pravda (Moscow)
The Quebec Gazette (Quebec)
El Republicano (Mexico City)
The Scots Magazine (Edinburgh)
El Siglo Diez y Nueve (Mexico City)
El Sol (Madrid)
Le Temps (Paris)
The Times (London)
The Times of India (Bombay)
L'Univers (Paris)
El Universal (Mexico City)
Winnipeg Free Press (Winnipeg)

Preface

American historical events come alive again in a different manner when one reads the accounts of them in foreign newspaper editorials. As an American reads in a Tokyo newspaper (dated December 10, 1941) that the attack on Pearl Harbor—which is so often described as a "sneak attack" in American history textbooks —is not termed an "attack" but simply the "Battle of Hawaii," and when he reads in a Berlin newspaper that now "Roosevelt Has His War," he becomes aware of a new perspective. History becomes more exciting when he reads a Madrid journal, published during the Spanish-American War, that says *Spanish* sailors should "Remember the *Maine!*" And when a Tokyo tabloid praises Lindbergh's famous flight but then laments that had he been Japanese, the government would have regarded him as too young for such an enterprise, American history becomes more meaningful. These topics, and the others in the pages that follow, tell us about ourselves and our neighbors during the last two hundred years.

In editing the newspaper editorials I have used the archaic spellings and capitalization in the early selections in order to retain the style of the era; misspellings and punctuation errors have been corrected for the convenience of the reader. For the same reason some abbreviations such as "etc." that appeared in the original account have been changed to their American-English equivalents. Capitalization of proper names from *The Times*

(London) follows its style. I also wish to acknowledge my gratitude to the newspaper editors for permitting me to quote from their editorials. Their prompt assistance proved most helpful.

Many persons have participated in the process of preparing this book and I am very grateful, not only for their assistance but also their encouragement. Professora Maria del Carmen Ruiz Castanēda of the Biblioteca Nacional, Professor Martin Quirarte, and Mr. Harry Wright II in Mexico City were very helpful. My colleague, Professor Thomas Hachey, and his wife, Jane, offered many thoughts and suggestions. Miss Elizabeth Devine and Reverend John Philip Talmage of the Marquette University Library provided truly pleasant and excellent assistance; they, together with the library staffs at the following institutions, made many foreign newspaper collections available: University of Chicago, University of Notre Dame, University of California at Berkeley, Wayne State University, University of Wisconsin, New York Public Library, University of Illinois, Bowling Green State University, Harvard University, New Jersey Historical Society, University of California at Los Angeles, University of Florida, University of Washington, the Newberry Library, the Milwaukee Public Library, and, especially, the Center for Research Libraries in Chicago.

In reading and preparing this manuscript, the following persons assisted greatly: Professor Anne Marie Poinsatte, Professor Louis Moulton, Professor Bernard Norling, Stephanie Loughran, Emma Geoghan, Paul Stuart, Kathy Kovacs, Fred Frey, Irene Zimmerman, Jenifer Boudnik, John Berens, Carol Kuechler, Ceil MacDonald, Susan Siefert, Dr. R. S. Gawkoski, and Mrs. Neil F. Hoyt.

And though listed last, my wife, Rosemarie, and our children shared this project from the beginning. They, together with my students and colleagues at Marquette University, have made this study most exciting and satisfying.

For this new edition (the title of the first edition was *As Others See Us*) I want to thank Ms. Ellen Murphy of Marquette University Library; also Professor Louis Moulton whose talents in translating are exceeded only by his generosity, and enthusiasm for learning.

Milwaukee, Wisconsin   R.E.W.

Contents

Volume I

*For the reader's convenience, these sections appear in both Volumes I and II.

Volume II

*For the reader's convenience, these sections appear in both Volumes I and II.

*Introduction

*A free Gazette is a sentinel
which watches unceasingly for the people.*
D. Jebb

From Paris in March 1789, *Le Patriote Français,* describing the crucial importance of newspapers, stated:

> Without the Gazettes, the American Revolution, in which France took such a glorious part, would never have been accomplished. All of them, for example, reprinted *Common Sense;* this piece of writing, in which reason triumphed, raised beaten spirits; without the help of the Gazettes, it would have remained unknown, and ineffectual as only a pamphlet.

The newspaper has served not only as the medium for disseminating the idea of liberty, but also as a vital source for tracing the history of a people.

As Americans constructed their republic in the years following 1776, newspaper editors throughout Europe and in other foreign lands observed this radical experiment in liberty. At first they were contented with reprinting brief articles from American newspapers. Indeed, in the early years of independence, the United States was all but ignored in the foreign press. The most notable exception was the publication of American commercial tariffs and regulations such as in *The London Gazette,* a twice-weekly journal in the 1780s, which carried accounts of events in Spain, Sweden, France, and other European powers, but very little about America. When John Adams was presented to the king in 1785 as the first American

---

*The Introduction also appears in Volume I

minister to England, the reception was reported in three lines! No reports of the American Constitutional Convention or the inauguration of George Washington appeared in the *Gazette.* The *Times* (London) often did little more than merely reprint verbatim reports of these events from New York, Philadelphia, and Boston newspapers. Clearly the United States stood on the periphery of the geopolitical power structure of the eighteenth century. English newspapers of this era usually averaged four to eight pages in length and were mainly informational in character. For example, *The London Gazette,* the century-old tabloid, consisted of four pages in March 1774: its first page carried such diverse notices as news about the king's travels and the average price of corn during the previous week; page 2 featured the proceedings of business meetings, while pages 3 and 4 were devoted to announcements of bankruptcy cases. *The Times,* founded in 1785, was more international in scope. The first page had dozens of one column-inch advertisements and a few editorials that invariably were related to events in European countries. Page 2 contained English and foreign news; page 3, financial reports and commercial statistics; and page 4, letters to the editor.

Allgemeinen Zeitung, the German newspaper, placed heavy emphasis on political affairs and paid scant attention to commercial items. Moreover, its focus centered on western Europe first, and then other European nations, Latin America, North America, Asia, and Africa, in that order. Early Mexican newspapers also concentrated heavily on political affairs and theory.

As the nineteenth century progressed and the commercial power and corresponding wealth of the United States increased, foreign newspapers reprinted articles from American sources with regularity. The arrival of packet ships from America in foreign ports always meant that recent events described in newspapers from Boston, New York, Philadelphia, and Washington would find their way into the foreign news columns of European and other area newspapers in the Atlantic world. In the first decades of the century, accounts of presidential elections in America and other significant news events in cities along the eastern seaboard of the United States appeared in European newspapers four to six weeks later. It took about the same length of time for such news to reach Mexico and several additional months before these events were reported in Chile or Asia.

As United States' frontiers expanded and her cities grew, new and popular American newspapers were founded. The development of the telegraph permitted eastern newspapers to gather and publish national news more quickly; consequently, foreign journals also published more American national news, rather than reports on just the Atlantic seaboard areas. And by 1866, the first permanent cable carried news to Europe (the first cable from San Francisco to Manila opened in 1903). Technology was rapidly uniting the world, a fact that Massachusetts' Senator Charles Sumner had optimistically predicted in his famous Boston Fourth of July oration of 1845, when he said that rapid communication would dissolve prejudice and provide a unity among all mankind.

British newspapers were influential, especially *The Times,* which had a circulation at this time of 60,000. It, together with other British papers in England and the colonies, exhibited a more friendly understanding of the United States. The *China Mail,* for example, on July 8, 1852, wrote:

> It is gratifying . . . that both countries are getting rid of their prejudices, and that time and more intimate intercourse are modifying John Bull's wrath against his firstborn for daring to break his leading-strings, and Jonathan's sense of parental harshness. When father and son have altogether forgotten ancient grievances, or, as they must, come to perceive that 'twas all for the best, they may hand in hand defy the world in arms—if they do not swallow it together.

British and French newspapers took the lead in the publication of thorough interpretive letters that were dispatched by their perceptive correspondents in the United States during these years. Although their opinions sometimes reflected national bias, especially during the crisis of war, these newsmen recognized certain traits typical of Americans, such as restlessness, energy, eagerness for commercial opportunity, violence, racial prejudice, and great mobility. Frequently these correspondents wrote of American pluralism and the paradoxical political and economic experiences of a people attempting unity while maintaining diversity. Moreover, some wrote with humor as witnessed by the following account in Victoria's newspaper, *The British Colonist,* on November 25, 1859:

> At twenty-five years of age . . . an American has practised ten trades, made four fortunes, one failure, and two campaigns, has conducted a law suit, preached a religion, killed six men with a revolver, emancipated a negress, and annexed an island. An Englishman has written two themes, followed an embassy, founded a bank, converted a Catholic, traveled round the world, and read the collected works of Walter Scott. A Frenchman has written a tragedy, contributed to two newspapers, received three sword cuts, made two attempts at suicide, persecuted four husbands, and undergone nineteen changes of political opinion. A German has wounded fourteen of his intimate friends, has swallowed sixty casks full of beer (besides the philosophy of Hegel), has sung eleven thousand songs, compromised one young lady, smoked a million of pipes, and dipped himself in two revolutions. . . .

During the remaining years of the nineteenth century, America's strengths and weaknesses were featured in the foreign press. *Le Temps* on November 9, 1886, reporting on the dedication of the Statue of Liberty, called America a ". . . great country, so full of life, so active, so generous, and so truly hospitable." The Chicago Fire of 1871, the Women's War Against Whiskey in 1874, the growing practice of divorce in Boston, the scandals of American politicians—these and hundreds of other topics received prominent coverage in the foreign press. By the end of the century, lengthy editorials traced not only America's domestic development but also her commercial and military expansion that contributed so significantly to the nation's meteoric rise to the status of a leading world power.

As the United States embraced global economic commitments at the turn of the century and gravitated away from political isolation in the decades following World War I, news stories from Washington, Chicago, or Hollywood figured almost as prominently in foreign journals as their own national news. Another World War and its aftermath brought America into the vortex of military and commercial power; and decisions in Washington, tragedy in

Memphis, successes at Cape Canaveral were quickly evaluated in the foreign press. A decade of domestic turmoil and international maneuvering by the United States began in 1970. Foreign newspapers reflected the agonies of the Vietnam War as many editors offered hopeful, and sometimes bitter, criticism of the American involvement. The war's sudden conclusion in 1975 provoked praise, anxiety and apprehension. A radically new balance of power in Asia became a likelihood and newspaper editors estimated the probable limits of American commitment after the military collapse in Vietnam.

The nation's Bicentennial Celebration provided abundant evidence that overseas observers recognized and respected the vitality and dream of the United States. Their congratulations and analyses frankly emphasized the promises and residual power of a nation weakened by internal discord and a disastrous war. The editorials differed considerably from those written in 1876. The Bicentennial commentaries reflected the American international alliances which provided military support and economic assistance.

President Jimmy Carter's decision to secure Sino-American normalization provoked a broad spectrum of responses: intense anxiety in Taiwan, anger in the Soviet Union, uncertainty in several other nations. The key question remained—would the recognition provide stability and peace in Asia and the world? The decision broke the traditional Asian policy pursued for decades by Democrats and Republicans. A strong and friendly People's Republic of China became a central feature in American foreign relations.

International views on American events enhance an understanding of the United States and the world. These overseas voices provide a fascinating perspective for the American past and present. More than this they remind the reader that the world is indeed a global village.

FROM THE
FOREIGN PRESS

Topic 14

THE CENTENNIAL CELEBRATION

1876

Almost ten million visitors came to the Centennial Exposition, held in Philadelphia from May to November 1876, to celebrate the nation's one hundredth birthday. The Exposition became the first in a series of world's fairs to be held in the United States. While delegates from thirty-seven foreign nations participated in the celebration at Philadelphia, centennial parties were also held in many countries.

PARIS. *Le Temps,* **August 1, 1876.**

The Exposition—Two important decisions were taken on the subject of the Exposition, but they will not be welcomed with the same response by the interested parties. The one is excellent. For a long time foreign hosts complained against the regulation that forbade them from selling their goods without having previously paid import duties for the whole of their merchandise. They addressed themselves to Congress and a law voted by the two Houses approved their requests. It remains to be discovered if, in practice, the annoying spirit of the American customs officials will not perceptively weaken the value of the concession obtained.

The second decision is a victory of the narrow and stupid fanaticism of the Puritan clergy over the good common sense of the public. You may guess already that it pertains to the question of Sunday. Workers' meetings, enlightened citizens of American and foreign origin, had energetically requested the opening of the Exposition on the day of rest that the "sabbatanians," fanatics, have succeeded in making a day of mortal boredom in the United States. The intelligent press, the *Herald,* joined itself to this crusade of tolerance. The Catholic Archbishop of Philadelphia, M. Wood, had declared that for his part he did not see any inconvenience in a diversion as moral and inoffensive as a visit to the Exposition. Finally, the reason which seemed to have surpassed all the others: it was evident that fifty or sixty thousand people of the working classes of Philadelphia had benefited every week from the measure being requested: and, as financially speaking, the Exposition at present is far from constituting a brilliant business, a sum of 25,000 dollars multiplied by the number of Sundays which remain until the closing, was not a windfall to disdain. The preachers began to thunder from the height of their pulpits, [and] the so-called "religious" press, where is daily exposed the most stupid and harmful things that are written in the territory of the United States, has declared that everything was lost if the Pharisees who consecrated the day of the Lord to laziness behind closed doors permitted the community of mortals to profane it by feasting their eyes on the spectacle of marvels contained inside the "centennial grounds." Meetings of old devout people and of howling ministers have stigmatized the attempts in this country blessed by the Lord for the "scandals" of European Sundays, and so on. In brief, the centennial commission organized a chorus, and by 30 voices against 9 decided that the Exposition would remain closed on the only day when a good part of the population would have been able to have the pleasure of visiting it.

The discussion moreover had been stormy. One member of West Virginia claimed that he was voting with the majority for fear of being tied up by the old ladies of his native town. Another delegate of the state of Alabama, having energetically upheld the right of the citizens not to be tyrannized by the fanaticism of a Puritan majority, received from one of his New England colleagues

the following characteristic response: "If you wish to revolt against
the will of the majority, your rebellion will have the same outcome
as that which you tried against the Union. You'd better vote for
the *ayes*." This is where we are in summary in the hundredth year
of independence. I recommend to our working delegates that they
meditate on this subject; they will without doubt recognize that it
is not only in Europe that abuses and prejudices have a durable
life, and perhaps then they will have a little more indulgence for
the imperfections of laws and the slowness of progress in their own
countries.

SHANGHAI. *North China Herald and Supreme Court and
Consular Gazette,* July 8, 1876.

[Two hundred foreign and American guests took an excursion on
the steamer, *Fire Queen,* for an all-day centennial party. After
lunch, a program of music and thirteen toasts followed. A part of
the newspaper account follows.]

The Consul-General [John C. Myers] then interpolated a toast,
prefacing it by saying that the first railway in China having just
been opened, he hoped they would all join with him in wishing it
success. He therefore gave them, "The first railway in China."
(Applause.) With scarcely any interval, he also gave "The United
States, China, and Japan," a trinity of nations, between whom he
hoped that peace, commerce, and prosperity would last forever.
(Applause.)

Mr. Tong-King Sing [a Chinese official], who was received
with much applause, rose to respond, which he did in very good
English. He thanked them for the way in which they had received
the name of his country. He also thanked them on behalf of the
people of China, and felt it to be his duty to say a few words in
reply. He said, a few words, because he did not feel himself able
to make a long speech. They must all agree with him that they
were met there to celebrate a great event—the Centennial of the
United States. Such an opportunity for celebration did not occur
very often, and only a small proportion, if any, of those now

living in the world, would live to enjoy the honor of such a day again. He did not think that even his youngest friend present, unless he lived to be nearly as old as Old Parr, would have the same honor again. It was a day "you Yankees"—(laughter)—had a perfect right to celebrate. Look at your country—what was she 100 years ago? Compare what she was then, with what she is today. And who had wrought the change? The people themselves. They had transformed wildernesses into cultivated fields and gardens. They had made farms where there were none before; they had made shallow creeks into navigable rivers, and driven roads for communication everywhere. The constitution under which they lived showed the nation would go on and prosper. Look at the development of her commerce. America supplied most of the nations of the earth with food—from her rich earth she supplied them with the corn they were all so eager to get. Again, look at the railways she had constructed. They amount to 70,000 miles in length; and all this has been done in less than 100 years. But while he could speak of America in that way, and was unable to allude to such progress in his own country, he had no right to be jealous. The statesmen of China were nearly all old men, and even such a change as that caused by the introduction of the Woosung road was too quick and sudden for them. They said, "Be slow; go slow; and make sure." There was another thing in regard to America and China to which he would allude. America did not like to quarrel with any other nation. She had quarreled with others, but she certainly had never quarreled with China. By late accounts, there did seem to be some ill-feeling among certain of the lower classes towards the Chinese; but he hoped they would see even such examples as those set right. In conclusion, he hoped that peace and concord would long continue to exist between the United States, China, and Japan. (Loud applause.)

LONDON. *The Times*, July 4, 1876.

The citizens of the United States will today rejoice, with much effusion of sentiment and of oratory, that they have become a nation great among the nations of the earth. . . . A group of small

Commonwealths has grown into a great nation which shall yet be greater. After the sturdy assertion of the liberty of self-government which caused the patriots of 1776 to repudiate the Sovereignty of George III, and their tenacity of resistance [that] enabled them to make good their resolution to be free, they did not close their frontiers so as to keep the territories they had won for the exclusive use of themselves and of their children. Immigrants from all the world were invited to come in and share their freedom. No nation ever offered the privileges of citizenship more liberally, and no nation was ever rewarded with such rich returns for its hospitality. The especial glory of the growth of the United States has been this, that the Republic has grown because refugees from all the rest of the world have flocked to its protection. Sometimes they have fled from the cruel conditions of overcrowded life at home, the blame of which could be laid at the door of no man, or class of men, since they were the necessary consequences of false ideas universally acted upon as if they were true; sometimes they fled from the tyrannies of conscription and of feudal law, which kept them bound from the cradle to the grave; sometimes they sought in the West a liberty to obey the dictates of their own consciences denied by Prelates and Governments of the European Continent. It is justly a matter of congratulation that a great people should have thus grown up. The troops of immigrants coming in year after year have traversed the continent, ploughed the prairie, bridged the mightiest rivers, thrown railways over and through mountains, and brought from the hidden depths of the earth those treasures of iron and coal which more than anything else increase the power of man to appropriate the gifts of Nature to his use. Of silver and gold we need not speak; the abundance of their production is comparatively an insignificant accident. The 100 years that have passed have seen a great industrial community developed with unexampled rapidity. Its growth would, indeed, have been still greater had not false and foolish notions of protective legislation deceived the Democracy of America, as they have deceived European Governments; but the productiveness of a virgin soil has been generous enough to hide this loss. The nation has not been so prosperous as it might have been; but the aggregate wealth it now annually produces approaches that of the oldest communities, and yet the mass of population remains so small compared with the capabilities of wealth-making that undeveloped lands afford that the wages of the labourer are higher than they are in any other part of the world. The English settlers and those who have come to share their freedom have brought the United States so far in the course of 100 years, and it would be vain to prescribe the limits of the growth to which the nation may attain in another century of existence.

The United States have become a great nation in numbers and in the production of wealth, and they have shown themselves great also in the capacity to free themselves, at the cost of much temporary suffering, from the great evil of slavery that was so long interwoven in their existence. The spectacle they present to the world of a vast multitude of people peacefully producing food and clothing, and ready to receive within their ranks immigrants from all lands who desire to join their freedom, is not unimposing. Although man does not live on bread alone, bread is one of the necessaries of life, and—speaking broadly and apart from special crises—in the United States bread may always be obtained. If we are impatient that the United States have as yet done so little for the world beyond increasing the affluence of the means of animal existence, we may, perhaps, see cause to restrain our discontent in thinking of the materials out of which were collected the armies of immigrants that have recruited the numbers of their citizens. They have for the most part come from those classes of Europe whose whole lives are given up to the daily struggle to obtain the means of keeping alive. By much effort, by savings that may almost be said to have been stolen from necessity, by resistance to temptation that has often been heroic, the few necessary pounds have been got together to enable the immigrant to sail from Liverpool or Bremen, from Cork or Hamburg, to an Atlantic port, and he has landed penniless to try his fortune in another hemisphere. If the times are fairly prosperous, he gets employment and wages that prove to him that he is indeed in a world which is new. The strength of character which brought him out remains with him; he saves, he becomes a householder, a house owner, a landed proprietor; but the memory of his own early struggles, and of the struggles of his father before him, does not pass away, and, if he were asked to speak of the land of his adoption and could put his thoughts into words, he would always describe it as "a land of fulness of bread." It takes a generation or two to raise the immigrant above the new satisfaction of material contentment, and the rarer development of the United States as a member of the elect nations that contribute something more than material wealth to the treasures of the world is yet before it. Into that future we cannot pry, though we have faith that it will come. Perchance a hundred years hence it will yet be only at the dawn.

The Times, July 6, 1876.

. . . All things considered, there has been no growth in the whole world equal to that ascribed in the last hundred years' history of the United States. . . . A hundred years ago, an infant Power asserted what might be called both the natural claim and the reversionary right to a whole Continent. In the name of justice, liberty, and equality it claimed the adhesion of those who could not otherwise win these blessings; and, whatever the Statesmen of the Old World may think of it, the United States were only applying Old World maxims when they warned the old leaven of European politics to beware of American soil. All the true interests of England were bound up in the cause of American Independence. . . . It is American Independence we have to thank for our tardy deliverance from a worse fate than despotism— tyranny and oligarchy under Constitutional forms. Upon the whole, and without a claim to deserve it, England may claim at least an equal, if not more than equal, share in the benefits of the great event now commemorated. Springing immediately from it, and with only the difference of a year or two, there then came into the very forefront of the world three new powers and influences—the great American Republic, the French Revolution, and the Free Press of this country. They started at once into being, and have respectively held sway over the whole civilized world. . . .

. . . A Century is a long time to look forward to, and the Americans are quite right in making the most of 1876, leaving

1976 to take care of itself. They have to make the flag of Independence a flag of unity as well, and to hold aloft that flag to the far-scattered and much-divided inhabitants of a realm that extends from ocean to ocean, and embraces every variety of climate and soil. . . .

Topic 15

THE HAYMARKET RIOT

1886

Saturday, May 1, 1886, was selected as the target date for nation-wide strikes and demonstrations in support of shortening the work day to eight hours with no reduction in pay. Members of labor organizations such as the Knights of Labor and the American Federation of Labor joined the movement as did Anarchists and Socialists. Chicago witnessed particularly strong tension as men in the meatpacking houses and railway yards joined brewers, bakers, cigar makers, and ironworkers in marching through Chicago streets on that day. Scattered strikes and demonstrations continued into the following week, and on Monday, several workers were shot by police during a battle between union and nonunion workers.

On Tuesday evening, at a protest meeting in Haymarket Square, some 1500 men listened to speeches against police brutality: more than 100 policemen marched to the square and ordered the crowd to disperse. When someone threw a bomb into the police ranks, the police fired their revolvers into the crowd. By the time the terror ended, more than eighty persons were killed and wounded. In the hours and days which followed, authorities arrested the editors and printers of the socialist newspaper, Arbeiter Zeitung, *and raided the socialist and anarchist meeting halls. The American press denounced the radical groups and demanded obe-*

dience to the law. Gradually the violence subsided. This tense episode in American labor history hastened the decline of the Knights of Labor and slowed the eight-hour day movement.

PARIS. *Le Temps,* **May 7, 1886.**

For several months, North America has been prey to a series of attacks of economic fever. All over the country, strikes were raging, sometimes limited in their extension and in their demands, sometimes aiming, like those provoked by the Knights of Labor, at involving the whole federal territory and at raising in one single stroke the whole social question.

After having affected the states of the South and Southeast and being particularly widespread over the network of railroads of the Mississippi and Missouri regions, on which Mr. Jay Gould possesses a preponderous influence, the plague was suddenly beaten down farther North. In the state of New York and in Ohio, entire corps of tradesmen suspended their work with a common agreement in order to demand an eight-hour day with maintenance of the actual rate of salaries, generally calculated on the basis of a 10- or 11-hour day.

These demands were complicated in certain areas with demands relative to the number of apprentices and to the use of workers not listed on the registers of workers' associations or *Trade-Unions.*

. . . For some time, in the United States, a parasitic plant of exotic origin developed in an extraordinary manner. At the beginning of this century the economists believed that the social question would not apply to the United States because of the abundance of land and because of the limitation of the number of the workers—in this country of election by the laboring classes, anarchy such as the *Freiheit,* organ of Mr. Most, preached, had won many adherents. At New York, Boston, Philadelphia, Cincinnati, Milwaukee, Chicago, everywhere that industry had accumulated its capital and its enterprises and assembled its workers, the doctrines dear to revolutionary Communism found a favorable audience and converts all prepared.

These last weeks, the crisis had taken a grave and urgent character. In Milwaukee, capital of Michigan, [sic] in the great center of the brewery of *Lagerbeer,* that is to say, in a completely German milieu, bloody conflicts have taken place on the subject of the eight-hour day. It is in Chicago, however, that the troubles have been the most serious. Several tens of thousands of workers were on strike for several weeks.

The anarchists, who brag about possessing in the commercial and industrial metropolis of Ohio [the writer believed Chicago was located in Ohio] a powerful organization, sought to inflame the conflict and aggravate the situation. A great workers' meeting was announced for the fifth of May [sic] at one of the public squares of the city, with a view to stopping the measures necessary for the immediate triumph of the socialist cause. The mayor of Chicago, responsible for order in the streets of the city, gave out a proclamation forbidding riotous assemblies in public places.

As the assembled masses did not obey the injunctions reiterated by the police, the chief commissioner believed it necessary to proceed to legal demands, while the anarchistic orators imperturbably pursued their inflamatory harangues. Hardly was the legal formula pronounced when a voice, which even up to now remains unknown, shouted: "To arms!" and three explosive bombs fell into the ranks of the police and made numerous victims.

In the presence of this aggression, the police agents believed they had the right to shoot. A lively fusillade occurred, charges were made from one side to the other, several dead and a considerable number of wounded were left on the ground. It was believed that such a catastrophe would spread terror among even the most evil-intentioned and that order, dearly bought with the price of such a day, would reign again in Chicago.

Nothing of the kind is happening. New strikes are conspicuous. Crowds composed of thousands of persons sweep into the department stores with the intentions of looting and are dispersed only by force of arms. In brief, the situation in Chicago as in Milwaukee, where similar incidents have taken place, remains imminently grave, and one asks if the state of Ohio, [sic] in the first place, and the power of the federal government, in the second, will not intervene in order to reestablish order in Chicago.

Violent socialism has made its burning entrance onto the stage in America.

Le Temps, May 9, 1886.

The troubles of Chicago appear terminated. The vigorous intervention of the police, the energy of the mayor, and the dispositions shown by all the classes of the population ended the insurrection without the governor of Illinois having called out the state militia. The police actively pursued their research, and discovered several depots of arms, munitions, and explosive materials, particularly in the localities affected by the meeting of socialistic associations and in the anarchist printing shops.

Since the greatest number, if not to say the total number, of chiefs and inspirers of the movement which just ended in these deplorable scenes carry German names and are emigrants of Germanic origin, the national sentiment of the native population is strongly excited against the invasion of pernicious foreign doctrines.

The chiefs of anarchism—at least those who are not directly compromised, as Schwabe and his associates, in the troubles of Chicago and of Milwaukee—Most and his consorts, pretend to defy in speeches the public conscience and to congratulate themselves for the success of their propaganda in the Northern states and in those of the West; but it is easy to see that at heart they are very afraid and simply hope, by force of defiance, to escape the legitimate resentment of a laboring democracy which does not joke with disturbers and abettors of disorder and crimes. The tone of those newspapers properly anarchistic—generally published in German and a few only in Swedish—which still appear, is perceptibly softened.

In Chicago, the mayor has declared that he would not hesitate, as a measure of public safety, to supress the organ of revolutionary socialism, the *Arbeiter Zeitung,* if it contained the least inflamatory article.

One indirect consequence of the bloody riots of Chicago and Milwaukee, which their instigators in Illinois and Wisconsin assuredly did not think about, has been to end several of the great strikes that raged over several places in the territory. The strikers feared seeing their cause confounded with that of the anarchists, and they abandoned their demands rather than share the anathema hurled against the agents of the revolution by the entire American democracy. In Chicago, the employees of the railroad *Lake Shore* have called off a great parade from which they were awaiting the most happy results for their cause. In New York, the employees of tramways signed an almost absolute capitulation.

It is a conclusion that comes to whomever has studied closely the conflicts of this year in the United States, which were even more grave than the ones ten years ago that brought out the masses of workers and militias in several central and western states: the young American democracy, like that of the old world [that] established itself and resisted the attacks of revolutionary socialism, knows how to display in the repression a vigor that is without equal and to prove an energy and a confidence which are incomparable by crushing the insurrectionist attempts while remaining within the law and not losing faith in her destiny and in liberty.

LONDON. *The Times*, May 6, 1886.

. . . The great mass of Americans are very tolerant of the expression of opinions, no matter how eccentric and violent. Even downright lawlessness is, up to a certain point, apt to be condoned. But there comes a time when all such forbearance vanishes, and when very sharp and summary measures are taken against rioters or marauders. When the New York policemen take to their clubs, which are formidable weapons, they use them with a degree of recklessness unknown to an English constable. More than once in the history of New York and Chicago it has been shown that nowhere is turbulence more sternly suppressed than in these cities. There are signs that the temper that has sometimes made the State militia mercilessly shoot down lawless mobs is aroused, and the Socialists will do well to take note of this.

No doubt, order will soon be everywhere restored. The men on strike will return to work, and boycotting will cease as soon as law-abiding citizens are roused to action. The country is, however, passing through a period of trial. In all the chief towns in the North, from Chicago and St. Louis to New York, and not in one or two industries, but in many, there are disturbances. The traffic of the railways is stopped or thrown into disorder. The tramcars in New York recently ceased to run. Many kinds of business have been brought to a standstill, and the loss of capital during the last few weeks of enforced idleness, restlessness, or uneasiness has been great. To some extent the strikes are the results of general depression of trade, from which the United States have not escaped. But in most instances the strikes do not put in the front of their claims any demand for higher wages; they wish a shorter working day, and ask eight hours' work and ten hours' pay. Not the least important fact connected with the strikes is the extent to which they have been brought about by Socialists, and it is a fact not calculated to recommend them to Americans, the last people in the world to appreciate theories which tend to put on the same dead level the idle and the energetic, the skillful and the incompetent workmen. Rarely has the world of industry been more disturbed than it is. Scarcely anywhere does the eye rest on a country where labour pursues its way tranquilly. . . .

. . . The disturbances at Chicago and Milwaukee are a sign that industry in the United States has now to contend with all the difficulties with which capitalists in Europe have had to battle. What has occurred in the Western States seems to show that Americans may have before them even greater troubles than those with which we are familiar. The labour market is not now, if it ever was, able to absorb an unlimited number of recruits from Europe. A witness giving evidence the other day before a Committee of the House of Representatives sorrowfully observed that the "American capacity to absorb Christendom seemed to be somewhat strongly taxed," and this is an inadequate statement of the facts. The hope that for many years to come the United States would know little of disputes between capital and labour has been long proved to be baseless. On the other side of the Atlantic are heard the same complaints as have been made here for years, and most of the States have become, so far as industry is concerned, old countries. The tendency to equalize the supply of labour has brought to America surplus workers, and the strikers are finding that their places can be filled without great difficulty. Some of the troubles of which European countries have had experience are making their appearance in Chicago and other large American cities in an aggravated form. It is remarked that the rioters are not, as a rule, native Americans. They are Bohemians, Poles, and Germans. They are strangers who are amenable to no strong public opinion, who have never been trained to self-control, and who are infected with the wild socialistic theories which find favour among revolutionists on the Continent. Some of them have left their native countries because they had given offence to the authorities. Not a few of them are familiar with the use of arms; and, unfortunately, there have been too great facilities in the United States for becoming acquainted with the terrible effects of dynamite. It is a grave fact that America yearly receives not only a vast number of labourers from Europe, but also many restless spirits, daring unscrupulous men, who are not content to make speeches and pass resolutions, but who would freely use the revolver and the dynamite bomb to gain their ends. If, as we are sometimes told, the era of labour struggles conducted by pacific means is over, if the future battles between labour and capital are not to be fought out on the field of political economy, but by material weapons, the outlook in some parts of the United States is dark. One source of safety, however, lies in the fact that Americans are not blind to these dangers, and that they nurse no visionary hopes about the best mode of averting them. The action of the police at Chicago on Tuesday and at Milwaukee yesterday shows that there is no disposition to parley with forms of Socialism which aim at a general upheaval, and which sanction every means of bringing this about. We may be pretty sure Americans will not be maudlin and weak in dealing with such an enemy.

Topic 16

THE HOMESTEAD STRIKE

1892

*At Homestead in southwestern Pennsylvania a strike against the
Carnegie Steel Company turned into one of the most brutal and
bitter struggles in the history of labor. Managing the company
while Andrew Carnegie was vacationing in Scotland, Henry C.
Frick brought in 300 Pinkerton men to protect company property
and nonunion workers: shooting broke out, and estimates of those
who died ranged from seven to thirteen. The Pennsylvania National
Guard, called out by the governor, restored order and enabled
nonunion men to continue working. In November, strikers returned
to work on the company's terms.*

LONDON. *The Times,* July 12, 1892.

It is stated that the GOVERNOR of PENNSYLVANIA
has ordered no less than 8,000 troops of the National Guard
to proceed to Homestead, the scene of the recent terrible riots.
The order comes none too soon, and its effect is instantly apparent in the announcement, on the part of the men, that they
will give up possession of the town and works to the troops.
Thus, it may be hoped, peace will be restored, and an end put
to one of the ugliest incidents of modern industrial history. Are

we to call it a riot, or an insurrection? Few of the elements of civil war are wanting, and many memorable historical outbreaks have begun in a humbler and less threatening fashion. The strikers —many of them foreigners, who have probably at home served as soldiers—were well armed with rifles and revolvers, and numbered some thousands. They stationed sentinels on the banks of the river to signal the coming of the "PINKERTONS," as they call those bodies of private police that are now so largely employed in the United States both for detective and for protective services. More than one attempt by the attacking party to land was repulsed, and the strikers showed skill as well as courage, for they planted a cannon upon a commanding position and opened a destructive fire on the police barges; they built, in accordance with the latest notions in fortification, a steel fort to protect themselves from the bullets of their assailants; and they attempted to set fire to the enemy's barges by pouring upon the river burning oil. When the fight was over, and the police, outnumbered, outgeneraled, and overpowered, were forced to surrender, the number of killed and wounded equaled the casualties in an ordinary South American revolution. Much is said in Fourth of July oratory about engagements less bloody than the conflict of last Wednesday at the Homestead Works. The strikers seem to have kept up in all things a semblance of actual warfare except in observance of its laws, for they shot down the bearers of a flag of truce and cruelly maltreated the police taken prisoners. "During the march," said our Correspondent at the time, "they were brutally beaten, stoned, switched, kicked, clubbed with muskets, and compelled to run the gauntlet of infuriated men and women." It is no consolation that the account of the doings at Homestead reads like an old story. In Pittsburgh in 1877 were much the same scenes. The mob got the upper hand, sacked all places where arms were stored, threw up earthworks, overpowered the troops and militia, plundered and fired buildings, public and private, as the passion of the moment suggested, and did as much mischief to the city as would have been inflicted by a bombardment. Nor have such things been peculiar to the neighbourhood of Pittsburgh. The riot at New Orleans is not in the remote past, and we do not know that any of the leaders of that outbreak against authority have had reason to repent what they did in the name of Judge Lynch. There are limits to the patience and tolerance of the law-respecting part of the community; and some fifteen or sixteen years ago Pennsylvania witnessed the good effects of wholesome vigour, when MR. GOWEN brought to justice the leaders of the "Molly Maguire" organization. The Anarchists who wantonly murdered several policemen at Chicago also met with their desserts, notwithstanding strenuous efforts to rescue them from the gallows; and Pennsylvania and Illinois were in consequence for all honest citizens pleasanter to live in. Such vigour, however, is a little too rare. Too often rowdies responsible for such outrages as those witnessed near Pittsburgh have had their own way, and have, in the end, been coaxed, not coerced, into decent behaviour.

No good is to be done by casting these things in the teeth of the American people. Next time that Congress is asked to give its attention to the affairs of Ireland, it is to be hoped that it will occur to some members that the savagery and lawlessness, of which the neighbourhood of Pittsburgh has been the scene more than once, have a prior and higher claim to consideration. The anarchy prevalent there might suggest the text that the foremost duties of us all are at home; that every country, however fortunate, will always have its hands full if it attends to its own affairs. That, however, is not the point which we press; we prefer to look at a danger concerning, more or less, the whole civilized world. The apologists of strikes like to dwell upon the tendency to get rid of the spirit of lawlessness, open or secret, by which they once were supported; and in fairness it must be admitted that it is rare to hear of the hideous outrages once common in trade disputes. But in the proceedings at Homestead there is foreshadowed a development of the labour question more alarming than any phase of it which has passed. MR. CARNEGIE, besides being an assiduous preacher of the superiority of all things American, would have the world believe that he is a generous employer. He has strong convictions about the duties attaching to the enjoyment of wealth; and his practice, let us hope, has tallied with his precepts. And yet in his works, in resistance to the policy of his company, a strike takes the form of a veritable insurrection. Modern industry brings together masses of workmen, as numerous as a small army, who often obey the orders of trade leaders as implicitly as if they were officers speaking to soldiers. These bodies, formidable from their number, may have weapons, if not in actual possession, within reach, and the workshop may be turned into a citadel or made to furnish materials for the construction of a fortress far harder to capture than a street barricade. We have been in the habit of assuming that the leaders of these industrial armies will not, if the worst comes, use their power to the utmost. The events that have occurred near Pittsburgh give a shock to that assumption. There the strikers stop at nothing to carry their point. They take the field against the police, offer battle, and defeat the authorities of the law in open fight. We must not be too confident that this audacity and licence are solely attributable to circumstances peculiar to America. No doubt the present state of things is irritating to American working men, especially those engaged in the iron and steel industries. Of late they have heard much of the blessings secured to them by protection. 'MR. McKINLEY and his friends have been descanting upon the good done by the tariff to their own country and the blow struck at the industries of others; and almost simultaneously with this vaunting talk comes the announcement by the employers that they must reduce wages. This vexes the workmen, especially such as were the dupes of the Protectionists' promises. But the whole story has far-reaching significance. What we have had to recognize is that, notwithstanding the improvement observable in the mode of conducting trade disputes, the incidents that have occurred near Pittsburgh may be repeated wherever law is weak, the number of its enemies is great, and arms are within their reach, and that we must not be too sure that industrial struggles will never in the future get beyond the stage of argument and passive resistance. Those who talk of a great strike as lightly as if it involved only so much holiday-making forget that it is but a step to scenes of bloodshed and anarchy such as have occurred at Homestead, and that there are never wanting designing men to counsel this step being taken.

Another reflection, and an obvious one, is that the employment of a private police force is a thing that should neither be permitted nor required in a civilized community. Such a force, at the disposal of any capitalist or any company that can pay for it, is a standing provocation to the labouring class. But in America it has been found almost necessary to have such a force for a very simple reason—a reason to which we desire emphatically to call the attention of Gladstonian members of Parliament, who will presently be asked to give the control of the police of Ireland and London to popularly elected bodies. The reason to which we refer is that in the United States the legitimate and regular police cannot altogether be trusted. It knows very well that its existence and its pay depend on the popular vote; that the people, the many, are its masters; and it takes care not to act too firmly against the people's wishes in times of excitement. The result is the demand for an extralegal force, like these "PINKERTON'S men," and, when the situation becomes strained, violence, bloodshed, and an outbreak of popular rage [occur], to find an analogy to which we have to go back to the Commune of 1871 and the massacre of the gendarmes in the Rue Haxo.

PARIS. *Le Temps*, July 17, 1892.

The workers' unrest, instead of decreasing, is only spreading in the United States. It is no longer a question of a simple strike, it is a real rebellion, and not only on one point alone but on several issues at a time, in the East, the center, the extreme West, in Pennsylvania, in Minnesota and in Idaho.

From the start, the strike of the Carnegie factories at Homestead was not an ordinary one. It was presented with very special characteristics; in the first place, in its causes.

There was doubtlessly in its origin a quarrel between employer and workers: the reduction of salaries was made more acute in the eyes of the workers by the fact that Mr. Carnegie is guilty of taking a luxury train outside of federal territory, even outside of America—in Scotland. But up to that point, it was only a strike, a peaceful and to some extent a passive strike, in which the adversaries observed themselves using up their energies and fighting with the one who would lose the most, that is, with the one who would yield first.

What changed it into disorder, with violence and massacre,

was that in order to replace the union strikers, the factory manager sent out a call for free workers, who did not belong to a union. From then on, it was no longer a war between two classes, employers and workers, but war between the same class and only between workers. Let us note, in passing, a customary trait. Mr. Carnegie proceeded straightforwardly, like an American. He applied to the Pinkerton agency, who sent him robust, well-armed companions. But the strikers were not less resolute; it was with gunfire that they welcomed the newcomers. It does not seem that this first attempt of private police was favorable to the theory professed by certain unorthodox economists: in having recourse to the Pinkertons, they have simply unchained anarchy.

After a few hours, Homestead was no longer habitable; the strikers had conquered the town; they had behaved like an unchained human beast.

Another customary American trait: in desolate and terrorized Homestead, the preachers went around on the streets, shouting that Jesus Christ and not Carnegie was the master; blowing [on] and stirring up the fire. But suddenly came an unexpected event. The militia arrived from Pittsburgh . . . Homestead is again kept in control . . . by itself.

Things happened exactly in the same way in the Far West, in Idaho. The situation there is perhaps even worse than in Pennsylvania. Blood flowed, and abundantly. About a hundred workers have been killed for having committed the crime of not belonging to a union and of having accepted the work that the others no longer wished to do.

In Idaho too there was insurrection: citizens imprisoned, telegraph wires cut, bridges destroyed, railroad tracks removed, mines dynamited, a whole region menaced with ruin. . .

What is the government of the Union going to do before this all too certain danger. It can only do one thing: cut short and clear, act fast and decide the amount of force necessary to repress the almost savage brutality of the riot. If the state of Idaho hesitates because of electoral considerations, the government of the Union should not hesitate long. An exaggerated patience would be neither worthy nor prudent.

It is to the honor of the United States that it permits to develop without hindrance the boldest initiative, to want strong and enterprising individuals, neither to ask the price of nor to measure liberty. But if this liberty befuddles it and drags it into shameful and odious excess one must find a remedy or a corrective in the law.

The American Union, while rigidly applying the law, will not be betraying its role, will not be lying to her principle, because it will be intervening here only as a guardian of all liberties, of which one is oppressed and crushed by the other. Its intervention, in this case, will not prove that the state, in general, must always intervene, that the scenes of Homestead and of Idaho prove that one must despair of the wisdom and of the good sense of the workers.

These are annoying accidents, the last ones even terrible, but they pass: notified in time by the law, the individual resumes his place; straightened accordingly by it, matters resume their course.

Topic 17

THE SPANISH-AMERICAN WAR

1898

Foreign relations between the United States and Spain deteriorated rapidly in the first months of 1898. The continuing revolutionary conflict in Cuba sent shock waves onto large eastern seaboard cities such as New York, Boston, and Washington, D. C., where they were made even larger by sensational newspaper stories. The De Lome Letter and the sinking of the U. S. S. Maine in February heightened the irritations of Americans against Spain and her seemingly oppressive policies, not only in Cuba and the Caribbean area, but also in the Philippine Islands.

Pursuing an antiwar policy, President William McKinley worked strenuously for peace in Cuba during his first twelve months in office. However, after considerable pressure from his advisers and Congressmen, he sent a message to Congress on April 11 calling for United States intervention to secure peace in Cuba. Congress replied on April 20 with a joint resolution that demanded the removal of Spanish forces from Cuba and gave the President the power to use military force if necessary; moreover, the resolution added that after the restoration of peace, control of Cuba would be left to the Cuban people. McKinley signed the resolution that same day and began a blockade of Cuban ports two days later. Spain broke diplomatic relations on the 21st and declared war on April 24; the next day, the United States declared war, making the declaration retroactive to April 21.

MEXICO CITY. *El Imparcial,* April 20, 1898.

The last indications in favor of peace have just disintegrated with the resolution of the American Congress, of which our readers are already familiar. Now war is inevitable as a painful consequence of the conflict between Spain and the United States. The armed intervention of the latter nation in Cuban matters, denounced strongly by the Spanish Government, will determine the rupture and after this, the initiation of hostilities.

As it seems that diplomatic recourses are exhausted, the question will be carried to the battlefield, and it will not be long before the first cannon shot is fired.

What road will events take to arrive at this first cannon shot? It seems that if the Spanish Government remains firm in its renouncement of the intervention of the United States, the Cortes of the Peninsula on the eve of their meeting may be the first to declare war, before the resolutions of the Legislative power of the United States, once signed by President McKinley, are carried out; that is to say, before the American army and navy begin to mobilize.

It is also possible that there will not be a declaration of war in the customary form, but that Spain, upon receiving the suggestion to abandon the island, may answer strongly in the negative and wait for the consequences, which would be an American aggression opposed by the Spanish army and navy in self-defense. . . .

El Imparcial, April 23, 1898.

The present circumstances are so delicate, that a good bit of prudence and calm is needed by anyone who because of education, feelings, or similar motives, sympathizes with one of the two nations who today find themselves face to face.

Today more than ever it is necessary that all men of good intentions maintain a fair measure of restraint before a situation as serious as the present, and adopt a calm attitude in the midst of various incidents which are bound to present themselves in this campaign.

This is the only way a disagreeable move can be avoided that would form a notable contrast to the conduct that the partisans of one cause or the other have observed up to now, and also the people who belong to one or the other colony.

Mexico sincerely esteems the two colonies, composed of hard-working people who conform to the laws of the Republic, and who to a great extent have formed families with the Mexicans.

Fortunately the old hatred for strangers has been extinguished in our country a long time ago, hatred that was reasonable at one time in the pages of our history. But at present this hatred has no reason to exist since the government and the people of both countries have extended a sincere friendship toward the Mexican government and people, and we are able to concentrate totally on the facts of the present situation.

On the other hand, there has never been a nation whose unalterable hatreds from past epochs were not totally dissipated by the effects of time and cordial relations.

In the Republic it is lamented that the Spanish-American conflict reaches for such a painful solution; we deplore the number of lives that will be spent in the battle, the blood and tears to be shed by one side or the other, the tragedies it is bound to produce, the intellectual and material energy that will be wasted in fighting.

In our opinion it is this very feeling of grief which should inspire a tranquil respect in anyone who sympathizes with one side or the other toward those who judge their adversaries in the campaign that has just begun.

This serene attitude of respect should be manifested precisely in those people who, by means of the publicity available to them, have the moral obligation not to provoke agitations, stir up passion, nor to provide elements of discord among the sympathizers of one of the two nations, or the individuals who belong to them.

LONDON. *The Times,* **April 26, 1898.**

Congress has passed and the PRESIDENT has signed the declaration that a state of war exists between the United States and Spain, so that the situation may be regarded as regularized.

Except as affecting some technicalities in the American prize Courts the declaration does not seem to possess any high importance. Spain had already declared that a state of war followed upon certain diplomatic steps taken by the United States, and all the world is aware that the capture of the Buenaventura last Friday together with the blockade of Havana by the American fleet are acts of war which speak more forcibly than any declaration. Congress, however, does not do things by halves. It has not only declared that a state of war exists, but that it has existed since April 21, including that day. This retrospective action may furnish some agreeable subjects of argument to the professors of international law, but its immediate and practical effect would seem to be extinction of all hope that the vessels captured before the declaration may be released. The protest of the American Consul and Commodore at Hong Kong against a notification calling upon the American squadron to leave the port in accordance with our proclamation of neutrality was funny enough in itself. But it becomes doubly amusing when Congress thus cuts away the whole ground on which it was made. We gather that correspondence setting forth the history of the case was presented to Congress along with the PRESIDENT'S Message, but Congress does not seem to have been greatly impressed with its importance, seeing that the House of Representatives spent about two minutes over the business of passing the declaration. The PRESIDENT appears to have said what he had to say in a businesslike manner, and probably he cares as little as people on this side of the water what inferences may be deduced from his expressions by fastidious constitutional critics. . . .

Those who regard war as a spectacle more or less devised for their amusement are likely to have to put up with a good deal of disappointment. Noble efforts have already been made by foreign correspondents and news agencies, in the way of rumours and denials concerning the capture of passenger boats and merchant vessels, to produce the illusion of a thrilling drama. We venture to think that the public will be very weary of all this long before news of real importance can arrive to stimulate its interest. This war, even under the direction of Congress, is not likely to be immediately fertile in striking incidents or sensational horrors. The Spaniards are already aware of the fact that it is not an affair of three weeks, and when the American people begin to see clear through the maze of blustering headlines, they will become aware of it too. . . .

To the American temperament an uneventful contest dragging on through weeks and months will prove rather trying. The PRESIDENT is not unlikely ere long to receive abundance of directions from Congress and elsewhere intended to make him "hurry up" and do something. Already there are cries that he is not sufficiently energetic. Party politics count for something even in a war, and we may take it that, if the Republicans are making capital out of the fight, the Bryanites will try to secure their share by protesting that they would have fought much better. It may even prove necessary to educate public opinion by engaging in a perfectly useless bombardment of Havana, although there is a risk that its inutility may be referred to anything but the true cause. The martial ardour that is now hurrying volunteers to Tampa Bay will probably chafe under the enforced delays due to the need for drill, equipment, transport, and details of that kind, which do not occur to the popular mind in moments of enthusiasm. Thinking people in the States of course perceive already that the war is not going to be a picnic, but it was not the thinking people who made the war, and it is not they who will bring pressure to bear upon those who conduct it. The popular orators are eminent patentees like MR. EDISON, who talk of swallowing Spain without an effort, and fire-eating officers who want to lay their ships alongside the Havana batteries. Of course it is possible that the Spaniards may blunder egregiously. They may do all the things they ought not to do, and deliver themselves into American hands. But it is not wise to reckon upon their dementia, and if they play their cards even fairly well the fight is likely to be one calling much more for calm determination and staying power than for excitement and enthusiasm.

PARIS. *Le Temps,* April 29, 1898.

The public is not satisfied. For a little while they were complaining that they had to wait too long. What especially annoyed

them is that the curtain rose and that nothing—or so little—
happened: war is declared and there has not even been a great
naval battle. It is hardly worth calling the bombardment of
Matanzas and the engagement of the *Cushing* with the *Ligero* a
prologue. Nourished, since the success of the famous pamphlet,
the *Battle of Dorking,* immediately following 1871, by fictitious
recitals of wars on land and on sea whose authors devoted only
a few pages to the preliminary operations, to all those slow preparations, to those thousand and one minute events that equate
what one calls testing the iron, this good public imagines that they
are duped and that they have the right to complain if a decisive
battle is not delivered within eight days.

In Spain, despite the ardor of the national temperament, one
is accustomed to a certain indolence, to a kind of fatalism which
willingly leaves to tomorrow all that which is not absolutely indispensable today and which has as an adequate enough expression
the adage so frequently repeated: *Mañana.*

In the United States, the disposition is less tranquil. Be it because of the harsh and dry climate that pulls the nerves like the
strings of a violin, be it because of the effect of a certain haste
in living that makes the race to riches especially rushed . . .

Who does not remember the terrible troubles caused to
Lincoln in the beginning of the war of secession, the feverish lack
of foresight with which a crowd of good citizens, without wanting
to hear, without taking any account of the circumstances, shouted
without respite or truce: *To Richmond!* Today an unscrupulous
press, a band of politicians whose aggressive jingoism does not
always have the excuse of a perfect sincerity, have done everything to exalt these dispositions.

To believe the yellow journals and their allies, it would take
only a snap of the finger to get the better of Spain. . . . Did not
an eminent fighter charm and win the enthusiasm of his followers
by saying that if he were sent to Cuba, he would make Castilian
the language most used by the majority of the hosts from the
infernal regions where Satan reigns?

Doubtlessly these are only the flowers of bellicose and brag-
ging rhetoric of which it would be only too easy to make a
bouquet for all the people, even the most refined and self-con-

trolled, when the approach of a great battle has loosened the bridle to all the murderous instincts. It is no less true that a sickly excitement reigns in the United States, and that it risks provoking, on contact with the realities of the slow evolution of the facts of war, a dangerous disillusionment.

The universities themselves, those sanctuaries of high culture and of the spirit of liberty, are affected by these influences. Harvard, the first establishment of this kind in America, sees its students leave their Alma Mater en masse in order to enlist: the juniors who have hardly attained adolescence as well as the sophomores who are perhaps going to compromise their final examinations; and it is in vain that an eminent professor, Mr. Charles Eliot Norton, the friend and editor of Carlyle, has the courage to protest against a craze that he estimates to be hardly patriotic. Has not one seen a millionaire of New York, Mr. John Jacob Astor, the actual head of that house which owns a good part of the apartments of the Empire City, after having offered to raise a battery at his expense, offer his personal services to Washington in order to be employed in the army in whatever post appeared suitable to his capacities.

Well! there is no doubt that an attentive and impartial examination of the situation would singularly dampen, if not this devotedness, at least the warm hopes which escort them. The idea of a happy surprise attack on Cuba is totally discredited. It is a question at this hour of a blockade—and of a long-term blockade.

The land forces of the United States will be able to carry military preparations only to the point where it will be possible to make use of it a few months later. Moreover, it would be a grave imprudence to engage in land operations in Cuba during the season of the year when yellow fever strikes there at its highest. There is a retarding force! . . .

. . . If the nine big Spanish battleships, against which America can oppose only five battleships of this rank, make their way toward the coast of the United States, the situation becomes serious at once . . . Even New York could become the objective of such an expedition [as the bombardment of coastal cities]. . .

All these hypotheses, it goes without saying, are dominated

by one question: that of fuel. In our days, the true nerve of the naval war is coal. However, it is to be noted that, on the one hand, several of the Spanish ships can carry with them in their hold, enough coal to suffice for a two-way crossing, and that, on the other, even on the terms of the proclamation of neutrality of the United Kingdom, they will be able to procure in the ports of Canada, at Halifax, for example, a quantity of coal sufficient to take them to the closest Spanish port, that is, in the case in point, to the Antilles.

No practical impossibility thus can be in opposition to a similar operation. It is possible that this conflict may see a Spanish offensive upset all probabilities and demonstrate to the American people, with the proverbial changing of fortune, the horrors of a war that demands not only the sacrifices of money but that comes to raise its hideous head on the soil itself at the hearth of one of the belligerents. . . .

MADRID. *La Ilustracion Espanola y Americana,* April 30, 1898.

As the use of lies is one of the maneuvers the enemy employs against us, they state that the castle Morro fired the first shots. What that fort did was to fire a cannon to advise peaceful ships of the appearance of the enemy's blockading squadron; that is to say, to give the signal of alarm to warn our ships that the Yankee squadron had begun the hostilities; and the capture without previous warning of some Spanish merchant ships that sailed ignorant of the state of war not only is an act of violence, but a thieving and villainous act against all morals. If it is true that the enemy admits to this act, and keeps these ships they kidnapped, knowing that they have no right to do this, it seems to us an even more villainous act than the capture itself. As to considering the signals from the Morro as the beginning of hostilities, this is as absurd as charging us with the negligence of the officers of the *Maine.* The United States is responsible for the provocation and the positive outbreak of war before declaring it. There is no doubt of this. That the declaration came late, after war had begun, is nothing but a cunning maneuver, rude as is all their conduct with which they, the unscrupulous lawyers, attempt to confuse a clear matter and force us to answer for their wrong doings. The blockade of a fort is an act of hostility, as is the capturing of ships: they don't even have the honor to accept the responsibility of their own actions.

. . . The motto "Remember the *Maine*," which the Yankees have taken to inspire their sailors, can serve to maintain a militant indignation among ours. "Remember the infamy of the *Maine*," we will repeat as long as the war lasts; see how those lives that you saved in the bay of Havana pay and [see] the dangers that you defied while the officers of the *Maine*, drunk with champagne on another ship, allowed their poor sailors to perish. Never forget the felony of the *Maine*, Spanish sailors. If in the hazards of war they seek help from your burning ships: Remember the *Maine!*

La Ilustracion Espanola y Americana, May 8, 1898.

. . . A sad day it was for us, the eve of May 2! General Augustin enlightened us as to the nocturnal entrance of the North American squadron into the bay of Manila and the following heroic combat, very unequal, of our principal ships that could oppose the armored ships of the enemy and their powerful cannons, their incendiary bombs, prohibited by agreements, with only wooden ships and antiquated artillery . . . The feeling was painful throughout all Spain: more a feeling of concentrated anger than one of fear: tears of powerless anger were those that came up to the eyes: machines making a joke of men: steel splintering wood: bombs smashing tile roofs, insolent wealth opposing honorable poverty: the healthy, fat pig trampling the moribund lion. Before long the cable was cut. Darkness, and long days without news . . . Only insulting laughter came from the Yankees in New York. But what is war? A mixture of happiness and pain. But those pains find us very tough. Onward!

. . . The Spanish residents of the Argentine Republic deserve a round of applause for their donations, as do those in Mexico. And the opinions of the Argentine general Mansilla that appeared in *Le Temps*, May 2, deserve to be read in all Spanish America. This general, now in his sixties, asks permission, giving up his military rank, to fight in Cuba on the side of Spain if only he will be allowed to retain his citizenship.

While the Cubans were procuring their independence, those who had done the same thing were on their side; but what we cannot permit is in procuring independence to seek aid from a foreign nation to oppose the mother country, mother after all is said and done, in spite of her wrong doings. The United States covets Cuba, and no protest from humanity will force them to desist from this object. And they desire Cuba not only for being a sugar factory without rival, but the key to the Gulf of Mexico and to the future interoceanic canal, and because its domination means the domination of the two oceans and hegemony over all the continent.

The war will create a strong North American navy, and once it is converted into a strong naval power, we will not be able to do anything in our own house without permission from the North Americans. Our police will not be able to detain one Yankee sailor without all their navy falling on our ports. . . .

Not only do we have to suffer from this protectorate; Europe, which continues immobile and impotent in the face of this intervention so contrary to the rights of men, also will suffer the consequences.

You probably haven't forgotten the plan which the United States proposed to us in the Pan-American Congress in Washington in 1889. Our delegate Sáenz Peña spoke to their egoistic and mistaken doctrine "America for the Americans" with another generous and suitable principle: "America for humanity."

We agree. Whether Spain is conquered or not, she will defend what is right for the universal cause. And as far as we are concerned, we feel great in our smallness.

La Ilustracion Espanola y Americana, **May 15, 1898.**

. . . There is an infamous crowd whose only ideal is egoism, who having forgotten what are propriety, justice, and human rights, and making use of material force, has at the end of the nineteenth century struck out to practice robbery, arson, and destruction. In the face of this cultural anarchism, the other civilized peoples have crossed their arms. The United States, or the United Scoundrels as they want to be called, since they behave like scoundrels, destroying us with an impossible war, they who have lived in peace throughout almost the entire century, against us who have not had one moment of tranquility, employ whatever means of destruction the satanic genius of arms has created to reduce the life of our overseas possessions to debris and piles of cadavers. This type of anarchism is worse than that of the fanatic or of the ruffian; this anarchism is a thousand times more criminal, and those who permit it will never have any reason to oppose the popular internal anarchism that tries to take possession of others' property and destroys whatever opposes them in obtaining it.

Today they want to rob from Spain, tomorrow, together with three or four powerful nations, they will rob from England; Holland will lose their island possessions in so far as Germany and Russia have a fancy for them; as Texas fell to the power of Yankee avarice, Mexico and Central America will fall and no one will be able to say they were surprised or fooled because the conduct of the United States with us today enlightens us as to the new international law that has legitimized robbery, sanctioned by the major powers by not opposing it; and upon beginning the twentieth century, after so much progress in the manifestation and practice of law, the effect will be that humanity has regressed to the age of Attila, and that what is actually beginning is the age of the barbarian.

And aroused by this barbarity we will concentrate all of our energy, or all our life, all our thought, the supreme ideal of Spain, in arming ourselves more and more every day in condensing anger and hate in our breasts and in taking revenge . . .

. . . The Yankees have added a vulgar fanfare to the customary Anglo-Saxon informality. For them the conquest of the Philippines, of Cuba and of Puerto Rico was a matter of song and dance. In Washington they had arranged to their liking the division of our colonies in both the new and the old world. Manila would be taken in three days, the Archipelago in twenty; governors and commodores, generals and administrators were ready in San Francisco, California, to present themselves at the edge of the Pasig

[river flowing through Manila] and erase the marks of our domin-
ion to the last footprint. Thirty expeditions of broken-down
Cubans and Yankees bolstered by three hundred cannons would
land and in eight days take Havana, Matanzas, Cienfuegos and
Santiago, with the help of Máximo and Calixto. One month is
about to be completed since the declaration of war, yet the marine
landing has not occurred, neither have Máximo or Calixto appeared. The program has become wet; it must be put out to dry,
and as long as the bad weather from the cannons of Cuba and
Puerto Rico blows on the coast postponing its completion to a
later date, and requiring the forces to regroup for a more propitious occasion, which the committees of Tampa and New York
will decide, we will see if the separatist rabble finds it more worthwhile in the next hundred years to fight face to face with our
troops. . . .

La Ilustracion Espanola y Americana, June 8, 1898.

One more very particular fact has attracted our attention
these days. The arrival of telegrams from diverse foreign capitals
that advise us to ask for peace by means of some neutral power
from Mr. McKinley, who declared war on us and who, according
to the telegrams would be willing to end this war if we would
agree to give Puerto Rico to the United States, give Cuba her
independence with a protectorate, and allow other foreign powers
to resolve the question with respect to the Philippines: this is
essentially what he proposes. Why all this? For the simple reason
that it is the most convenient to our enemies and to the tranquility
of the world, as those nations who feel themselves bothered would
no longer be disturbed. We refuse to injure any Spaniard by agree-
ing to such a foul idea: from the offices in North America they
ordered us, and their President suggested that we renounce completely our authority in Cuba and withdraw our land and naval
forces from that ancient possession. We have been even more
offended by the question of the generous blood spilled in Cavite,
the capture of peaceful merchant ships before the formal declaration of war, the unwarned bombardment of our cities, the use of
our flag to attack us, and the use of forbidden projectiles. There-

fore, it is not necessary to ask for peace by reason of gratitude. Will we ask for it by reason of fear? We were either unafraid or very ashamed when we rejected, come what may, many lesser suggestions. And since then, what has occurred aside from the matter of Cavite, which is the beginning of an uncertain entry? Until the time of this writing, their squadrons have been set back and damaged in Cardenas, Matanzas, Cienfuegos, Guantanamo, Santiago de Cuba and Puerto Rico. We are the attacked and the insulted, not the conquered who must accept intolerable conditions.

That disgraceful peace would only be acceptable after terrible disasters that would prove us to be helpless. It is up to McKinley, who expelled us from Cuba, to make his threat effective, to close our ports with his squadrons and to conquer our soldiers: until now his famous peaceful intervention has only managed to augment what evils there are in Cuba and to spread them to the other islands; our batteries in Spain and the Antilles are solid, and the hearts that defend it are full of fire. Are we to betray all these by proclaiming them powerless? Who is this imbecile who still speaks of such a shameful thing?

If we should do this, within ten years we would say goodbye to the Canary islands, soon to the Baleares and soon we would be exiled from Africa . . . as this is the fortune of those people who do not know how to defend themselves. As long as Spain is strong and hard, other nations, even those that are strong, will think twice before daring to oppose us. If not for patriotism, or loyalty, then simply for mercantile reasons we must defend our rights.

TOKYO. *The Japan Times,* **April 26, 1898.**

Editorially the *Kokumin* is the only metropolitan journal which has taken up the Hispano-American hostilities, since the severance of diplomatic relations between the two countries. Says our contemporary, it will be impossible to pass judgment on the conduct of the two powers for having precipitated the present rupture; but geographically Cuba is to the United States as

Tsushima or Iki is to this country, and prolonged disorders in the island cannot but be harmful to the interests of the American Republic. On the other hand, however, Spaniards may attribute the prolongation to American filibustering and the moral assistance which Americans are extending to the rebels. Indeed in his last message to Congress, ex-President Cleveland declared that America did regard the rebels as belligerents; but that if Spain so wished, the United States might negotiate for the purchase of Cuba. The message further intimated that the United States should insist on Spain's granting autonomy to the island, and that America should see that this was done; but if Spain failed to restore order even after this the United States would be obliged to resort to a decisive step. Subsequently Spain introduced some reform on the island but this action only ended in eliciting ridicule of the rebels and was able to effect nothing. Instead, things grew more complicated, until as the upshot of all, America had to send the ultimatum, which on Spain's noncompliance became the immediate cause of hostilities. Coming to the conduct of the Cuban campaign, our contemporary is rather severe on Spain. She has plunged the poor island into great misery, and after sending over an army of 200,000 troops, she has not succeeded in quelling the rebellion of 40,000 men, thus betraying her utter incompetency. . . . Then on the side of the Americans there may be some who have been inciting the rebels to resistance with the hope of first securing independence for the island and then annexing it to the Union. Nevertheless, thinks our contemporary, Spain is altogether behind the times in her colonial policy, regarding all her dependencies as so many sources of revenue for the home government. Her administration in Cuba in consequence has been one of tyranny, and it was only her deserts to have invited American interference. On the whole the *Kokumin* expresses itself in favor of annexation by the United States.

The Japan Times, **May 12, 1898.**

Next to the continental question, the Philippine situation, thinks the *Nippon,* has the most important bearing on the peace of Eastern Asia. It will be an easy work for Americans to subjugate the whole group, in the present circumstances, but the journal does not believe that the Republic would care to retain but a small portion of it. As for the remaining portion, our contemporary doubts whether it will consent to remain under Spanish rule as soon as it becomes aware of the really helpless condition of the Iberian Kingdom. That the revolutionists who may then rise will succeed in establishing a successful government again appears problematical to our contemporary, and the natural sequel to such an event, it thinks, will be interference on the part of European Powers, such as France, Russia, and Germany. Should the turn of affairs take such a course, it will immediately become another cause for the disturbance of the peace in these parts. In case of interference, the journal would not like to see the group come under German or Russian or French control, while in case of a partition, it wants Japan to be right on the spot with watchful eyes.

Topic 18

THE REVOLUTION IN PANAMA

1903

According to the Hay-Herrán Treaty, passed by the United States Senate in March 1903, Colombia would receive $10,000,000 together with a $250,000 annuity for a six-mile-wide strip of land across Panama to be used for building a canal. Accustomed to years of discord and tension, particularly on the canal issue, Colombia rejected the treaty in August by a vote of 24 to 0 and requested more money. Anxiety increased in Panama as reports indicated that an alternative canal route through Nicaragua would be selected. On October 30, five days before the revolution, the U. S. S. Nashville received orders to prevent the landing of armed forces and to seize the Panama railroad in case of an insurrection. Through efficient planning revolutionary leaders, including the French entrepreneur, Philippe Bunau-Varilla, brought about independence, gained recognition from the United States, and secured a new treaty by November 18. In 1921, the United States Senate approved a treaty granting Colombia $25,000,000; in return, Colombia recognized the independence of Panama.

LONDON. *The Times,* **November 5, 1903.**

A revolution against the Colombian Government has broken out at Panama. There is nothing surprising in the fact itself, nor would it have been likely to arrest attention on this side of the Atlantic were it not for the close relations with the United States into which this South American republic has been brought by the negotiations as to the Isthmian Canal, and for the influence which any political convulsion within its borders may exercise upon the fate of that momentous scheme. Any European State might reasonably expect to settle down to peace and quietness for a long period after such a condition of things as has lately been prevailing in Colombia, but the South Americans know no lassitude. A Colombian envoy who appeared in the United States last month with instructions for the representative of his republic there, admitted naively that his fellow-countrymen had just finished 37 months of war; and whether this was an accurate estimate or not, there is no doubt that last year the Colombians kept up a lively turmoil of intestine discord, which fairly challenged comparison with that indulged in by the Venezuelans beyond the frontier. There have been signs of late that fresh trouble was brewing in Central America. . . . The United States Government, our New York correspondent tells us, has been long aware that a revolt was impending in Panama, with the object of severing it from the Colombian Republic. Now the revolutionists have proclaimed the independence of the Isthmus, thrown the Colombian officials at Panama, naval and military, into prison, and proclaimed a Government consisting of three Consuls and a Cabinet. A similar rising seems to have been projected at Colon, on the other side of the Isthmus, but the town appears to be at present either in the hands of the Colombian Government troops or of American marines landed from the gunboat Nashville. The only fighting so far reported is the bombardment of Panama by the Colombian warship Bogotá, which has resulted in the death of eleven Chinamen. No notice was apparently given of what was going to happen, and the United States Consul has been instructed to protest against the violation of the rights of war.

Colombia seems to have brought the revolution on her own head by her wanton procrastination in the matter of the Isthmian Canal Treaty. A good many Colombians were no doubt opposed to the treaty, partly because they did not understand its terms and partly because they may have feared that it heralded an encroachment of American power. But the people of Panama themselves seem to have supported the scheme, their interests being, as our New York correspondent points out this morning, really American and not Colombian. The Canal Treaty was ratified by the United States Senate as long ago as March 17. Ratification at Bogotá was still required, but ever since Colombia seems to have been doing all she could to avoid that consummation. The actual position at present is by no means clear, but the period within which the Colombian Congress might take affirmative action with regard to the Canal Treaty has expired without result, while the amendments to the treaty made by the Colombian Senate demand, among other things, more than double the price agreed upon in the original agreement. Colombia, in fact, has been frankly obstructing, and there seems every justification for our correspondent's remark that she tried to blackmail the United States, on the one hand, and the French Panama Company, whose rights the United States have bought, on the other. She appears, however, to have reckoned without her host, in the shape of the people of Panama themselves. The revolution may take the decision as to whether Colombia will have an Isthmian Canal or not out of her hands, by simply severing Panama from the rest of the Republic on the South American mainland. Even if it should fail in its main purpose, it may so far succeed as to force the hand of the Colombian Government and oblige it to accept the treaty, and to accept it at its original valuation.

Besides her prospective interests in the peace of the Isthmus as a builder of the canal, the United States is, by the treaty of 1846 with New Granada, under an obligation to preserve tranquility and protect traffic there, and she still, we are told, recognizes this obligation as binding. American warships have consequently been ordered to proceed both to Panama and Colon with a view to protecting the railway and maintaining free transit across the Isthmus. The Admiral commanding the American Pacific squadron has been ordered to hold his vessels in readiness, and there is much activity at Washington. The attitude of the United States Government is studiously correct. American naval officers are enjoined to protect American interests at all points and do everything possible to avoid bloodshed. The revolutionary Government has not been recognized at Washington. But, though the Americans of course abstain from assisting the rebellion, they are not likely to go out of their way to range themselves on the side of Colombia. The presence of their warships may act as a check upon the progress of hostilities, though a good deal will depend upon the spirit in which the American officers interpret the general language of their instructions. If it is a fact that Colombia only has a force of 300 troops or less upon the Isthmus, the revolutionaries ought, at least in the early stages of the rising, to have matters more or less their own way and to obtain possession of the province of Panama with little bloodshed. Should they succeed in doing so, the Colombian Government will probably find it difficult to reconquer their refractory department, with its population completely hostile to the policy of their rulers in Bogotá. The revolution, which at first sight only seems to interpose one more barrier to the realization of the Canal treaty, may in the end secure the great waterway for Panama.

MEXICO CITY. *El Imparcial*, **November 4, 1903.**

We have just received notice that the Republic of Colombia . . . suffered a grave revolutionary movement with the result that independence of the Isthmian Republic has been declared under the name of "Republic of Panama."

The news has caused an indescribable sensation in Mexico, certainly in the Americas, and especially in Latin America. Not only is it a matter of a formidable revolution, which unfortunately has bloodied the Colombian ground; but also the notice has come in a manner absolutely unexpected. Unfortunately, similar news relating to countries of Latin origin in America are quite common.

However, in this movement, which has just profoundly affected the entire hemisphere, there are circumstances which have given it an importance of the first order in regard to the historic events of the era. It is not just a pronouncement among the long list of rebellions; it is not one of the frequent uprisings to overthrow a weak government. It is so much more. It is a prologue to a great drama which will end more or less in a definite division of the Spanish American Republic.

. . . the wealth of Colombia remains unexploited. The majority of the four million inhabitants, poorly productive, are dedicated to the questions of politics. Colombia's territory, somewhat less than that of the Mexican Republic, remains virgin. The continual revolutions impede the development of industry, which could be a primary fountain of strength. Likewise, due to the same causes, the financial situation has reached an extreme state.

. . . If the Colombian people had not been devoured by revolutionary rage; if the Colombian politicians had been more capable and their patriotism less warlike and more practiced, they would have conceded to the matter of the Panama Canal the tremendous importance that in reality it has. They would have understood the situation, calculated the interests placed in perspective to the problem and they would have tried to find a convenient solution for everyone, but especially for Colombia.

But, far from any such consideration, the people in revolution and the government involved in its own defense have ignored the problem, left it unsolved to a point where its solution is going in a manner quite tragic for the Colombian nation.

Undoubtedly, the origin of the revolution of the Isthmus lies in the question of the canal. The Colombian Parliament definitely rejected the treaty, through which the United States compromised in order to build the Panama Canal; an act, of course, that will be of primary benefit to American commerce, to Colombia and principally to the Isthmus region, which with the building and the subsequent traffic will receive a considerable growth.

On the rejection of the treaty, the Colombian Government has hurt several interests, among them those of the people of the Isthmus, who in revenge have decided that they owe no obedience to a government that has hurt their interests, and they have proclaimed themselves independent with the objective of negotiating the treaty themselves.

How will the drama unfold? It is difficult to be precise. However, Colombia, its government drained by its previous revolutions, and by the operations of parliament; without foreign credit, . . . not . . . able to stop the uprisings in spite of the fact that they were a logical consequence of the circumstances; finds it difficult to suffocate this revolution in its cradle. Moreover, the fact that the United States has recognized the provisional government of the Isthmus can be said to cut, once and for all, the union between that region and the rest of Colombia.

PARIS. *Le Temps*, November 8, 1903.

It could well be . . . that the conditions placed with a rough and awkward covetousness by the Congress of Bogotá on the acceptation of a treaty without which the canal will never be achieved had brought to a climax the measure of irritation and provoked the rebellion that just triumphed. The Colombian legislators apparently imagined that they could indefinitely pull on the cord, that they had the good end, that the United States and the French Canal Company would give in on all points and the only thing necessary was to formulate the demands. They just learned, at their expense, what such politics can cost.

It is here that the action of the government of Washington fatally intervened. In spite of an attitude full of serenity and dignity that it observed following the recent vote of the Congress of Bogotá, the United States, after the long and difficult efforts it had exerted to get its program sanctioned by the two Houses of Congress, had nonetheless faced a serious check.

It seemed equally difficult that President Roosevelt and Secretary of State Hay should accept without stumbling this defeat, that they should raise the price on their propositions and that they should find a way of making their project at Bogotá triumph.

It is not in Europe that the idea was born according to which, at the bottom of the events of the Isthmus, there could be the secret spring of a sort of American complicity. Even in New York, *The Times* and the *Herald* have expressed from the first day their suspicions in this regard with an incomparable candor.

It is fitting, doubtless, not to lose sight of the fact that people have often accused these newspapers—like certain Senators and members of [the] federal Congress—of being the organs of interests opposed to the completion of the Panama Canal—whether they represent the rival line through Nicaragua, or whether they serve the interests of transcontinental railroad companies threatened in their lucrative transportation advantages. Thus one should only attach a mediocre value to their imputations if two types of accompanying action did not seem by nature to confirm them.

The role of the *Nashville* in the troubles of Panama has been assuredly in conformity with the obligations of the navy of a civilized State, which must intervene in that case, even by force, in order to protect the life and property of its nationals. Admiral Glass and his squadron [and] the movements of this naval division seemingly give credence to the hypothesis of familiarity with the designs of the revolutionaries of the Isthmus that only a gift of prophecy—to which the federal government does not pretend—or a preliminary proposition similar enough to a complicity would explain.

Whatever the case may be, the cabinet of Washington acted quickly in recognizing the new Republic and its provisional government, in making it known in Bogotá and in counseling the unfortunate Colombians, awakened from their golden dream, to a most prompt and complete resignation. Whatever judgment one can try to make on the operation itself, one must affirm that it is a task well done and properly expedited.

The governments of Europe—who are not offended . . . have kept from taking . . . an attitude that could shock the susceptibilities of the United States without tending the wounds of Colombia. They are preoccupied before everything else with the completion of this canal, the great work of civilization that will cost not only hundreds of millions, but also weighty crises in the old and new world, individual catastrophies and dismemberments of States.

Le Temps, November 13, 1903.

. . . Colombia cannot be under any illusions. Everything indicates that Mr. Bunau-Varilla, minister of Panama whose powers are many and regular, is going to obtain the opening of negotiations with the commissioners announced by the Isthmus and that this will reinforce his mandate.

No one knows if they will estimate that the treaty of Hay-Herrán holds good or if it is necessary to renew it. In any case, they think that there is no turning back on deeds already done, and that the best thing for Colombia is to resign herself to a result that her political folly made necessary, at least as much as the combinations of diplomacy and big business have been able to make it possible.

It is not the explosion at Bogotá of troubles without doubt natural but inopportune, nor the demonstrations directed against the residence of President Marroquin and of his family that will give to the Colombian Republic the prestige and moral force that she is not able to do without, not even to succeed in the insane and bold adventure of reconquering with her army a region that wants no more to do with her and whose independence is protected by a great power, in the name of great cosmopolitan interests, but simply in order to subsist and escape from the process of deadly decomposition.

Between this Republic in decadence, divided against itself, reduced to her resources alone, and a State maintained by the United States and by the complicity of the interests of international commerce, a contest is not and could not be equal.

Topic 19

THE INAUGURATION OF WOODROW WILSON

1913

The election of 1912 found the loyalty of the Republican party split between their candidate, President William Howard Taft, and their former leader, Theodore Roosevelt. After Roosevelt lost his party's nomination to Taft, he became the nominee of the new Progressive party. Woodrow Wilson, born in Virginia in 1856, a graduate of Princeton and Johns Hopkins (where he received his Ph.D.), and first nonclerical president of Princeton, became governor of New Jersey in 1911. Considered a conservative Democrat, Wilson won his party's nomination on the forty-sixth ballot.

Wilson and Roosevelt both campaigned as progressive candidates; while their platforms did not differ greatly, their personalities and campaigning certainly did. Roosevelt, with great emotion, reminded his audiences of their great heritage and the vigorous life, while Wilson spoke calmly of new horizons and freedoms for America.

The only man with an earned doctorate to win the presidency, Wilson received 42 percent of the popular vote; Roosevelt, 27 percent; Taft, 23 percent; and three other candidates shared the remaining 8 percent. The electoral votes went overwhelmingly to Wilson: 435 to Roosevelt's 88, and Taft's 8. Democrats won both houses of Congress as well. The election, a pivotal one for the

*twentieth century, brought the Democratic party into the mainstream
of endorsing domestic reform and international leadership.*

MEXICO CITY. *El Imparcial,* **March 4, 1913.**

The triumph of Wilson marks the victory of the democratic
interests in the entire country. There are Democratic majorities
in the governments and legislatures of most of the States and in
the Senate. A radical change has been initiated both internally and
externally in the United States.

Through his authorship of six or eight works of history, economics, pedagogy and politics, Wilson has become well known as
a serene historian and a wise jurist. His works on economics,
politics and sociology are being used as texts in several professional
schools; his political works have an unusual importance and are
superior to others of their kind. He is, moreover, a member of
a great number of political, scientific as well as educational
organizations.

Since the beginning of the election campaign last year, comments have been made regarding Wilson's affability and smile.
Beneath that smile is an educated, mature and disciplined man.
Already well known are his rare energy and a high standard of
principles, qualities which have astounded and even alarmed his
fellow politicians, for he is a man not guided by private interest,
a man who does not seek consultation once he is convinced of a
solution that he feels must be carried out.

The simplicity of his habits, his scholarly ideas and his reserved
character make him less appealing to the traditionalists. Since
his election he has caused a series of surprises in the American
political and social world. He began by clearly rejecting a sacred
custom and announced who would be his cabinet members. Later
he declared that he was going to dispense with the inaugural ball,
a traditional ceremony held at the White House. He insisted on
this despite the protests and astonishment of Washington social
circles.

He has caused other surprises, which indicate that the future
character of his administration is not at all bound to the elements

of tradition. Instead it is evident that there is a radical element in the hands of this sincere, energetic and powerfully talented man; a man of great ability, upright, and with ideas and principles, unknown in our times.

TOKYO. *The Japan Times,* March 4, 1913.

Today Dr. Woodrow Wilson will enter his great office as the President of the United States of America. With an area of over 3,700,000 square miles and a population of more than 100,000,000, with its exchequer overflowing and its diplomatic counsels received with respect everywhere in the world, the United States of America has never been so great as it is today. And to stand at the head of affairs in that great country—to be the sovereign, in all but name, of that country, if for only a limited term of years—is a very high honor indeed, and it carries with it a great responsibility.

While all the world congratulates President Wilson, it will be with the greatest interest that other countries will observe the lines of policy the new President will follow in regard to some of the great pending questions in which the United States is concerned. The question of the regulation of trusts, on which the new President is expected to take a strong stand, is entirely an internal one and does not directly concern other countries. But there are certain great questions—the independence of the Philippines, the Panama Canal tolls, Navy expansion and tariff revision—to which other countries cannot be indifferent. It is concerning these and similar other questions that their interest and curiosity are aroused.

To the independence of the Philippines, the Democratic party is pledged by its past declarations. The instant the report of Democratic victory in the presidential election reached the Philippines, there was great rejoicing in the islands. At one time Dr. Wilson was reported to have expressed himself in favor of giving immediate independence to the islanders. But that report has never been verified. President Taft was recently reported to have expressed himself in favor of the continuance of the present regime in the Philippines on the ground that the inhabitants are not yet ready for complete independence. It is a question of time. The Republicans are also pledged to give independence when the conditions of the islands make it safe to give complete freedom from American control. President Taft has advised his successor in office to be guided by the opinions of the civil administrators of the islands, who were all strongly opposed to the immediate withdrawal of American control. The very fact that America has already spent hundreds of millions of dollars on the islands—in building a magnificent harbor, in constructing railways, of which not a mile existed when they passed under American suzerainty, in making sanitary provisions throughout the territory, and in opening schools that are now attended by 520,000 children [sic]. The Democrats opposed the annexation of the Philippines at the time, but after fifteen years of American occupancy, during which so many valuable undertakings have been commenced and so great an amount of money, both national and private, has been invested in undertakings, the situation is apparently very different. We doubt very much, even with Mr. Bryan in the State Department, whether America will give immediate independence to the islands. But something will doubtless be done to reassure the Filipinos that the United States Government will keep its original pledge of giving them independence.

In regard to the Panama Canal tolls question, we are already informed that Dr. Wilson has expressed himself in favor of Senator Root's proposed revision, which aims at removing all cause of grievance to Great Britain. In the meantime the British Government has sent a second letter to the United States Government further explaining its position. It is not impossible that with President Wilson's strong approval, Senator Root's proposal may after all be accepted by the Senate. If not, we believe that the American Government will agree to some form of arbitration, so that this vexatious question will be disposed of in a way honorable to both countries.

What will be the outcome of the present disagreement between the Senate and the House of Representatives in regard to the Navy, it is difficult to forecast. It will probably end in some kind of compromise. That the Democratic House of Representatives is determined to essentially reduce the ambitious scheme of navy expansion formed under the Republican regime, there is little room for doubt. There is no country which has hostile designs against the United States, and we believe the Democrats will be wise if they carry out their more peaceful policy. Another question and one of immense difficulty, because of the great complexity of interests involved, will be the revision of the tariff. It is believed that President Wilson will convene an extra session of Congress for the purpose. How far he will succeed in fulfilling the pledges of his party for a tariff for revenue only remains to be seen. That there will be a general lowering of the rates there is no doubt. Japan will benefit thereby if not directly, at least indirectly, in her great trade with the United States.

That President Wilson will succeed on the whole in carrying out his peaceful policies seems assured from his reputation for wisdom, decision, and high purpose. In his noble efforts, the new President will certainly have the sympathy of the peoples in this part of the world.

LONDON. *The Times*, March 4, 1913.

On March 4 Dr. Woodrow Wilson assumes the presidency of the United States. It is recognized on all hands that his task will be one of surpassing difficulty. "We stand," he said not long ago, "in the presence of an awakened nation impatient of partisan make-believe." Yet if ever there was a party that is a party only in name, it is the Democrats. They are disorganized by years of opposition and erratic leadership. They have been brought into office not by the championship of some great cause, but by the mistakes of their opponents. It was doubtful until the last moment whether they would fight the recent campaign on a Conservative or Radical platform, under Radical or Conservative leadership. They have been handicapped during the last decade by a curious mixture of settled traditions and empiricism. Thrice they enlisted under Mr. Bryan's Radical banner; but when Mr. Roosevelt adopted many of the mottoes with which the banner was emblazoned they fought his proposals as the champions of states' rights and the Constitution. Since the Republican party broke over the tariff, hope of victory and of place has been their only real bond. That bond no longer exists. There are today Democrats as protectionist as the average Republican, as well as revenue-tariff Democrats. There are even a few Imperialist Democrats, though the bulk of the party are what at home would be "Little Englanders." Some Democrats would be happier in the company of Mr. Roosevelt; others are in essential sympathy with the political philosophy of the "bosses."

. . . The new Administration will, moreover, be confronted with difficulties that were spared to the Republicans. Since last the Democrats were in power the United States have assumed imperial and foreign responsibilities. External affairs are no longer dismissed in a casual passage of the annual presidential message. There is a general feeling that the days of self-centered isolation have gone. There is even an advanced school which thinks that the United States cannot afford to remain forever indifferent to the great issues of European politics. The Democrats have made no official effort to modernize their old conception of foreign policy, which is, in effect, that the United States shall have no foreign policy. They have opposed every forward movement that the Republicans have been forced to make. The Spanish war left the nation with extra-American obligations. The Democrats fought their assumption. They would, if they could, have set Cuba adrift without a lesson in self-government. They will enter office . . . pledged by their platform to grant independence to the Philippines. A bill is before Congress to free the islands eight years hence. While criticized for obvious reasons even by some of the more enlightened Democrats, it is clear that with Dr. Wilson's support it can pass. If Dr. Wilson is faithful to his platform he will lose caste with responsible opinion; if he is faithless, he will make enemies within his party.

Mexico may present an even more urgent problem. The average American, though he dislikes the idea, admits that in the last resort it will be "up to" the United States to intervene. Nevertheless, since civil strife broke out, Democratic politicians in Congress have deprecated intervention as contrary to American tradition. It may be the same with Cuba and some of the Central American Republics. There are around the Caribbean Sea half a dozen countries where the sword may at any moment be substituted for the ballot. The belief grows that ultimately the United States will be forced to become at least their suzerain. It is argued that it would be impossible to tolerate a zone of chronic unrest so near the Panama Canal. It is feared that if the United States refuses to intervene at the appropriate moment some foreign Power may be compelled either to collect the debts or protect the persons and property of its nationals. If that were allowed to happen, there would not be much left of the Monroe Doctrine. Hence, Mr. Taft's proposals to refund the debts of Honduras and Nicaragua, placing the custom houses under the control of American officials so as to secure loans advanced by American bankers. The idea was simultaneously to satisfy European bondholders and to render politics more stable by neutralizing the customs, the receipts of which are in those countries often almost the only thing that makes a revolution worthwhile. The Democrats in the Senate killed the requisite treaties. It was argued that they contravened the tradition that the United States should not meddle in the affairs of foreign countries. There was opposition to the Government's "turning bagman" and using diplomacy to place and secure the money of New York bankers. It had been the same in regard to the Government's support of the American group in the "Six Powers" loan negotiations with China, though, luckily for Mr. Knox, Congress never had a chance of interfering.

Dr. Wilson will have, in fact, to adapt the principles of the nineteenth century to meet what many Americans call the "manifest destiny" of the twentieth. It is not only that he may at any moment be confronted with a situation which will require the prompt sacrifice of party policy to national prestige. The Panama Canal would not, from the selfish point of view, have been worth building, the Monroe Doctrine would not be worth maintaining, had they not the sanction of an economic necessity. The United States are yearly becoming less self-sufficient. They already need markets for their manufactures and are reaching abroad for food supplies. Their foreign policy consequently grows less idealistic and more material. The Monroe Doctrine is no longer a vague declaration of independence for the Western Hemisphere against European political institutions. It is primarily a declaration of

American trade ambitions. To put it differently, its defensive value is military rather than political—a safeguard for the Panama Canal, which symbolizes commercial Pan-Americanism. It is the same in regard to the Far East. Idealism about the "open door" is yielding to a definite policy of financial adventure. The United States, in a word, are determined to secure betimes the share that they deem they may need in the division of the world's markets. From the European, and especially from the British, point of view, the importance of this change cannot be overestimated. The Canadian reciprocity project, the entry of Americans into the South American meat trade, the invasion of England by the American motor car, the ubiquitous activities of the Standard Oil Company and of other producing establishments, are all symptoms of the tendency that has during the last decade forced the Republican party to adopt something more than a negative foreign policy.

In domestic affairs . . . there is a somewhat similar process of transition. The United States are undergoing a kind of twentieth-century socioindustrial revolution. As at home, there is a tendency to look to the Government for help. There is a demand, and a logical demand, for an increase in Federal power. The Democrats are by tradition a party of individualism. The old Jacksonian party has been rightly called an individualistic democracy. So, too, the Democrats are the champions of states' rights. In the sixties the majority of them fought for the right of states to leave the Union; since then they have constantly opposed in practice the extension of the authority of Washington. Yet the social welfare calls for a measure of Federal paternalism, and business itself admits the need for more comprehensive Federal regulation. So far as can be gathered, the average Democrat is hardly better aware of this than he is of the need for a clear-cut and decisive foreign policy. It is a case of new wine in an old bottle, and to Dr. Wilson will fall both the making of the wine and the patching of the bottle. . . .

The President-elect has thus not only to formulate a comprehensive policy, but to keep his party in line behind it. He will have to steer a middle course. Too much Radicalism would drive his Conservative followers into revolt. Business would be alarmed, and "hard times," with their almost inevitable political results, might follow. Too much Conservatism would tend to produce a repetition of the Republican fiasco under Mr. Taft. Nor have the Democrats only to keep their stock at a better figure than that of the Republicans. They are confronted by a third party flaunting a definite social and political programme concocted with especial reference to the "spirit and needs of the times," and led by the man who more than any one else has taught his countrymen to think about the changing needs of the new century.

. . . In all phases of national life the next few years promise to be of the greatest interest and importance. The last of the old parties is on trial. If it fails it is at least possible that the last of the links that bind the country to the old order of government under a rigid Constitution and its attendant traditions will have been snapped. Small wonder, therefore, that a revelation of Dr. Wilson's policies and political capabilities is awaited with the utmost tension. Never has a President-elect so successfully kept his own counsel. Beyond the fact that he had reiterated his intension to be "progressive," he remains with his Cabinet the only unknown quantity in a situation the difficulties of which are manifest.

Topic 20

THE UNITED STATES DECLARES WAR

1917

When war broke out in Europe in July and August 1914, the American government adopted a policy of neutrality, although many public figures expressed sympathy and support for the Allies (notably England, France, and Russia) rather than the Central Powers (Austria-Hungary and Germany). In the first months which followed, President Woodrow Wilson and his Secretary of State, William Jennings Bryan, maintained a studiously correct neutral posture. However, as German submarines began torpedoing merchant and passenger vessels and American lives were lost as in the sinking of the British liner, Lusitania, *in May 1915, Wilson demanded, sought, and eventually obtained commitments from the German government that she would abandon unrestricted submarine warfare. Bryan resigned at this time for he feared that Wilson's demands might take the United States into the war. During the remainder of 1915 and through 1916, relations between the United States and the Central Powers remained strained, while commerce between America and the Allied Powers expanded at an astonishing rate.*

In January 1917, German military leaders made the decision to achieve victory more swiftly by resuming unrestricted submarine warfare. In early February, Wilson broke off diplomatic relations with Germany. On March 1, the State Department released the details of an intercepted diplomatic note from the German foreign secretary, Alfred Zimmermann, to the German Minister in Mexico urging that in the event the United States declared war on Germany, Mexico should join the German cause and reconquer her former territory in Texas, New Mexico, and Arizona. The note also urged Mexico to encourage Japan to switch from the Allied Powers to the Central Powers. Tension, war fever, and the loss of additional American lives at sea continued during March. On April 2, Wilson, in a message to Congress, called for a declaration of war. The Senate (82 to 6) approved on April 4, and the House (373 to 50) on April 6; Wilson signed the joint congressional resolution that same day. (On December 7, the United States declared war against Austria-Hungary.) The crusade by the United States to make the world safe for democracy entered its violent stage.

MEXICO CITY. *Excelsior,* **April 6, 1917.**

The foreign newspaper that we have just read fully confirms the effort put forth by the German Government concerning Count Bernstorff's arrival at an alliance with Mexico and Japan should the United States enter the war. . . .

. . . German diplomacy shows itself as misinformed regarding Mexico during the present conflict, and in its orientation to international politics, Mexico has maintained and maintains a strict neutrality . . . although, being a country of relatively small importance, it cannot help but have its interests in the war divided, feeling sympathy for both sides. It would depart from neutrality if it favored one to the detriment of the other, showing preferences or making distinctions.

. . . Mexico has as its tradition a principle which serves as a base in international affairs, and as a product of the past, strengthens us in the present and will serve us as a guide for the future: the defense of its own law which necessarily brings forth a respect for foreign laws.

. . . Mexico lost those territories [Arizona, Texas, and New Mexico] in an unjust war, in which, once more, rights were conquered by force; but even keeping in mind the injustice, the country has not shown signs of that state of latent hostility which still keeps some people awake at night. We have not cultivated hatred against our conquerors. This also is in view. Have we done well? Have we done badly? Time will tell. But the truth of the matter is that Mexico has never exhibited a desire to revive old conflicts, always keeping in mind the judgment of history.

Given this state of a national conscience—which German diplomacy has not been able to penetrate—the proposal of the imperial government would come to show us, not only in the eyes of the world, but before our own eyes, as being forced by an imperialist desire. But no! Mexico is not an imperialist nation, nor is it spurred on by imperialist sentiments. . . . The annexation of Arizona, New Mexico and Texas, our old provinces—oh, how far spiritually from us—would have all the appearance of a program of conquest so foreign to our national sentiment that we have done well in judging this proposal as absurd. Our peace and our neutrality shake hands. Both serve as a base for our law.

As for the rest, to make New Mexico, Arizona and Texas become part of our national domain—many, many thanks! It would be the raffle of the elephant.

BERLIN. *Neue Preussische Zeitung*, April 4, 1917.

The pretense, which lay over the recent episodes of the apparently self-contradictory policy of America vis-a-vis Germany, is now conclusively revealed in Wilson's war message to Congress. For us, certainly, the speech of the President, which makes war between Germany and the United States unavoidable, is no surprise. Wilson, wanting to have the American people behind him, was only hesitant of going too fast; his will for war was present at any moment. Nothing justifies the assumption that Wilson honestly sought to avoid war; even less the assumption that he has done anything positive to prevent war. The act of breaking off relations with Germany in a moment of ignorance over the submarine question; his attempt, to muster the neutrals against us, advocating for them the policy of "armed neutrality"; the arming of American merchant ships; his announcement to the neutral governments that these ships, without being attacked, would immediately open fire if our submarines revealed themselves—in short, all his actions and proclamations were only pretenses on his way, since the beginning of the war, of adhering to policies which in reality were never neutral, but terminated in prejudice toward Germany and a one-sided, striking support of our enemies. During the entire war Wilson has termed all Germans as wicked enemies: after we took up arms, and our chief foes collapsed from our blows, he treated this collapse as if it were the collapse of all civilization. "Nothing was able," so declared Wilson in the speech, "to change our apprehensions of our lives. There is no more to surrender." Already then it was clear that Wilson's policy, when Germany would not yield on the submarine question, must in the short or long run lead to war. The decision was only a question of time. In the end, Wilson had to resort to the "moralistic" platform, to be able finally to take up arms against us. His war-grounds are not valid, and none of the communicated speech to Congress says anything new; at best, it demonstrates still his prevailing manifestations of insincerity, hypocrisy, and distortion of true facts. Nevertheless, a few of his lies cannot be permitted to remain uncontradicted. When Wilson said that the German government had given the United States a promise in April 1916, it negotiated only a conditional promise—subject to the assumption that America could and would bring England to a cessation of her internationally hostile naval behavior, failing which we would reclaim our freedom of action. Just as much a lie is his assertion that ships of all kinds were sunk without warning—our declaration of the prohibited zone contained a general warning for all in that prohibited zone. Let Wilson stop Ambassador Gerard's insolent diatribes against the Kaiser, which at present he has not, in which he, despite better knowledge, accused the Kaiser of having to affix the war on false grounds. When Mr. Wilson dared to assert that the German government had begun the war without the referendum, knowledge or approval of the people, and that the war is perpetuated by the rulers, provoked and led in the interests of the dynasty and a small group of rulers, it is familiar; calling us tools, the desire is to have his countrymen fall in with the Entente, and not Germany. A contrast between the German government and the German people does not stand the test, and the attempt is not only unserviceable, but shocking. Meddling in the affairs of the German people cannot be repudiated sharply enough. When Congress joins the viewpoint of the President, which cannot be overcome, Germany and the United States will find themselves in a state of war, and therewith will happen what we knew must occur after the resumption of unrestricted submarine warfare, which we have brought about. Whether a declaration of war follows, or whether in the House of Representatives a resolution of a state of war is introduced, without a declaration of war following, is a question of unimportant significance. Contrary to Wilson's interpretation, America has "imposed" the war (it cannot be enjoined that Germany has attacked America); a firm protest must be entered to this distortion of the facts. Germany, in bringing the submarine war against its enemies, has in no way injured the vital interests of America, and this also was evaded, when Wilson insisted on carrying on business dealings with our enemies and on opposing the German blockade with force. Wilson's design, therefore, was to bring about war not over the vital interests of the American people (of which we had no separate, opposing interests) but solely over a questionable point of law, the submarine strategy. This point of view certainly fades more and more into the background in Wilson's war message; meanwhile, he behaves from the first line as the "Champion of Human Rights," and as an ally of our enemies, "to force Germany to accept terms for the conclusion of the war." If Wilson supposes with these terms to bring about negotiations, it is not evident, but still that seems to be the end. "The military situation forces us to accept all results which unrestricted submarine warfare can cause," said the Chancellor in the session of the home commission of the Reichstag on January 31, in anticipation of the state of affairs which at present has commenced. Certainly, we do not underrate the accession of America as the eleventh enemy in the order of our hostile foes, but these facts cannot in any way alter our unshakeable confidence in the happy results of our mighty peoples' cause. The participation of America will exercise no critical effect on the state of the strategic war situation. The arms preparations on the other side of the ocean, the union of the

American navy with those of our enemies, the possibility of the dispatch of an expeditionary force—these can frighten us just as little as the moralistic action of America can exert on the remaining neutral states and on our enemies. America can extend to our enemies no foodstuffs and no supplies; our excellent submarines guarantee this. What the working of support by America to our enemies relates to finally (let it not be misunderstood) [is]: on the one hand, that this rich land through its nearly limitless financial resources has powerfully strengthened the resistance of our enemies, and on the other hand (which we reprimand), that the participation of America in the war, walking next to England as a new, extremely strong member in the ranks of our enemies, will require of us an indemnity of significance.

FRANKFURT. *Frankfurter Zeitung,* **April 7, 1917.**

The war seems like a terrible whirlpool little by little pulling all the people of the globe down into a crater, and the tremendous measures of this occurrence put before our eyes frightening images of the blindness that the deity allows among men, which lives again today. The perceptible motives, the reasons for reaching this view, earlier the treason of the Italians and the Rumanians, [are] now the intervention of America and the hostile attitude of China. One would have thought that a state whose chief and official spokesman has in thousands of solemn declarations made known his love of peace and his sickness over the horror and devastation of this war would permit himself to know no higher aim than to work for the termination of this war, which now has already lasted 32 months. Yet we live to see the great republic across the Atlantic Ocean pouring new oil on the fire of world-conflagration (that he [Wilson] pretended to want to extinguish), thereby increasing this consuming fire. If the reasons should lie this way—and President Wilson as a statesman and spokesman of the Entente gives it this appearance, as if that sufficed for a reason—then it is to be very differently viewed as an attempt to change very significantly us and our national life. Thus, apparently today we would be foolish to believe that a bridge between such opposite positions could again be forged. In reality the reasons are not humanity and justice (which our enemies in this war have put forth), but rather nationalistic passions; aspirations to power; the desire to repress and crush Germany; the inability to understand that we as a great people seek to maintain ourselves, our lives and our customs . . .

This lie [that Germany was the aggressor in the war] has indeed received so universal a currency, that all who march in the ranks of our enemies, have acquired it,—also the last of our enemies, President Wilson, who has decided that America will furnish the Entente with a million soldiers and other requirements of war, and that Germany, through sanctions, is cut off from overseas supplies, which could threaten starvation—he moves with these absurd accusations against us . . .

In America, where the only principles of war that anyone knows are that of bloody profits from war supplies, Wilson and the Congress are laying new fires on the funeral pyre. In Europe all the people are weary of the war. Peace is overdue. When it comes, the present blockade of our enemies will be taken away. But we do not delude ourselves—the sounding horns of the men of war in the Entente are no more than the blaring tones of three months ago. But even though the accession of America should increase their eagerness for the war, we shall succeed.

VIENNA. *Neue Frei Presse*, April 8, 1917.

It will be presented as a war of a democratic people against Germany. The claims which they boast of, the arrangements the democracy has described, are directed against the Central Powers. They want to hoist up a flag, on which is written, "The Entente fights in the name of Freedom." But these men who, day and night, always were led by the hope that their shining light would disperse all darkness, that it could only rejuvenate their country, want no freedom brought by a stranger or a rival. Woodrow Wilson, the oppressor of our allies, worked with the cunning but vain expectation that he could push a weary people to the ground; and presumed that the Central Powers were dependent on the graces of this cruelest conqueror. What an infamous disregard of his opponents by this self-complacent man, who sets himself up today as judge of the world. The arrogance, with which Wilson shifts between the German people and their political leaders, proves that he himself really lacks the deepest comprehension of freedom. It begins with tolerance, with the understanding that in the twentieth century and with this war—as Kaiser Wilhelm says in his communication to the Reichschancellor—a new era has begun, which must result in the public life of each nation being based on its particular character. A freedom, which would rise in Germany and the Monarchy over the smoking ruins of peaceful communities, would be a mockery and a humiliation . . .

The American freedom does not hinder the plundering of peoples' property, or corruption in many branches of the administration and municipal machines, or the exhaustion of poverty and economic horror, as Aristophanes has described the demagogical era of Athens. We do not have the freedom that the packing houses in Chicago have, where meat is prepared for shipment. Upton Sinclair has painted this murderous pit in words, infused with horror, which report on this degenerate democracy. The official silence in a democracy, which passes by with downcast eyes the poisoning of a people, hardly bears imitation in this land, where the sense of honesty has strong roots and where a living conscience remains in business. The American democracy described by Tocqueville is no more . . .

PARIS. *Le Temps*, April 3, 1917.

. . . It is a great date in the history of America [April 2—Wilson's War Message], a great date in the history of humanity. The will not to mix in with the quarrels of Europe dominated the American political scene for more than a century. German violence has been stronger than this will and a new ally comes to our side. Despite the Monroe Doctrine, despite immigration, despite the ties of all kinds which bind the two nations, the political aggression of the Hohenzollerns has obliged a people to go to war who were resolved most firmly to remain neutral and whose leader said less than a year ago: "Too proud to fight."

It is not the moment to specify in detail what this collaboration of America, the general lines of which we have recently indicated, will be. Today it is the moral import of the event which captures the world's attention. Mr. Wilson, from the first day, conducted his politics as a man of law. His impassiveness, his refusal to judge, his fear of sentiment sometimes surprised us. But this attitude itself gives to his present decision the value of a verdict. It is neither the desire for territory, nor nationalist feeling which throws the United States into the war: it is the affirmation methodically established that Germany violated systematically the laws of war and of peace and that her defeat alone can assure the repose and the dignity of peoples.

The Germans, contrary to all truth, were able to accuse us, despite the evidence of the facts, of having desired a war of revenge. History actually showed on our side a painful wound opened by the former aggression. They were able, despite the texts and the strongest certitudes, to impute to Russia, so deeply delivered to their influence, designs which were nonsense. They were able to attribute to an unforeseeing England, who confided the care of her defense to six divisions, the absurd project of crushing their military power formidably accrued for a half-century. They were able, because the intercrossing of European interests awoke the hereditary transmission of conflict where the lie had a good chance. What will they be able to say of America?

The United States only wanted peace. . . . They found through it a guarantee in the situation of their frontiers. The war unchained in Europe through the will of Germany only touched their interest economically. They claimed for the American citizen only these three indefensible rights of neutrals: the right of trade, the right of traffic, and the right to life. They know that the first of these rights is, in war, an awkward exercise and they were ready to defend it through a watchful diplomacy. They know that the two others, even in the least civilized of times, had never been menaced and they feared nothing for themselves of the terrible events which the old world was shaken by.

It belonged to Germany to proclaim at the threshold of the twentieth century the principles of barbarism which past centuries had not known. To all neutrals, to the small as well as the great, it was reserved to them to learn that when Berlin decided the war, there was no longer dignity, nor independence, nor security for anyone in the world. One day across the ocean, there came to the American coasts the cry of the drowned ones of the *Lusitania*— old people, women, children, assassinated by Germany; and if that day, America did not declare war, if more than twelve months have passed before she declared it, her conscience did not wait to condemn irrevocably those whom her armies will fight tomorrow.

When the starry flag of the Union will wave on our battlefields, it will be more than a great military, naval, and financial cooperation that will come to uphold our cause: it will be, anticipating the judgment of history, the decision of the human conscience. As atrocious as was the unpublished horror of it, the heinous offense of the *Lusitania* is not worse in fact than the violation of Belgium or the surprise invasion of our peaceful France. It is the same conception of the relationships between peoples which is affirmed in the one and in the other crime. It is the same amorality which is written in the backwash of the torpedoed liner or in the smoking ruins of burned villages. Here and there, it is always the avid and bloodthirsty Germany, to whom nothing human is accessible and who, deifying her strength, believed herself able to divinize her crimes with the same stroke.

The France of the past formerly fulfilled toward America the duties which her ideals dictated to her. To the United States, which comes today to pay its debt to the same ideal, we offer, at their entrance into the ranks of the soldiers of law, the fraternal salute of a people who have illumined thirty-two months of sufferings in the service of liberty.

Le Temps, April 7, 1917.

. . . The Americans have never forgotten that at two decisive hours of their history, France was for them the friend liberator. They remember that, without the aid of France, the thirteen revolting colonies would without a doubt not have achieved their independence. They know that the day when France offered to the United States the sale of Louisiana, the unity of the newborn Republic achieved its enduring foundation. . . .

. . . If the United States is hereafter on our side, despite the bonds of interest which were formed between Germany and themselves, despite the German immigration, despite their aversion for any intervention in the quarrels of Europe, it is because we are right. President Wilson said it and Congress repeats it after him: it is a question of putting down the natural enemy of liberty. For this effort of public preservation, the most powerful democracy of the world had to, when the hour came, answer: "Present!"

With a refortified zest we are going to pursue our war and hasten the hour of punishment. The fight now has its full meaning. It is no longer the defenders of the right who are fighting against the preying nations. It is the democracies who are leading the game against the despots. France, the United States, Russia, England, Italy—these are the free people, masters of their destinies, who are going to found peace on the ruins of autocracies. Never has a more beautiful sight been offered to the eyes of humanity. Never has the law of progress affirmed itself with more brilliance against the survival of the past.

LONDON. *The Times,* **April 7, 1917.**

We publish today the text of President Wilson's formal declaration of war against the Imperial German Government. It is based upon the resolution which both houses of Congress adopted by immense majorities, and which includes a solemn protest that the struggle has been thrust upon the United States by the repeated acts of war already committed by Germany against their Government and people. The insistence of a handful of pacifists only served to demonstrate the extent and the fervour of the war temper in the legislature and in the nation. It resembles with remarkable closeness the temper in which this country took up the challenge flung down to her by the rape of Belgium. It is in no joyous or lighthearted mood that the Great Republic departs from her oldest and her most cherished traditions and commits herself without hesitation and without reserve to a tremendous conflict in the Old World. She draws the sword reluctantly, as England drew it. Like England, she is not moved by greed, or by ambition, or by hate. One passion only fills her, but it is the deepest and the strongest of all: it is the passion for justice amongst States and peoples which compelled us to stake our all against the would-be oppressors of mankind. We have known from of old, and the Germans have now learnt at our hands, how fierce and how unquenchable is the flame it kindles in the hearts of free nations. That it is this unslaked thirst for right, for law, and for humanity which has forced the United States into war is proved by every word, written or spoken, which reaches us beyond the Atlantic. America has no sordid interests involved; she has not even to think of any immediate menace to her shores, such as the seizure of Belgium by a Great Power would constitute for us. She has come forward to defend the right and to overthrow the wrong. That is what lends its moral greatness to her action. That is our surest pledge that there will be neither stay nor limit to her action until the high end she has set before herself is achieved. There was no hint in the speeches of the majority, or in the measures proposed by the Government, of a "limited war" or of a "peace without victory," and a motion seeking to hamper the dispatch of troops to Europe was at once voted down. By a sure instinct, the speakers did not fasten upon the specific crimes of Germany for denunciation, but upon the spirit and the system from which they spring. It is to deliver the world from Prussian "militarism" that the peaceful Republic, in which so many Germans have sought and have found freedom from all that "militarism" means, now takes her place side by side with the democracies of Europe. The manner in which she will begin to aid them has still to be settled in detail. What is certain is that within the shortest possible time "Prussian-Germany" will have to confront all America's limitless reserves of men, money, and material, combined with those of her present enemies. Her old foes will henceforth be animated by the new and immense confidence which the support of the United States already brings them; her new foes, by a generous rivalry with those who have borne the first and the most terrible burdens for the common cause.

The intervention of America as the champion of right in a European controversy is an event so great in itself, and so pregnant with inscrutable results for the whole world, that it baffles understanding on both sides of the ocean. We feel with Mr. Lloyd George that "at one bound" America has become a world power in a sense in which she has not been a world power hitherto, and we feel with him that she has waited to renounce the advantages, real and fancied, of her historic isolation "until she found a cause worthy of her traditions." She has found that cause, and, with the chivalry and the courage her people have always shown in great crises, she has dedicated herself to it. . . .

TOKYO. *The Japan Times,* **April 14, 1917.**

AMERICA has come in! What a dramatic sound the words have! For weeks it has become a foregone conclusion that the great Republic would sooner or later be drawn into the great European war to make it a veritable world war. But now that she has actually unsheathed the sword, the fact freshly awakens the mind of all to the tremendous international changes the war is working. Albeit her traditional policy of keeping aloof from European quarrels, albeit her time-honored policy of barring entangling foreign alliances, albeit her glorious history of self-contained isolation, America has been forced to throw in her lot with the warring nations on the side of the defenders of civilization, humanity, justice and liberty. The ice has been broken. The great Republic will probably never again be the Republic of Washington and Jefferson. Not that we have not seen America in evidence in the Far East, but Europe in all likelihood will henceforth have to count her in its affairs. This opens a long vista of possibilities, which but for the war would furnish a theme for high flights of imagination. Even as it is, some minds, the moment the American intervention became inevitable, have already turned their thoughts to those possibilities. . . .

The Japan Times, **April 21, 1917.**

When the United States declared war against Germany, it was commonly believed in Japan that the entire wealth of the United States would be used for war expenditure, and she would not be able to make investments in the Orient, and that as the United States will undertake to supply England and France with all necessary war articles, Japan will not be requested to send supplies to the Entente powers. But the "Tokyo Nichinichi" [a newspaper] opines that the situation will be entirely contrary to the above prediction.

While it is not yet known how far the United States will participate in the war, the United States Government has decided to float bonds to the extent of 6,000,000,000 yen, and to send the war supplies to England and France as much as possible. The "Nichinichi" believes that when the United States begins these activities, the industries of the country will make tremendous development and the financial condition of the country will be more favorable than before.

A war is considered by economists to cause unproductive expenditure, but there are often cases when a war has developed industries and commerce on the contrary. Japan is a good example of these rare cases, and while she is participating in the war, her commerce and industries have made unprecedented progress by the effect of the war. The United States also harvested a tremendous profit out of the war, while she remained neutral. When she actually enters the war, she will utilize the accumulated wealth obtained by her trade activity in the past three years.

The "Nichinichi" believes that the participation of the United States will not bring any change to the financial situation of the world. She has supplied the Entente powers with war funds and war articles even while she was neutral, and although she will endeavor to give more assistance to the Entente powers, it will not mean that she will give unlimited support to England and France.

What Japan is doing to help the Entente powers is small, but it is, however, necessary for the Allies, and, despite the supply from the United States, Japan will keep on sending supplies to the European powers.

The possible investment of the United States in China is so small in amount compared with the national wealth of the country that it will not be hindered by her participation in the war. Especially regarding the plan of cooperation between Japan and the United States to develop the Chinese resources, the war will not cause any difficulty. The paper concludes that the participation of the United States in the war will not affect international financial relations.

Topic 21

THE SENATE REJECTS THE TREATY OF VERSAILLES

1919

In January 1918, President Woodrow Wilson delivered his famous Fourteen Points Address to the Congress. Prepared as a statement of war aims, this blueprint for peace listed both specific and general objectives for the postwar world such as the return of Belgium to her people, an independent Poland, and the formation of a general association of nations that would provide large and small nations with assurances of territorial integrity and political independence.

A month after the armistice in November 1918, Wilson sailed to Europe where the French, English, and Italian people welcomed him as the American messiah. The Versailles Peace Conference, under the special direction of the United States, England, France, and Italy, developed plans for ending the war; moreover, Wilson carefully wove a Covenant for a League of Nations into the fabric of the peace treaty. Germany reluctantly signed the treaty in May 1919.

More than two hundred pages in length, the Treaty of Versailles was hotly debated in the American Senate where political bitterness and apprehensions, together with Wilson's stroke and stubbornness, added to growing public weariness. The vote for Senate approval failed on November 19, 1919; the Treaty was rejected a second time in March 1920. Finally, the United States signed separate treaties with Germany, Austria, and Hungary in August 1921, and these met with Senate approval.

PARIS. *Le Temps*, November 11, 1919.

When will one finally know the outcome that the United States Senate reserves to the Treaty of Versailles? Perhaps in a few days; or at the latest in three weeks. . . . At Washington this last phase of battle excites political passions. But this is no reason for us Frenchmen to lose our tempers.

One makes a lot of noise about the "reservations" that the American Senate has started to vote for. To read certain commentaries, it would seem that these reservations really upset the whole treaty. That is an interpretation which perhaps is accorded to the election period but which the facts and the texts do not justify.

First of all, by rejecting the "amendments" and in consenting to vote only some "reservations," the United States Senate has indicated very clearly that it demands no modification of the treaty. It simply wants to register with the Allies the sense the United States attaches to certain clauses, or rather, the conditions under which they will participate in certain measures of execution. If these reservations restrain the scope of the treaty, it is only in theory. In fact they are limited to affirming restrictions which already exist in reality.

According to the first reservation, which is henceforth adopted, the Senate and the House of Representatives will be able to decide by a common accord that the United States is withdrawing from the League of Nations. The two parliamentary assemblies of the United States would therefore have the sovereign power, without referring to the council of the League of Nations, to decide the question of knowing if the United States is fulfilling the conditions necessary to retire; that is to say, if it has acquitted herself of all the obligations imposed by the pact. From the theoretical point of view, this is diminishing the jurisdiction which had been accorded to the council of the League of Nations. But in practice, how would the council hold the United States in the League of

Nations if the American public was in such a frame of mind that the two parliamentary assemblies of Washington could vote the denunciation of the pact?

The next reservation stipulates that if there is an occasion to apply Article 10 of the pact—that which guarantees the independence and the integrity of all the states adhering to the League of Nations—it will be necessary to obtain the authorization of the American Congress before employing the military and naval forces of the United States. Even if this reservation were not formulated, how could one dispense with the authorization which it prescribes? The Constitution of the United States declares black on white that the right to declare war belongs to Congress.

One could make analogous remarks on each of the other reservations proposed to the Senate. The most serious of all, perhaps, is that which allows the United States not to accept for the moment Articles 156, 157, and 158 of the treaty—those which return to Japan the rights that Germany possessed in Shantung. But what is really the situation? China has not signed the Treaty of Versailles. So long as China has not signed, the question of Shantung remains in suspense, since Shantung is a province of China. If the United States reserves provisionally its acceptance, what is changed actually?

Will one say that the Republican majority of the Senate is looking to transform the spirit itself of the treaty? Will one say that the Republican party, which is actually the master of the legislative power in the United States, and which perhaps will be the master of the executive power in sixteen months, wants to ruin the idea of international solidarity on which the whole treaty rests? That again would be an interpretation contrary to what one knows.

In matters of international solidarity, the doctrine of the Republican party has already been enunciated in 1899 by Secretary of State Hay, in the instructions which he gave to the American delegates before the first conference of the Hague. He wrote:

> The duty incumbent on the sovereign states and which consists in making international justice prevail through all the wise and efficacious means, can only be ceded by the fundamental necessity of preserving their own existence. Imme-

diately after their independence, the most important fact is their interdependence.

Nothing can assure to a human government, and to the authority of the law which it represents, a respect as profound and a loyalty as firm as the spectacle offered by sovereign and independent states, whose duty consists in formulating the laws of justice and in punishing the violation of the laws, when they bow with veneration before the august supremacy of these principles of right which give to the law its eternal foundation.

These lines are twenty years old. What is the spirit which inspired them if not the same spirit of international solidarity that the Treaty of Versailles is trying to make prevail?

This is not all. The doctrine of Undersecretary of State Hay has been upheld again in 1910 by one of his successors, a Republican like himself, Mr. Knox. The words of Mr. Knox are the more interesting since he is today one of the Republican members of the Senate. Here is what he said in stating the foreign policies of the United States in a solemn assembly given by the University of Pennsylvania.

We have attained a point where it is evident that the future holds in reserve a time when wars will cease; a time when the nations of the world will realize a federation as real and as vital as the bonds actually existing between the parts composing one same state; a time when, in virtue of an international and deliberate cooperation, the strong will help the weak everywhere.

The role of this country is always to maintain her politics and her historic attitude and to be faithful to her greatest national duty, a duty which entirely accords with all her external duties. This role is to advance the epoch which is portended by the whole course of history as well as by the divine prophecies and all revelations.

As the War of 1914 demonstrated in a tragic manner, this ideal was farther away than Mr. Knox believed it to be in 1910. But did not the horrors of the war give to the recommendations of the Republican Secretary of State a greater price and a greater urgency?

It is then reasonable to hope that the Senate of the United States, in which the Republicans dominate, will want neither to "kill" the treaty nor to disband the League of Nations. And we will do well, in commenting at Paris on the debate at Washington, never to deny these principles of international solidarity which remain alive in our American ally. . . . They are necessary for the security of our country.

LONDON. *The Times,* **November 17, 1919.**

. . . The truth is that the majority of the Senate hold American opinion to be strongly opposed to the assumption of real responsibilities in the Old World. Our Washington correspondent has little doubt that in this they are right, and that their opposition to the Treaty represents the national feeling. It is, as he has often explained, a natural feeling for a community in the stage of political development in which Americans now stand. . . .

We cannot but deplore the situation which has arisen. We deplore it rather for its moral than for its immediately political consequences. We have always shared PRESIDENT WILSON'S conviction that if ever again the aid of the United States is needed to save Europe, that aid will be given, League or no League. But the moral consequences are undeniably serious, and cannot be contemplated without real concern. If America "takes the heart out of the League"—that League which was lately hailed as her chief contribution to the salvation of the world—the Allies will have to regret a loss much more serious than the loss of her material help, invaluable though this would be in securing the settlement which she has done so much to mould. Her example cannot fail to have a very bad effect upon other States and peoples. Many of them, it is to be feared, who would have joined a League of which America was a leading member, might hesitate to join a League which she refused to enter. The whole moral status of the League must be impaired by such a refusal.

. . . If the moral engagements into which the CHIEF EXECUTIVE of the United States entered in the name of the United States are not confirmed, a certain revulsion from American ideals and a certain diminution of American prestige, in the Old World at least, would seem to be inevitable. We should deeply regret such a calamity to the cause of civilization. We decline to draw any positive conclusions from the present situation. We shall hope against hope that rejection and the consequences of rejection may be averted. But it would not be right to conceal from Americans or from ourselves the existence of the considerations to which that situation is giving rise.

. . . There can be little doubt that the Republicans do represent the national instinct. Everything goes to show that a League of the ambitious type established at Paris stands farther along the road of internationalism than Americans with their traditions and training are prepared to go. It would be so even without the distrust bred by a constant advertisement of the flaws in the Treaty, and without the industrial turmoil which so insistently pulls the vision down from the international horizon and, as MR. HOOVER said the other day, tends on account of the part which foreigners are playing in it to create a positive aversion for Europe.

This does not mean that the lessons of the war have been forgotten. The Americans are a practical race. They do not feel it would be sound policy to be committed to a routine of meddling in European affairs. They believe for one thing that such a policy runs in principle counter to their cherished Monroe Doctrine. They fear that it would react in an unhealthy manner upon the assimilation of their polyglot population.

But they are neither a heartless nor a stupid race. They realize they must play their part in smothering offhand the beginning of another world conflagration. They think this can best be done by a policy of intelligent and beneficial isolation, such as was for so long our pride, and by the solidification of the commercial and financial rather than the political world.

It can, for instance, be said with confidence that the credits that Europe needs and that America so far is inclined to hold back, will more likely be forthcoming when the country feels that the Treaty is disposed of and can make a quiet and nonpolitical survey of the reasons which must logically decide it to lend.

The Times, November 21, 1919.

... MR. WILSON was too confident at Paris, too confident on his return home. Instead of trying to propitiate and educate the Senate, he consistently antagonized it by sneering at their attacks. Instead of patiently explaining the League and the Treaty to the people, he took too much the line that they should accept what he deemed good for them. Had he been willing to compromise some months ago, the United States would and might now be a member of the League, subject to reservations which really would not greatly matter.

American reluctance to enter the League unreservedly and to bless a peace settlement whose wisdom they question in many respects is due primarily to causes which we have no right to criticize. The United States is in somewhat the same position towards the Treaty of Versailles as we were towards the Holy Alliance after the Napoleonic Wars. Her tradition and training alike make her doubt the advisability of a routine interference in European affairs. She prefers to continue a policy which corresponds closely to our policy of glorious and beneficent isolation during the last century. The Atlantic, she thinks, is even in the 20th century as broad as the Channel in the 19th.

The idea may be wrong, but it is natural. It does not of necessity connote an unfriendly aloofness from us or any other Power. But there can be little doubt but that its force might have been much weakened had the President been more conciliatory to the Republicans and had he taken more pains to educate both them and public opinion about the broad significance of the changes wrought by the war, and about the impossibility in the circumstances of making a utopian peace settlement.

BERLIN. *Neue Preussische Zeitung,* November 23, 1919.

It has been made known that Wilson will discuss the entire theme of the Peace Treaty of Versailles in a message to Congress on December 1, and until then nothing will be said about the rejections in the Senate. The *New York Times* writes that it is as clear as ever that the American people wish to ratify the Treaty and join the League of Nations. The American people have always wished ratification in a form that is not in contradiction with the Constitution and that does not hinder the nation's freedom of action. In the whole country the aversion is great towards an American intervention in European affairs.

In Wilson's background is the view that direct negotiations between Germany and America are impossible. But so long as no peace is concluded, the resumption of trade relations also remains impossible; also a designation of consuls is unthinkable. The plan of Senator Lodge to let both houses declare that the state of war has ended will likewise be labeled as inadmissible. The Constitution, of course, gives the right to make war and conclude peace to the President [*sic*]. The Supreme Court would also have the right to nullify Lodge's wishful resolution. Wilson himself will probably now turn to the other great powers and discuss with them which reservations he can accede to that would not necessitate a second treatment of the League Constitution.

MEXICO CITY. *Excelsior*, **November 21, 1919.**

President Wilson has died. He has died if not physically, certainly politically: the failure of the Peace Treaty in the Senate chamber has ended his life which had begun to decline, ironically, in spite of the applause which he gloriously received from a delirious Europe.

The defeat in the election for representatives last year was a difficult blow from his country at a time when he most needed the support of his fellow Americans. But Mr. Wilson had superseded the limits of the American tradition, and since that time he remained erased from the hearts of many of his fellow citizens. He was a dictator who tried not to summarize the spirit of a people but to replace it with his decisions. From that very moment, the solution could be logically inferred.

. . . Mr. Wilson's defeat has been still more sensational and depressing than what we judged it to be [in December 1918], since some Democrats have taken part in the repudiation of the Treaty. Does this mean they have considered that the only way of saving the party was to divorce it from the conduct of the President? We have at times asked ourselves precisely this—whether Mr. Wilson's attitude would not prejudice his party. . . .

The seriousness of the matter for the American President is that if his hour has already sounded in the United States, he will have no better luck in Europe. The enthusiasm of his first reception dying out, he slowly began losing ground among the governments and people, and the opinion which followed is that many of the postwar difficulties are due exclusively to him. In this tremendous fall, the man who yesterday appeared to be the arbitrator of the world, falls into a sad and silent decline, in the midst of the indifference of his own people and of the indifference of foreigners.

Here, in Mexico, the figure of President Wilson is little pleasing; even his admirers—who can be counted, for passion speaks loudly—show themselves to be lukewarm and reticent. We note simply the fact—as in parentheses—because the moment of a complete and calm judgment in respect to our country has not yet arrived.

But whatever may be the significance, from an international point of view, of the repudiation of the Treaty, we cannot pass by inadvertently one of the reservations made by the Senate: referring to the Monroe Doctrine it is stated . . . "The said Doctrine will be interpreted completely outside the limits of the jurisdiction of the League of Nations and under no circumstances will the clauses of the Treaty with Germany be able to affect it."

It really is unnecessary to underline the importance of this amendment.

The United States reaffirms its right to establish itself as arbitrator for the American continent. Unfortunately, the Monroe Doctrine has undergone so many interpretations that it is no wonder that this insistence on withholding the Doctrine from the obligations of a Treaty (viewed as a definite promise of world peace) is provoking mistrust.

We do not know the effect which this amendment will have on the governments and peoples of Europe, on those who have been called upon for a common cause under the names of justice and liberty; we shall ignore the interpretation given by those governments and peoples to that desertion of a compromise based on a generous and honest basis which pretended to be uplifting. But we do feel it necessary to state that the reservation made regarding the Monroe Doctrine, which almost appears as a "mental reservation," brings with it a fright. We shall say further, regarding Mexico, the aggravation of the fright is keeping us sleepless in the midst of the misfortunes of our country.

SHANGHAI. *Chung-hua Hsín-pao.** [n. d.]

The American Senate has passed the reservation vetoing three articles of the Peace Treaty concerning Shantung. Let us drink to the health of the victory of right and justice. China feels gratified that by such action the United States has demonstrated its readiness to uphold the attitude of China, namely, the Shantung settlement is an injustice to China. It is certain that the reservation will not be accepted by Great Britain or France, to say nothing of Japan. Hence it affects not only the peace treaty but also the League of Nations. If President Wilson cannot find a satisfactory solution his only course is to withdraw from the world power organization. Hereafter the solution of the Shantung question must be attended to by China. The situation in the Far East is, therefore, entering upon a critical stage. It is to be hoped that the people of our country will rise to the occasion and act in a manner worthy of the friendly attitude of America.

. . . The world is as much in confusion as it was during the war. The reason for such continued disturbance is injustice. The Peace Treaty of Versailles is by no means a document of justice. If the Great Powers were united it might have passed for the time being but the right attitude of the United States has thrown a dark shadow over it as a whole. We regret, therefore, that the people of Great Britain and France do not agree with the people of the United States in this matter. The possible breaking up of the big Powers is not the cause, but the result of the injustice done to

---

* As reprinted in *Millard's Review,* December 6, 1919.

smaller nations by the Peace Treaty, which is the making of the big Powers. To expect good results after sowing the seeds of injustice after the defeat of Germany is like climbing a tree in quest of fish. Peace will only come with justice for all. Without it the world will never be peaceful. Statesmen who depend on maneuver for success are bound to fail.

SHANGHAI. *Millard's Review,* November 29, 1919.

The American Senate after adopting a number of reservations to the peace treaty and League of Nations Covenant, including one on the Shantung matter, finally by a large majority rejected the treaty altogether and adjourned. Thus, on the face at least, the work of President Wilson at Paris has been nullified. A Reuter dispatch of exactly four lines brought this significant news to the millions of people living in Asia this week. Thus America finds herself in much the same status as China. She has refused to sign a document in which she does not believe. China's representatives at Paris and China's officials at Peking dared not sign the peace treaty because it ratified an immoral act—a theft of Chinese territory—by a country that had posed as an ally. To have signed would have provoked a revolution in China that would have been worse than the Boxer uprising magnified a thousand times. In America where the people are articulate, they have prevented their officials from signing the treaty because they did not believe in it. The Shantung reservation to the treaty by the U. S. Senate was but one of the details, but it typified all that was wrong and rotten in the secret bargaining and trading that went on behind closed doors at Paris. There will be those who will ascribe the Senate's action to pro-Germanism; others will ascribe it to internal politics warming up for an approaching national election; while still others will say that an ungrateful people have thrown over a leader that almost gave his life for a cause.

To answer the last point first, the rejection of the treaty will not in the long run injure President Wilson's place in history. Mr. Wilson opened the eyes of people everywhere to a newer and better system. He did more perhaps than any other lone man could have done. His mistake was that he attempted to do too much alone. His theories could not stand up in the face of the fearful practicality he found in Paris. He went to Paris with a theory and a hope, but without a plan. He did not understand the inside politics of Europe—who does for that matter? He aroused the people of Europe, but as yet the people of Europe are not running their own political affairs in the same measure that the American people are directing theirs. And the next point, internal politics: America has a national election next year. Until the peace treaty and the League of Nations Covenant became known to their last item, comma, and period, the Republican opposition had nothing to hang their opposition on. Then came the details of the treaty to be closely followed by a searching into the underlying motives that caused certain things to be said and to be incorporated into the treaty. The Shantung matter crystallized the opposition. President Wilson, the advocate of righteousness and open covenants, was forced into a defensive position. He had to admit that expediency forced his hand; that he got the best he could; that he hoped the thing he brought back with him would, although imperfect, be better than nothing. Then came the President's tour and its dramatic ending. Had the President been able to stand the strain, he would have carried his point. But his enforced retirement from public affairs lost him the support of his people and the opposition won. The Republican Senators are not without the support of the American people—they are too close to the votes to be far afield. Recent Republican victories in various parts of the country prove that. As to the last point, pro-Germanism: that may be dismissed without discussion. Three million American troops in Europe for an ideal is the best answer to that.

Topic 22

LINDBERGH'S TRANSATLANTIC FLIGHT

1927

Born in Detroit, Michigan, in 1902, Charles A. Lindbergh spent his boyhood days in Minnesota, studied at the University of Wisconsin for two years, and then took flying instructions in Nebraska. After additional studies as a cadet in the United States Air Service Reserve, and commissioning as a first lieutenant in the Missouri National Guard, he acquired fame as an airmail pilot between Chicago and St. Louis. Determined to win the $25,000 prize offered in 1919 by New York hotel owner, Raymond Orteig, to the first aviator to make a nonstop New York-to-Paris flight, Lindbergh landed at the airport at Le Bourget, a suburb of Paris, after a flight of 3700 miles.

TOKYO. *The Japan Times,* **May 23, 1927.**

The dauntless spirit of the American people was again demonstrated by the daring achievement of a young son of the great republic, Captain Charles Lindbergh, who recently crossed the vast expanse of the Atlantic in a nonstop flight from New York to Paris in the record time of 33 hours and 31 minutes.

It is not so much the actual success in flight as his daredevil spirit that impresses our mind. Two French flyers, Captain Nungesser and Major Coli, had attempted to cross the same ocean before him and have been missing for more than a week, the general belief being that their lives were lost in the heroic attempt. This disaster could not dampen the enthusiasm of the intrepid young American birdman, and he calmly smiled as he mounted the plane on his death-braving journey.

It is this American spirit of fearlessness which enabled the Thirteen Colonies to rise in an open revolt against their mother country, to fire the "shot heard 'round the world," and to address themselves to the gigantic task of empire-building, basing it upon the new principles of liberty and humanity, thereby contributing toward the general well-being of the human race.

The special interest and lesson for us Japanese regarding the success of Captain Lindbergh is the fact that he is only 25 years old. Had he been a Japanese, he would have been regarded by the Government as too young to engage in such an important task. Young William Pitt became the Prime Minister of England when he was 25. The youngest premier in the history of Japan was the late Prince Hirobumi Ito, the father of the Imperial Constitution, who formed the first ministry when he was 45. It may be safely conjectured that no man who is under sixty can hope to become a Japanese premier in the near future. Our overemphasis on seniority has been a veritable monkey wrench in the machinery of our national progress.

In America, age is no limitation, for men. If one has ability, he is entrusted with any task however gigantic. He is unmolested with tradition or the sense of juniority and he can make success as brilliant as that which was made by Captain Lindbergh.

PARIS. *Le Temps*, **May 23, 1927.**

It was an old woman who, yesterday, on the boulevard, when the news spread of the happy arrival of the American aviator Lindbergh, went away repeating: "The brave little boy! The brave little boy!" And she cried among the enthusiastic crowd.

We beg the Americans to receive this simple exclamation as homage from the French people themselves. The courage and youth of the victor are both honored in this way. The joy and heroism of his exploit had to touch the Frenchmen to the bottom of their hearts. This daring man is only 25 years old and that makes our admiration mingle with tenderness. We still fear that several of our brave compatriots have perished in an enterprise similar to that of Lindbergh. Didn't people insinuate that we would feel some resentment at seeing Americans succeed where ours have failed? May free America look at us and listen to us on this day when she experiences so much just pride. In the multitudes of Le Bourget and of Paris, last evening, there is only one great cry of joy. Tens of thousands of Parisians massed in the streets asked that American flags be draped from the windows of the boulevards. In Le Bourget, French aviators have, so to speak, received in their arms the young hero and have surrounded him with brotherly concern. There is only one sentiment in us before the success of this courageous aviator: we admire him because he was intrepid and we love him because he is young.

"The brave little boy!" The French woman who saluted so simply his triumph in this way spoke as mothers speak. She had trembled at the thought that this young man could have had the tragic end of some of those who went before him. She had experienced the anguish of Mrs. Lindbergh who, stoically, pursued her habitual tasks over there while waiting to know the sentence of destiny. It was in some way her child, the child of this French mother, who ventured between two worlds above the oceans. And when she knew that he was finally among us, that his courage had received the reward that she herself so much desired for him, there came from her heart the only word with which she would have received her own son escaping from danger: "The brave little boy!"

At Le Bourget, it was under the coat of a French aviator that Lindbergh was able to escape from the delirious bravos of the crowd. May the Americans see there a symbol. Their hero is well with them; he is at home with them in his audacity, his optimism, his perseverance. But his victory, which honors them, makes all of us glad at the same time. It realizes our wishes to see the nations renounce their useless rivalries. Every man who is distinguished by genius or valor becomes our friend, and we thank him for the part that he takes in our task of equitable peace.

Also, when the citizens of the United States again hear us accused of practicing, openly or in secret, a jealous and suspicious chauvinism, they will answer our accusers by describing the spectacle that Paris offered on this night of the 21st of May, 1927, when the Frenchmen, unanimously, joyously, affectionately, acclaimed the American aviator, Lindbergh, the 25-year-old hero.

BERLIN. *Neue Preussische Zeitung,* May 22, 1927.

. . . How much the danger of his attempt was clear to Lindbergh is shown by his remark: "When I crawled into my plane, I felt the same as if I had entered a cell as a man condemned to death. And when I landed the plane in Paris I was so happy to have been pardoned at the last moment."

Lindbergh's cockpit was comparatively speaking confined; and the pilot, a tall slender young man (in his outer appearance entirely of the Scandinavian-Germanic race), had trouble accommodating his long legs. For this he moved the instrument panel, but then he was not able to see ahead, for the seat lay too far back. He "flew blind," say the experts, only able to obtain a view to his right and to his left through use of a periscope. In such a position Lindbergh had to remain nearly 40 hours! No companion was in his sight who could sustain him, if he lost courage. At no time did he permit himself the prospect of turning back—a trial of strength, which required a true man.

Swedish papers bring interesting information about the ocean-flyer Lindbergh, who is only 25 years old. He was born in Detroit, the son of a Swedish patriot. His features are typically Nordic: blonde hair and blue eyes . . .

Neue Preussische Zeitung, May 25, 1927.

A sea of enthusiasm is raging in Paris. America is filled with jubilation over the brilliant deed. Charles Lindbergh has landed his single-engine plane in Paris after a 33½ hour journey over the ocean. His achievement is unprecedented. The technical equipment of his plane was a glaring problem and his warning devices primitive. But the gods have not allowed the daring Icarus to suffer for his presumptions. Besides clinking gold, Lindbergh brings home the proud knowledge of having achieved a record performance; he has now mastered the longest distance that has been achieved in a plane without an intermediate landing. The faces of the great discoverers and pioneers have admitted a new hero into their Pantheon, who by his subjugation of the ocean enters with equal stature.

   . . . Germany is also gloriously represented in this heroic gallery of the great pioneers and pathfinders [Columbus, Vasco da Gama, Magellan]. There were the two great, unforgettable performances of the Z. R. III, which in October 1924 flew over the ocean, and, eight years before, Captain Paul König's voyage to America in a submarine. The distance which the Z. R. III in its 80-hour voyage covered has still not been surpassed. Captain König twice took his commerce-submarine "Deutschland" from Germany to America, a feat which at the time made an enormous impression on friend and foe and which they by particular circumstances placed on the side of the greatest maritime achievements of all time. A success in which Germany likewise participated was the flight accomplished last year by the Spaniard, Franco, who flew a German Dornier-"Whale" from Spain to Brazil and Buenos Aires and which covered a distance of 10,000 km.; also, the similar flight in England of the airship R. 34, a copy of a German Zepplin, which flew from Edinburgh, Scotland, over Newfoundland to Long Island in 59 hours, and back to Belfast in Ireland in 61 hours.

   . . . When Lindbergh soon leaves for the port of New York in the stateroom of a passenger liner, and when all the reporters in the new world interview his happy mother, when the day the entire United States echoes with joy over the achievement of their Lindbergh arrives—what man will then still remember that not too long before a Gertrude Ederle [the first woman to swim the English channel–1926] was received and carried through the streets of the metropolis of the Hudson in triumph by 100,000

people. And who, enjoying in the morning his comfortable break-
fast and hearing the report of the youngest ocean-conquerer—
will think of the North Pole-flyer Byrd, who was cheered by the
world last year; of Amundsen, the discoverer of the South Pole; of
Peary's journey of discovery to the North Pole; of the men who
want to uncover the secrets of Mt. Everest; of Sven Hedin, who
opened up forbidden lands and discovered a whole gigantic moun-
tain range; of the German African explorers, who ventured into
the unknown and explored the deserts and jungles; of the great-
hearted performance of a Stanley, who went in search of Living-
ston; of all on whom the veil has descended—whose chances then
are so small as that of Captain Lindbergh?

Topic 23

THE KELLOGG-BRIAND PACT

1928

In June 1927, Aristide Briand, the French Foreign Minister, proposed a treaty with the United States which would outlaw war between the two countries. Frank B. Kellogg, Secretary of State, suggested that all nations be invited to condemn "recourse to war for the solution of international controversies." On August 27, 1928, in Paris, fifteen nations signed the multilateral agreement which specified that all conflicts, regardless of origin, would be settled by pacific measures. However, no means of enforcement were provided. Ultimately, sixty-two nations signed the pact.

PARIS. *Le Temps,* **March 1, 1928.**

. . . if the response of Mr. Kellogg to the French note of January 20 affirms that the correspondence exchanged until now between the two governments provides evidence that France and the United States desire equally to create an international movement for effective world peace and that they are in agreement on the eventual principle of the procedure to follow this effect . . . the one obstacle . . . is the fact that France doubts that she can, as a member of the League of Nations and party to the Treaty of Locarno and other treaties guaranteeing neutrality, engage herself with the United States and other principal powers in not having recourse to war in their reciprocal relations without violating, even there, her international obligations. Mr. Kellogg considers that if these international obligations permit France to conclude a bilateral treaty with the United States, they will permit her also to unite with the United States in order to propose the conclusion of a multilateral treaty with the other major powers, because, in his opinion, the difference between the bilateral form and the multilateral form of a treaty having as its goal the renunciation, without reserve, of war is a question of degree and not of substance.

Right there is the error of the American Secretary of State. France can, without inconvenience, conclude an unconditional bilateral pact with the United States, all eventuality of a war between the two countries being outside of all credibility, just as no one can seriously consider that the League of Nations could ever be led to decide on an international action against the great American Republic. To be convinced of it, it suffices to reflect on the geographical, political, and economic position of the United States in the world. All objection of this kind to the French proposition is therefore without practical import. But, on the contrary, the case is totally different with the other powers held, like France herself, by the decisions of Geneva. When Mr. Kellogg declares that he can hardly believe that the clauses of the pact of the League of Nations constitute an obstacle to the cooperation of the United States and of the member states of the League of Nations in a common effort to abolish the institution of war, and when he recalls the recent adoption of the Sixth International Conference of the American States, at Havana, of a resolution "expressing in the name of the American Republics the condemnation without reservation of war as an instrument of national politics, in their mutual relations," when seventeen out of twenty-one of these states represented at the conference are members of the League of Nations, the American Secretary of State commits a grave error. In fact, it is war of aggression—that even which France proposes to repudiate solemnly—which has been condemned at Havana, as the text of the adopted resolution proves, a text which says notably that "the war of aggression constitutes an international crime against humanity" and which proceeds from the same spirit as the resolution of Geneva of September 20, 1927. The American Republics represented at the Conference of Havana conform themselves strictly to the resolution which binds them as members of the League of Nations and which, in fact, did not permit them to subscribe to another formal condemnation than that aimed at the war of aggression.

Moreover, the question is asked in the same manner for all the powers belonging to the international institution of Geneva and it cannot be any other. It is not a question of weakening the positive value of a multilateral pact while stipulating reservations and exceptions for the cases where nations would be justified in having recourse to war, since these reservations and these exceptions are in the nature of things, because if all war of aggression is criminal, all war of defense against unprovoked aggression is legitimate. The American government itself formulates some reservations for the cases that are able to come up from the Monroe Doctrine—which is, however, one knows, only a unilateral declaration, as the delegate from Argentina recalled yesterday at Geneva. It would be, therefore, inadmissible that one should wish to obtain from France that she not specify the capital qualification which is imposed from the fact of her international obligations and which moreover the other principal powers would not fail to use in their turn if they had some foreknowledge of this fact.

LONDON. *The Times*, **April 4, 1928.**

The correspondence between MR. KELLOGG and M. BRIAND on peace and war continues, and, for the present, that fact alone is of greater importance than anything else. It cannot be altogether in vain that France and the United States, at this stage of slow reorganization after the destruction of so many old values by war and revolution, should exchange views on the possibility of preventing a relapse by some general agreement . . . Since the war there has been a gulf, wider than the Atlantic, between the prevailing European and American conceptions of the new order of things. To some extent the British Empire has served as an intermediary between these two contrasted worlds, and at times the strain has been severe. With the departure of lingering European illusions about America, a change is coming over the whole prospect. The gulf itself was, if not an illusion, perhaps a provisional working hypothesis useful while each side was recovering breath. But the gulf has lately been perceptibly narrowing. A sharp division between the two great areas of modern civilization cannot be maintained indefinitely. The United States cannot for ever insist on an isolation in which, through repeated disappointments, she has made the rest of the world half believe. She cannot because the daily incidents of an inevitable American expansion belie all theories of isolation. Intercourse between America and Europe is assuming after an apparent interruption a thousand new forms. Can it be reduced to new terms of law and policy? To take the issue at its broadest, can the United States cooperate systematically with Europe in the general work of ensuring peace? Will she only cooperate occasionally and at discretion? Or will she deliberately choose a way of her own, apart from the network of commitments and responsibilities in which the other civilized nations are involved?

All these very general but critical questions lie at the root of the exchange of views that is now developing between the AMERICAN SECRETARY of STATE and the FRENCH MINISTER of FOREIGN AFFAIRS. For that reason the correspondence is hopeful. Direct contact is officially established, and is being maintained, between two states of mind that until lately seemed utterly opposed. France is firmly set in the framework of the new European system as defined in the Peace Treaties, the League of Nations, her own alliances, and Locarno. She is most distinctively European, distinctively continental. She stands, more than any other Power, for those conceptions from which the United States has carefully held aloof for seven years or more. Yet it is a movement on the part of France that has brought to light a new tendency of American opinion. M. BRIAND proposed to the United States last year the conclusion of a pact repudiating war as an instrument of policy between the two countries. The proposal attracted little attention. It seemed hardly more than an amiable gesture, the embodiment of one probability out of many in a form of words. MR. KELLOGG did not reject the proposal. He expanded it, and in so doing revealed the changing temper of his country. He suggested, instead of the bilateral pact proposed by M. BRIAND, that France should join the United States in proposing to the other Great Powers a multilateral pact repudiating war as an instrument of policy, and this at the very time when proposals were being brought forward for a large increase in American sea armaments. The immediate effect was disconcerting. America was returning into world politics under two contrasting aspects. Yet both the naval programme and the peace proposals indicated most clearly that the Great Power beyond the seas was reaching out towards a more active participation in the world's affairs and must seriously be taken into account. . .

BERLIN. *Neue Preussische Zeitung,* August 18, 1928.

Information . . . puts it as a confirmed fact, that Dr. Stresemann has accepted an invitation to Paris for the signing of the "War-forbidding Pact." . . .

We view the Paris journey of Dr. Stresemann as exclusively an act of courtesy towards the United States, with whom the suggestion for the Kellogg Pact originated; so we can expect little solid operations from this new instrument for the prevention of war, against which no one has anything to object. Since bitter sentiments still prevail, the German foreign minister shows himself studiously eager to document explicitly the German readiness for peace; while on the other side, in France and England, it will also contribute to the cleansing of the political atmosphere. Yes, it is on the contrary entirely possible, through a whole series of tactics and skills, to remove every doubt of their true disposition toward Germany. The two-bridging incident, the Franco-British maneuvers, the shameless works of espionage—all these embittering and shocking incidents should have served to manifest, to cool down, the all too exuberant hopes of uninformed information-fanatics. First, as in the German publicity of this pronouncedly hostile treatment, yet the "Locarno-joy" was finally so great, that the journey to Paris for the signing of the Kellogg Pact could appear as just reduced to a visit to the Seine. The "official" German circles see the atmosphere as cleared, so that the Paris journey no longer stands in the way. The French were anxious at the beginning to prevent a German signature of the Kellogg Pact. They have themselves reached out to make illusory any practical applications with regard to eventual arms reductions. But for Germany the accession to the Kellogg Pact signifies indubitably more than just a bond. However, in truth, the poisoning of the political atmosphere which was aimed at shortly before the meeting of the Entente state-minister with Dr. Stresemann in Paris clearly is evident. We have from the first, then, no doubt what the prevailing theme in Paris will be, if by chance Dr. Stresemann intends to bring up the chief problem of Franco-German relations, namely, the evacuation of the Rhineland, at his Paris stay. In appreciation of this fact, we can only view Dr. Stresemann's journey to Paris for the signing of the Kellogg Pact as exclusively an act of politeness vis-à-vis the United States.

TOKYO. *The Japan Times,* August 24, 1928.

When the U. S. Secretary of State left New York to go to Paris in order to sign a treaty denouncing war, a group of people calling themselves the "Anti-Imperialist League" paraded along the pier bearing banners inscribed with such slogans as "Hands off China," "Hands off Nicaragua," and so forth. To the general public, it would seem curious that any body of men should think it necessary to heckle a statesman bound upon such a truly charitable mission as that aiming at the abolition of war, much less that they should "denounce the Kellogg antiwar treaty." The Anti-Imperialist League has more than once come into conflict with the New York police, the last occasion being an attempt in Wall Street during the noon hour, when they endeavored to harangue the crowds. On this occasion they received short shrift from the police who, whatever the Constitution may say, have no use for free speech. Their enemies say they are Bolsheviks, and no more serious charge can be leveled against a good American than to call him by that name. It immediately sets the watchdogs upon him, and there is an end of the appeal to reason.

Still, it seems passing strange that as Mr. Kellogg is departing to perform what, on the surface, at least, appears to be a most exalted and humane act in the true interests of mankind, any body of men should bodily gather at the pier and denounce him and his treaty. What is wrong with this prospective treaty; what can possibly be wrong with it? The whole world seems to have expressed approval of it—what can there be about it that is possibly misleading?

Almost ten years ago, another American statesman, at that time acclaimed as a god by war-ridden Europe, left American shores to take his part in European affairs, with still greater promise for the regeneration of mankind. The panacea then was "self-determination," and the whole world acted as if the mere declaration of the phrase automatically effected the salvation of misgoverned and oppressed peoples. None dared denounce President Wilson at that time, and few are prepared to denounce Mr. Kellogg at this time; if they do, they are treated as the anti-imperialists were at New York, and ignominiously dispersed.

What is there in the coming treaty against which the reasonable and humane man may lodge objection—on the surface, nothing. Why is it, when this much-discussed treaty is about to be signed—and a great ceremony is to be made of it—two friendly powers are making a private agreement of a naval character which is considered prejudicial to the interests of a third party? All will be signatories of the new treaty to abolish war. What is at the back of all this friendly profession and secret suspicion?

Time will provide the answer. The Powers have to their credit a treaty forbidding the use of poison gas in warfare, and in the United States today the use of deadly chemical fumes is being advocated to combat the bootleggers. Humanity is in the discard. It is notorious that every nation has its military chemical laboratory, some being much more advanced than others in the preparation of deadly gases. Every nation has pledged itself not to use poison gas in the next war, and every nation is ready to follow the example (in "self-defense") of the first nation that violates the agreement; the most solemn agreement—the language is extremely dignified, and should be read.

There has been much reasoned consideration of the benefits of the new treaty denouncing war. It is argued, and no one will combat the view, that every little [bit] helps, every step forward is a step forward. Mr. Wilson's doctrine of self-determination was received with the same feeling of elation and hope; the world felt that such a praiseworthy idea could not be wrong. Nor can it; but its application may be disastrous. Without instilling into backward peoples the capacity to govern themselves, the new universal remedy stiffened their determination not to be governed by others. It brought more bloodshed and confusion into the world, and proved the great ally of the Bolsheviks in their policy of universal disruption. The world was not (and is not) ready for Mr. Wilson's excellences, and it became an easy mark for Bolshevik aims. Confusion in many states was the unforeseen result of the declaration of a panacea for world peace. The reformers were too hasty, and the peoples were unready. The present condition does not justify hope of immediate universal peace, which must come from within, and cannot result from outside pressure. In many parts of the world, injustice and misgovernment are triumphant. The noble efforts of the best part of mankind may be crowned some day, but flagrant injustice is still rampant. This being the situation the world must not believe that war has been so easily banished by the new treaty and thus permit itself to be lulled into a false sense of security. Behind the antiwar pact must be continued to be marshaled all the forces for international understanding and comity; the doctrine of cooperation rather than competition among the peoples of the world must be taught to the masses so that behind the high pronouncements of statesman may be formed a body of world opinion which will make the violation of the peace a psychological impossibility.

LONDON. *The Times,* **August 27, 1928.**

. . . it is a notable fact that MR. KELLOGG, the Secretary of State in the United States Government, which has for years held aloof from the intimacies of the peace struggle, has himself crossed the Atlantic on the eve of a presidential election to sign the Pact, in association with the representatives of fourteen other States, including all the members of the British Empire, Japan, and the leading nations of Europe. The terms of the Pact are very broad. They may fairly be described as vague or nebulous. But if this general affirmation of a new principle of international order may in itself appear slightly indeterminate, if the price of signing it appears to be a somewhat sceptical commitment to a nebulous ideal, the price is more than worth paying; and the commitment may be most hopefully undertaken if the signing of this treaty by the assembled nations means that the United States is really coming in, that the great, wealthy, rapidly rising American Power which lies between a straining Europe and an East in turmoil will at last really lend a hand, in MR. KELLOGG'S sober phrase, to render war more difficult.

In this treaty the backing of America means everything. Without that backing it has little more significance than such as may be implied in the resolutions of a Peace congress. The ratification of MR. KELLOGG's signature by the Senate at Washington will mean that the power of the United States is enlisted in a definite movement of world policy, that what may now seem a faint breeze will fill the flapping sails; that what in the meantime appears to be almost a platitude will acquire a most practical significance. The movement away from war has been hampered hitherto by the negations or the relative inertia of large tracts of the world. The force of that dragging, delaying, inconclusive tendency will be greatly lessened if the signature of the Pact means that the United States is loosed from her temporary moorings and is prepared to join in the active search for peace. The Pact is being signed at a critical moment in the life of the American nation. Public opinion is deeply moved on a variety of issues before the election of the new President. Domestic issues naturally hold the first place, but even amid the clamour of the primaries, the conflict of personalities, and the struggle between town and country interests, it can hardly escape the notice of the electors that the chief nations of the world are associating themselves with a new and distinctively American initiative to promote and assure peace. It is not the League. America rejected the League for reasons of her own, and the rest of the world has learned not to insist upon or to hope for her participation, or even to complain of her abstention. A second failure on the part of the United States could with difficulty be borne, but that, happily, is not anticipated. The new treaty will, in effect, mean much or little to the extent that it has or has not the ardent support of its American authors. In the confidence that this support will be really given our Government, the Governments of the other member States of the Empire, and several Governments besides, will sign today.

. . . For this Pact, this joint affirmation of a new type of policy, suggests the possibility of a movement of wider scope towards a goal at which British policy has steadily aimed since the War. In such a movement we are in hearty agreement with America, and once it receives the full support of the American people the international prospect will be clearer than it has been for a long time past.

BERLIN. *Neue Preussische Zeitung*, **August 16, 1928.**

. . . Then frankly we ask: what is there in this Pact and treaty to insure that peace will not be just redefined and interpreted? This is the sense of the whole Pact-comedy: the men, and nations, wish it to narcotize [their opponents]; but they themselves, unchecked by any ridiculous no-more-war sentiments, are stronger to defend and build.

In September the League of Nations moves on to disarmament preparations. For Germany the treatment of the disarmament question is decisive. It also must soon be demonstrated whether the Kellogg Pact is more than a "very good fraud"; more than "a poisonous snake," . . . And whether from this comes "the only possible and correct" German foreign policy,—a policy of self-consciousness.

Topic 24

PRESIDENT FRANKLIN D. ROOSEVELT AND ECONOMIC CRISIS

1933

The presidential campaign of 1932 focused sharply on the causes of the economic depression which had engulfed the United States and threatened the political and economic foundations of the nation. Campaign oratory by Republicans for the incumbent, Herbert Hoover, and by the Democratic contender, Franklin D. Roosevelt, outlined possible changes but few specific commitments. Winning all but six states, Roosevelt swept the electoral college vote by 479 to 59, and won the popular vote by 23,000,000 to Hoover's 16,000,000. Moreover, Democrats won majorities in both houses of Congress. On Inauguration Day, March 4, the world's most powerful industrial system verged on collapse.

TOKYO. *The Japan Times & Mail,* **March 4, 1933.**

Today, Mr. Franklin Delano Roosevelt assumes the Presidency of the United States of America. He is the first Democratic occupant of the White House since President Woodrow

Wilson and the victory of the party of which he was the standard-bearer was a veritable landslide, showing without doubt the desire of the American public for some change.

The Presidency of a country like the United States is far from being a sinecure. It is undoubtedly one of the highest positions the world has to offer, is a place of great honor, but it also carries with it many weighty responsibilities, both material and spiritual.

Mr. Roosevelt inherits, with the job, a host of momentous matters to which he and his official family will have to bend their energies and their full capabilities. Perhaps the greatest of these questions is the vexed problem of war debts and what intentions, what line of action, the new incumbent of the White House will take in this matter is still not definitely clear. It is an intriguing question and the nature of the discussion foreshadowed at the forthcoming World Economic Conference will largely depend on the American attitude with regard to war debts. Consequently, this attitude is one which is pregnant with importance for the entire world, so that Japan, for one, cannot merely look upon the settlement of this American-European question as one that merely concerns a part of the Old World and the New World.

Recent reports stated that Mr. Roosevelt was carefully guarding his own solution of the problem, but the news that his advisers have been talking of a preliminary moratorium on war debts, and that too for an unspecified period, will put heart into America's debtors. If a temporary respite is to be found along these lines, there is the possibility of the whole question's being discussed in an atmosphere of goodwill between the debtor nations and their big creditor.

In Senator Cordell Hull, whom Mr. Roosevelt has chosen as his Secretary of State, the President will have a man of wide experience and a veteran in politics who, without the adventitious aid of wealth or social position, has been able to climb to the top through sheer grit and merit. Senator Hull, too, will find that many responsible tasks devolve on him. Here in the East, we will naturally be carefully watching the nature of the policy that the new Administration will take towards the Sino-Japanese problems. Mr. Roosevelt himself is known as being a keen student of Eastern affairs, while both he and his Secretary of State have been hailed as men with open minds who will view things in their stern realities rather than committing themselves to legal and other technicalities. If this be so, then will there ensue further harmony between Japan and the United States, and it must be the earnest duty of our statesmen to convince the United States that Japan's policy in the Far East is dictated by one compelling urge—the absolute necessity of maintaining the peace and order of this part of the world. Such will redound to the benefit of all the world, particularly of the order restored, new and wide fields will open out in this portion of the globe for American investments and initiative.

At home, too, the new Administration will have a deal of work to do and much new ground to plough. A recent New York report intimated that Mrs. Roosevelt, who has been one of the most active women in the States since her husband was elected President, is of the opinion that the women of America will have a great task to do in devising practical and effective means to bring about better conditions not only in America itself, but also elsewhere. She expressed the hope, at a speech delivered to a gathering of prominent women of the land, that the day of questionable over-freedom in personal conduct has passed. She is a believer in and practices the virtues of plain living and high thinking, and this expression of her hopes may be regarded as an indication of the manner in which the First Lady of America will proceed to work to ensure that the members of her sex do their bit in bringing about better material and healthier spiritual conditions.

This aspect of the efforts that will be made by the new Administration will also be carefully watched here, all the more so as the more progressive of Japanese women have made true American womanhood their model and hope to fashion the new Japanese womanhood from the best of the West, particularly of the United States, and the best of the East.

The Japan Times & Mail, March 5, 1933.

Influential and observant Japanese who keep closely in touch with foreign affairs in general and those concerning the United States in particular are fully convinced that President Roosevelt will inaugurate his assumption of office by the adoption of policies so spectacular that they will rivet the attention of the world.

In the economic field, for example, Mr. Yunosuke Yasukawa, a director of the Mitsui Bussan Company, one of the greatest business organizations of Japan, expects Mr. Roosevelt to place an embargo on the export of gold from the United States—a step which has been rumored here occasionally, but which heretofore no one of importance has attached any importance to.

In diplomacy, Mr. Yusuke Tsurumi, liberal publicist and former member of the lower house of the Imperial Diet, who has recently returned here from an extended tour of America and Europe, anticipates that the new President will extend formal recognition to the Soviet government of Russia, and greatly reduce the war debts which European countries owe the United States, as well as placing an embargo on gold exports.

. . . According to Mr. Tsurumi it will be well-nigh inevitable for Mr. Roosevelt, who, he says, is fond of playing to the gallery, to make some dramatic gestures in the effort to retain his present high level of popularity, which, as a matter of fact, is due largely to the rather negative cause of disappointment with Mr. Hoover.

This being the case, Mr. Roosevelt must do something vital to turn the current of American economic life in the direction of prosperity, and one of the first steps toward this, Mr. Tsurumi thinks, will be to grant the Soviet government of Russia what it has been so eager to obtain for so long—formal recognition by the United States—which, it is anticipated, would open up a vast outlet for American manufactures.

Mr. Tsurumi believes that other urgent measures that will appeal to Mr. Roosevelt's statesmanship—which he praises highly—will be to relieve Europe of its pressing burden of war debts to the United States, and the imposition of an embargo on gold exports, to stimulate purchases of American goods by other countries which are already off the gold standard, and to contract the present inflow of the goods they sell to the United States under cover of the high exchange value of the dollar.

Mr. Tsurumi thinks that the Secretary of State Hull, under President Roosevelt's directions, will discard the hectoring policy that Mr. Stimson has adopted toward Japan, and that the Japan-China dispute will not continue to occupy the major position that it has assumed under the Hoover administration—with the result that the American attitude generally toward Japan will be much more friendly with consequent improvement in the relations of the two nations.

MADRID. *El Sol,* March 7, 1933.

All the banks of North America find themselves affected at this time by a legal moratorium, which cannot be motivated by anything else other than a suspension of payments, a cause for financial panic. To have this happen in a country that has become the banker of the world constitutes a terrible shock. . . .

. . . Why has a phenomenon of a universal character had such catastrophic characteristics in the United States? Because of a moral process which is bound to that golden fancy that was America and that now seems to crumble in trembling. England paid a similar tribute a year and a half ago because of a lack of trust in a restless universe. But what in England was a mechanical pressure of foreign capital, in North America is moreover a moral disintegration of the very nation. That is why in England the situation was able to be saved: suspending the gold standard, declaring a partial banking insolvency before the foreigner; that is, returning in depreciated pounds the reclaimed capital. In the United States, the suspension of the gold standard would only solve the situation partly, for the entire nation has lost its faith in its economic destiny.

America—all of America—has been a land of an exultation of a cult of wealth. It has been socially saturated in a lucrative aspiration without restraint. This radical inclination of the American was based on a firm conviction of limitless natural resources, easily accessible with financial aid. And so, European capitalists came to America producing magical results. It is not strange that when the Great War moved the gold in the world toward the United States, the infinite financial possibilities which accompanied the phenomenon were calculated by a secular capitalist fervor which grew as the hour of promise arrived. And the North American businessmen began frantically to explore and organize such a lucrative illusion.

Although excellently endowed for the merely instrumental and technical, North America was launched by capitalists of a primitive and overwhelming spirit into excessive consumption in which by means of credit, material ventures which normally would have required many years of savings and work were anticipated and obtained. Each worker—or a countless number of them—had his own house, car and radio. The middle classes saw thousands reach the same status. The powerfully wealthy hoisted the sail of extravagance—and went throughout the world squandering and behaving contemptuously like roguish millionaires. The entire country became enveloped in a speculative fire. The bankers conceded much more credit than was prudent; the industrialists produced much more than was discrete; the merchants expanded their businesses as much as possible; the gamblers converted the Stock Exchange into a speculative tumult.

The national territory was not enough to relieve that enterprising nature that had become inflamed and had multiplied in the United States. And that Yankee credit—that credit which seemed unending because of the booty of gold taken at the grief of Europe—bought mines and constructed factories and spread promises of fortune throughout America. It came to Europe; it helped Germany rebuild its industry; it provided checkbooks to several Governments so that they would draw on the banks of New York.

But in all this, financial foresight was lacking as well as a prudence to fear what was happening in the world. The authorities of the banking systems tried to control the expansion of credit, but this overflow continued as long as possibilities were available. It became impossible for the Federal Reserve to continue to enhance the money. There existed a bare margin of benefit for all. The restraint of the expansion began too late.

And so the first surprise to the Stock Exchange of New York occurred in 1929. There was a great depression of all stock values. What had happened? It was blamed on a liquidation occurring in London and thus was ignored as not important. Later it was said that the great European production of grain had been an unforeseen blow to North American agriculture and had alerted something of a panic. The depression in New York affected other international exchanges and the result bounced back to New York.

The North American banks began to become congested with depreciated values as their debtors could not reimburse the banks for their debts. The availability of credit began to disappear. Industries reduced their production. The prices of raw materials went down. The need for the purchase of these raw materials diminished. Values decreased, prices fell, production lessened. The American faith began its decline as extremely as had its illusions been created.

Simultaneously, with the misfortunes of business in America came the catastrophes of Europe: the moratorium of Germany, the suspension of the gold standard in England, the breakdown of Ivan Kreuger. Everything reverberated to the United States with depressing insistence and enormous losses, accelerating the inevitable crisis.

The North American government made unheard-of efforts in the last three years to contain the avalanche, and they succeeded at times to create periods of calm. But they made the big mistake of believing that they could save the nation in isolation. The connection of American business with world affairs and the condition of America in a state of inability to react morally made this impossible. The American dream had been deflated and the entire country was disenchanted, torn with violence and infected with despair.

Now, minor incidents otherwise looked upon with serenity, new exports of foreign capital, liquidations of some enterprises, have determined the fate of these days. Panic has broken loose without restraint. People have rushed to the banks in search of the savings they had left. And so has come the moratorium, and probably the abandonment of the gold standard and, who can say, maybe even an international moral awareness in America.

PARIS. *Le Temps*, March 5, 1933.

. . . Four months of insolvency of power in the United States have resulted in singularly aggravating the universal malaise. The fact that the President in action, Mr. Hoover, no longer had the necessary authority to engage the politics of the Union, while the President-elect was not yet in the situation of taking his responsibilities, totally paralyzed the government of Washington. Mr. Roosevelt . . . is a new man with new ideas who enters the White House, and his coming to the presidency of the Union must, by the force of things, determine profound changes in the American political scene. President Roosevelt must face, from the first day, grave difficulties both at home and abroad. The banking crisis, which is entering its acute stage, the fight against the strike, the recovery of the financial and economic situation, the problem of debts, the problem of tariffs, the necessity, more urgent than ever, of a straightforward international collaboration, in full union with the European powers, for the consolidation of the peace which alone can reestablish confidence without which there is no restoration of a balanced world economy possible, such are the essential aspects of the immense task which awaits the host of the White House.

This task is so much the more delicate and more difficult because the President of the Union is obliged to deal with a public opinion that is often badly informed about international affairs or misled by systematic campaigns. The initiative taken by Mr. Roosevelt to prepare his political action by engaging in conversations with the ambassador of Great Britain and with the ambassador of France on the question of debts and that of the world economic conference marks well enough that the successor of Mr. Hoover has a very large conception of the orientation which is actually imposed on American politics. From all evidence, he realizes that America cannot remain obstinate in a "splendid isolation," that she must frankly assume her part of the responsibility in the political, economic, and financial activity of the civilized world, that the surest way of reestablishing her own prosperity is to help in the restoration of the prosperity of all nations, especially of Europe, and that the solution of the American problem remains subordinate to the solution of the world problem. From the point of view of the American interests, this is a fundamental truth which makes the initiatives taken up to now by President Roosevelt entirely acceptable in the eyes of the American people and invites a policy of loyal collaboration.

This policy has already been tested in some restricted areas and has given results which promise that it is possible to obtain increased collaboration in the international domain. It can be practiced usefully only through the concerted efforts of the United States, Great Britain, and France for the maintenance of order and peace in the world. France constantly applies herself to favor such a collaboration which is within the logic of her doctrine. Between the Americans and us there is no true opposition of interests, no profound divergence of goals. . . . In order to remedy efficaciously the world crisis from which she suffers so cruelly, America needs the cooperation of France and England; to secure order, peace and prosperity in Europe, Great Britain and France need the cooperation of the United States. The common cause to serve is so great, so vast, so urgent, that it is well that each one sacrifices a few particular preoccupations.

So urgent, we say, because it suffices to consider what is happening at this moment in the world—the actual war in the Far East, the threat, more precise each day, of a halting of the disarmament conference, the malaise which weighs on central Europe, the breath of Hitlerian folly which blows on Germany—in order to be convinced that circumstances are pressing and that it is becoming urgent to act resolutely against the international disorder which dangerously compromises our civilization. Our English friends, sometimes so slow to be roused, are starting to discern the realities of the hour clearly. It suffices to read the commentaries in the London newspapers about the drama which is actually unfolding in Germany to affirm that the danger which Hitlerism is creating has opened eyes on the other side of the Channel. . . .

. . . Vigilance is demanded of all people animated with a sincere desire for peace, and it is necessary that the powers which can actually set up obstacles to every real danger should exert themselves at a useful time there where one must make it understood that Europe needs confidence and serenity of soul in order to work for its rising again and that these are adventures about which Europe cannot be complacent.

LONDON. *The Times*, March 6, 1933.

MR. ROOSEVELT has made an admirable beginning. In his inaugural speech on Saturday he candidly reviewed the difficulties of the position in the United States, accepted the responsibility for dealing with them, outlined the policy which he intends to pursue, and promised to shirk no part of his duty, even if he should have to ask Congress for "broad executive power to wage war against the emergency as great as the power that would have been given me if we were in fact invaded by a foreign foe." In the four-month interregnum since his election the situation, bad as it was then, has grown steadily worse and at an ever increasing pace, until at last something like panic seems to have taken control of large sections of the American people. On the very morning of his inauguration the State of New York itself was driven to decree a temporary suspension of banking facilities, thus following the example set by the State of Michigan three weeks ago and since then by many other States. There is now no part of the United States where depositors are permitted freely to withdraw their own money from the banks as they require it. The bank crisis, with its inevitable paralyzing effect on an already stagnant trade, and even on the everyday activities of life, has now enveloped the whole nation and has compelled the shutting down of all exchanges dealing in securities and commodities throughout the country. When the news reached Washington that the great metropolitan banks had been compelled to close their doors, the thousands gathered together for the inauguration must have felt that the very hour of the crisis had struck. They must have prayed that, as so often before, the country's urgent need would bring forth a man who was capable of meeting it. And certainly the speech which they heard was a heartening response to this unspoken appeal. Taking upon his shoulders a burden of power and responsibility as great as has ever rested on any one man, at a time moreover as critical as any in the history of his country, MR. ROOSEVELT has addressed himself to his colossal task with candour, with courage, and with determination.

There is no need here to summarize a speech which is the shortest ever made by an American President on taking the oath of office. . . . What is important to note is the spirit which inspired it throughout. A high and resolute militancy breathes in every line. Speeches are not actions; but here at any rate is a speech which promises action and which is instinct with confidence that the action promised will be successful. Many who read it in this country will hope that the new PRESIDENT will infect not only his own countrymen but others on this side of the ocean with something like his own confidence in "waging war against the emergency." In his references to the causes of the depression he does not shrink from unpleasant truths, though perhaps he oversimplifies a complicated story and dwells too exclusively on one set of its many origins. But, even so, he is sure of a response from the American people, especially in their present mood. . . .

. . . His most urgent task, as he recognizes, is "to put the people to work," a problem which he is convinced can be solved if it is wisely and courageously taken in hand. He is even prepared to adopt the method of direct recruiting by the Government for carrying out "greatly needed projects to stimulate and organize the use of our national resources." He proposes to redress the "overbalance of population" in the industrial centers by endeavouring to provide on a national scale for a better use of the land and by "definite steps," which he does not particularize, to raise the value of agricultural produce. He is convinced of the necessity of the "national planning and supervision of all forms of transportation and communication and of all other utilities which have a definitely public character." In giving effect to this conviction he is likely to rouse the opposition of a good many vested interests, which will only be partially reconciled by his insistence on a drastic reduction of expenditure by all governing bodies, Federal, State, and local alike. Nor will they be any better pleased with his declaration that there must be "safeguards against the return of the evils of the old order."

. . . Not only is immediate and, it may be, drastic action required if catastrophe is to be avoided in the United States. To set America on the way to recovery is itself an important and necessary contribution to world recovery. And America, less dependent on international trade than almost any other country—certainly far less than Great Britain—is by so much the more capable of winning her way back by independent action to a measure of her former prosperity. MR. ROOSEVELT did not confine himself to giving the broad outlines of his plan of campaign against the depression. He announced that a special session of the new Congress would be called immediately to consider the detailed measures which he would present, and nothing in his speech was more significant or called forth greater applause than his plain intimation that he would seek wartime emergency powers to carry out his plans if he should fail to secure the necessary cooperation from Congress. The tone and temper of his speech must have a bracing effect on American opinion, and its good effects will not be confined to one side of the Atlantic. If his courageous words are followed by equally courageous action, then he may lead not only his own country but the whole world with it back to sounder and more secure prosperity.

Topic 25

THE ATTACK ON PEARL HARBOR

1941

Negotiations between Japan and the United States grew tense and cautious after July 1937 when Japanese forces advanced into north China. President Franklin Roosevelt's "Quarantine Speech" in October 1937 urged peace-loving nations to quarantine aggressors: this speech probably increased American efforts to boycott Japanese goods. Sensitive to the power and fury of isolationists, and the increasingly critical position of Great Britain, Roosevelt sought limitations on Japanese expansion without resorting to war. On September 27, 1940, Japan joined Germany and Italy in a Tripartite Pact: the members pledged assistance to the victim of an American attack. After Japan obtained bases in southern Indochina from the Vichy French government, Roosevelt, in August 1941, froze all Japanese assets in the United States and warned the Japanese against military advances into other countries. By November 3, the Japanese government had decided to attack Pearl Harbor if negotiations in Washington failed. Refusing to accept State Department proposals that she withdraw from Indochina and China, Japan set in motion on November 29 the final countdown for a carrier-based attack on Pearl Harbor. At 7:55 Sunday morning, December 7, Hawaii time (Monday morning, December 8, Japan time), the attack began. When the fighting ended, American military casualties exceeded 2,200 killed, 1,100 wounded; 19 American naval vessels were sunk or damaged, and 188 airplanes destroyed. Japan lost twenty-nine planes and pilots. On December 8, the United States declared war on Japan; on December 11, Germany and Italy declared war on the United States, and that same day, Congress declared war against them.

TOKYO. *Japan Times & Advertiser,* December 10, 1941.

BATTLE OF HAWAII

It is still too early to observe in true perspective the results and significance of the battle of Hawaii which the Imperial Navy opened on Monday morning. However, the facts and figures already given out by official quarters are quite sufficient to show the turn of the war which has been staged with dramatic suddenness, which is explainable only by the magnitude of the decision Japan had been forced to take.

. . . Of the entire American fleet based at Pearl Harbor, something like 70 percent has been disposed of on the opening day of the Pacific battle.

. . . the result of the battle of Hawaii is already quite decisive in character as far as the opening phase of the Pacific war is concerned. It may also be appropriate to point out the magnitude of the strategic conception of the present Hawaiian battle. Honolulu is 6,286 kilometers from Yokohama. The assault on the island was opened in concert with the attack, from the air and sea, on Guam, some 2,400 kilometers, Davao 3,456 kilometers, and Singapore some 6,000 kilometers from Yokohama. In the sweep of conception, in its bold character, the present strategic plan of the Imperial Navy has nothing to compare in the naval annals of the world.

However, it is one thing to conceive such a strategic plan and quite another thing to execute it. The results achieved at Hawaii and other points of attack even at this early stage prove that the men and ships of the Imperial Navy are quite equal to the task with which it is charged. Their work and spirit are true to the tradition of the Navy whose early chapters were glorified by admirals like Togo. Their present success bears, as nothing else does, testimony to the state of efficiency attained by the entire Navy.

For this supreme hour it has drilled and trained, sparing of words but always steadfast to its great purpose. Their training began, it may be said, when the Imperial Navy had to suffer humiliation at the Washington conference of 1922–1923. In that hour it decided that inferior tonnage could be made up only by one thing, namely training. That they have lived up to this resolution, and that their idea was infallible is proved by feats that have glorified the opening page of the Pacific battle and justified the faith that the Japanese nation has always unquestioningly reposed in its Navy.

AMERICAN RESPONSIBILITY

A perusal of the memorandum and summary of the diplomatic conversations at Washington . . . ought to be sufficient to show how Japan strove to the last moment in the cause of Pacific peace. However, it is pertinent to enlarge on this point.

In the note presented to Washington on November 20 the Japanese Government indicated the limit to which it was ready to concede in order to reach an amicable understanding. This was shown by five points: namely,

(1) Both Japan and America undertake not to send troops into any of the regions, excepting French Indochina, in the southeastern Pacific area;

(2) Both countries cooperate in the Netherlands East Indies to secure those goods and commodities of which they stand in need;

(3) Both countries undertake to restore commercial relations to those prevailing prior to the freezing of assets, and the American Government consent to supply Japan with oil as required;

(4) The American Government undertake not to resort to measures and actions prejudicial to the restoration of general peace between Japan and China;

(5) The Japanese Government undertakes to withdraw troops from French Indochina upon either restoration of peace between Japan and China or establishment of an equitable peace in the Pacific area; and to remove the Japanese troops from the southern part of French Indochina to the north upon the conclusion of an agreement with America as then proposed.

The rational and well-considered features of the Japanese proposal must be apparent to any student of East Asian affairs in the light of reality or to those who were disposed to weigh the Far Eastern situation in fairness. However, the American Government rejected the proposal on the ground of being only a modus vivendi, saying that it would be futile to try to settle the situation by such means as long as the two governments failed to agree in fundamental points.

It was made quite clear that the American Government was consistently motivated by the desire, not to secure peace over the Pacific by adjustment of relations, but to consolidate its own position in China and in other parts of the Far East. Dipolmatic conversations, from Washington's standpoint, were only a process leading to the action for achievement of the end it had always held in view regarding the Far East. It became conclusive that the American Government had interest for Far Eastern peace only so far as it assured its own position in that part of the world.

No less serious an error was committed by the American Government when it underrated the fighting power of Japan and believed that Japanese submission could be wrested by threats of force. This attitude only drove the Japanese nation into the last resolve of taking up arms in the cause they were prepared to defend to the last.

The aim of the war is clear as far as Japan goes. It aims at the ultimate object of a new order for East Asia. Under this order all peoples of the East are to have fair opportunity and shares in material welfare under reasonable conditions. Its achievement means a new East Asia no longer working at the behest of foreign taskmasters or sweating for their interests only. It will indeed be a new chapter in the history of East Asia which is now promised, a new era of peace of such a pattern as only the true spirit of humanity and progress can conceive.

PARIS. *Le Temps*, **December 10, 1941.**

The war has become worldwide. It has made the world tour and the celebrated, peaceful roundelay evoked by Paul Fort has become an apocalyptic roundelay, an immense round of death and destruction. The war is spreading and prolonging itself and many men could be tempted to despair. When will they again find enough wisdom to stop before the abyss where civilization risks disappearing? Before this event the French obviously have to fear an increase of their misfortunes, an infinite prolongation of the bloody crisis which has struck them and from which they laboriously recover. They have to fear for the continent with which they feel bound up through physical privations that are becoming more and more painful.

Nevertheless, let us not hesitate to write it: perhaps this sudden extension of the plague over the whole surface of the globe is preferable to its slow propagation which would no doubt last for years.

In this total war all problems present themselves at once. They will have to be resolved all together. An enduring peace will have to be established not only between the countries of a single continent, but between the continents themselves, and without doubt this last task will be the most important, that on which the first will depend. The immensity itself of the war, the number and diversity of nations which are engaged in it, will demand that one take the eternal human values into consideration. The peace will have, like the war, a character of universality.

Will this extension of the conflict not be the most convincing and the most evident proof of the interdependence of nations and of continents themselves? The era of little national wars seems closed since 1914. Interests, however, are too tangled for it to be possible to limit the conflagration as one likes. No one, powerful as he may be, is able from now on to say to the war: "You will not go any farther." Let us keep from speaking about the fatality of the war. Its development is only the consequence of this union, through multiple and sometimes invisible bonds of nations on the whole surface of the inhabited globe. One may try to hide these bonds under the veil of opposing ideologies. Doubtlessly, diverse conceptions of the world are sometimes opposed to the point of giving vent to force; but above them is found the complicated and tight network of interests which, despite their apparent contradiction, are nevertheless common to all peoples.

Total and worldwide war will one day make clear the necessity of a total and worldwide reconciliation. One will see then that a continent, as evolved as it is, cannot live without communicating materially and spiritually with other continents; that America is not able to do without Europe any more than Europe can do without Asia or Africa. So then this great crisis such as the world has never known will inevitably have a universal solution, and we cannot prevent it from being so. We will all have to suffer further. How many generations will be sacrificed! But we must, nevertheless, raise our souls above these sufferings and think, before the rage of the torrent, of resurrecting our murdered fatherland, assured of living in a renewed world and of holding there the place that its past, its traditions and genius have fixed for it.

BERLIN. *Deutsche Allgemeine Zeitung,* **December 9, 1941.**

ROOSEVELT HAS HIS WAR

As is so often the case, the discretion of criminals has backfired. Roosevelt now has his war, which he had sought, but it has come in another form and another fashion from what he had wished. He managed everything most slyly. He knew of the obligations of Japan under the Tripartite Pact and so worked with all his power on a war plan which was already a reality through his infamous order to shoot of some months ago. The scheme of his criminal calculations was to creep into war with the Axis Powers without great formalities, but first of all through use of the stick and the carrot to avoid war with Japan. He would kill two birds with one stone. Because this refined plan truly gave him the potential to deceive the American people, it led to a war without Congress and against the election campaign promise of 1940. Moreover he thought in this plan to carry the war to the powers of the New Order "one after another." He had everything nicely reasoned out. But in this one thing he was in error, and truly the destiny of a criminal usually depends on a particular fact, which his discretion has overlooked or falsely assessed. President Roosevelt himself, and those with him, have deceived the American people and gotten into a war, which his own war plan was to prevent.

So completely was he entangled in his own ideal, that he completely misunderstood the attitude of Japan. His judgment of Japan rested on a selected circle of Japanese opinions, and not on a knowledge of the Japanese people, their honor and vital necessities. This Rooseveltian judgment wanted an agreement of businessmen, and in this assumption the warmonger Roosevelt began his fatal mistake. Through an economic war against Japan, through an embargo of cash transactions and oil imports, he thought he could so break the Japanese will that in the long run a businessman would take over. However, he has obtained the opposite. Indeed in the transactions with the U. S. A. the Japanese have displayed an infinite patience. Prince Konoye sent his personal letter to Roosevelt. The new government of Tojo moved the transactions forward and besides even sent Special-Ambassador Kurusu to the assistance of Ambassador Nomura in Washington. But the men in the Roosevelt camp only considered all this signs of weakness. The special session of the Japanese parliament did not open their eyes. Roosevelt still always believed he could impose dishonorable conditions on the Japanese. . . .

. . . The Quarantine Speech of Chicago already showed the war designs of Roosevelt against the Axis powers and Japan. Still in peacetime, he conspired with Churchill behind the back of the British government of that time. His ambassadors in London, Paris and Warsaw, on his instructions, gave rise to the impression of American assistance for the war and for forcing peace on all of Germany. In 1940 we captured documents containing details of the steps the American ambassadors undertook, and the promises they gave, notwithstanding the fact that America was still bound by the law of neutrality. So Roosevelt strongly pushed Belgrade and Athens to resistance, and soon he gave away promises of lend-lease to all possible states, in the same manner in which he had earlier guaranteed the English that he would plunge the entire [German] people into misfortune.

So today Roosevelt is the guilty person not only for East Asia, but for the entire world conflagration. But for him the European war would have ended long ago. For had Roosevelt not broken and gone around the Neutrality laws, the English could have purchased no war materials after December 1940, and could have paid for no foodstuffs. Roosevelt was throughout the guilty person and will be for the now certain collapse of the British Empire. His whole war policy is a single chain of deceit and fraud to the Congress and people of the U. S. A.

In the beginning of 1941 Roosevelt raised the cash clause. He abandoned it through the authority given him in the lend-lease law to give away American war supplies. He succeeded in overcoming the doubts of Congress with the explicit promises that American ships would remain outside of the blockade zone. Then he began a search for incidents to catch Congress unawares. Without the consent of Congress he issued in July 1941 the shooting order to the American fleet. Without the consent of Congress, he occupied Iceland. American destroyers engaged in active war actions. The shooting war which the President of the U. S. A. inaugurated here was illegal by constitutional and by international law. The dispatch of Harriman to Moscow, the extension of lend-lease to the Bolshevik partner, the shipment of war material to Vladivostok, all showed that the President sought war on land and sea, and undertook war acts that certainly were outside international law.

Surrounded by Jewish counselors and influenced by businessmen, Roosevelt extended a covetous hand for world domination. He took the British possessions in the West Indies, seized, through the occupation of Dutch Guiana, for the first time a military base on the South American continent, to subjugate it and as a springboard to abuse Africa. This is his world war. The frustrated plan to defraud Japan now gives to him a different end to his provoked altercation than he had ever dreamed. Through his false assessment of Japan he has confirmed that he had no idea of our powers at this time or in the future. It sounds like a myth that he once wrote a book that bore the title, *Looking Forward,* that he once attempted a New Deal.

MEXICO CITY. *Excelsior*, December 8, 1941.

THE WAR IN THE PACIFIC

We are, without any doubt, confronted by events whose consequences it is impossible to foresee nor to calculate in all their scope and repercussions. We are referring to the sensational news that moved the world to pity and especially the American nations: the aggression of the Japanese forces against the Philippine and Hawaiian Islands. This is the clear technique, already known, of the undeclared war; of the deceitful, unexpected attack when all the diplomats and statesmen of Japan and the United States could be found in negotiations to avoid that which today fatally has happened.

The Empire of the Eastern Sun, before the demands of our northern neighbors to withdraw from the military alliance with the European nations of the Axis and to desist [from] the always growing expansion of African conquests, is answering with undercover preparations of the terrible surprise, and is working precisely in the most wearying manner in the civilized world—attacking without warning and without cutting the bridges extended by themselves in order to avoid the war. The Japanese were the inventors of the formula—wholly exempt from the principle of justice, Machiavellian—of the undeclared war. They utilized it for the first time in Korea in the face of Russia to attack its squadron without a previous declaration of war at the beginning of this century. It has been only a few years since the bloody chapter was opened which today darkens humanity, that is, when the Japanese militarists wrote the tragic prologue with the undeclared wars against Manchuria and China.

Today began what has to be the conclusion of the Asiatic technique already described. While Roosevelt and Cordell Hull declared that they would never go to war if Japan abstained from attacking Siam and Burma, and while they made the last desperate attempt at conciliation apparently seconded by the Hirohito empire, this one (the Hirohito empire) has preferred the red road of the war with the typical system of all militarisms: aggression—mortal, brutal and hypocritical.

Of this event, which in International Law constitutes the most difficult problem, that is, the demarcation of the conflict and its authors, in this case one finds it very clear. The aggression has split the Japanese nation and the United States finds itself in a defensive battle, imposed by necessity and the spirit of conquest by another power. Ethics and the law assist them, in undoubtable form, by reinforcing the attitude of the champions of liberty that they have followed gracefully in the last years. They themselves are setting forth the example in America, by the Good Neighbor policy, which is now solid and productive.

The war, which now is a crude and imperious act, knocks therefore at the doors of Mexico, which finds itself in the center of action, and as it is the direct route by the way of its coasts to the Panama Canal, key point for the North American continental defense. We are used to being spectators and because of that tend to be uninvolved in our sympathies and antipathies; with the judgment of one who is limited to observing, the war is a phenomenon that until now has not affected us in a direct way, and for that we give ourselves the luxury of continuing our discussions, of deeply involving ourselves in international discord, of not being prudent, and of even being disorderly. Today before the evidence of a battle that has galvanized and agitated our powerful neighbors, that has caused the mobilization of the navy, army and the people of the United States, we Mexicans ought to modify our mentality as spectators, understanding that the actual events have definitive characteristics superior to the strongest human wills; wanting to or not, we are now among them. And the indisputable realism is that our individual and common actions ought to be dedicated to the national good.

The first and logical thing is to continue without hesitation or vacillation the international policy that the President of the Republic adopted [the breaking of diplomatic relations with Japan] since the latest events. The time of disputes and antagonisms has been superseded by the events. Each and every one of us Mexicans ought to understand that our best help to the nation and to the country in this grave, decisive crisis will be the intimate and profound conviction that only our spirit, united and national, only discipline accepted with spontaneity and liberty, will help us to frighten away the irresistible whirlwind that so nearly catches us.

This is the minimum that Mexico can hope for from her children. The irresistible enslaving reality imposes a conduct very different from the norm. Without self-defeating exaggerations but with firmness and serenity, we will have to go forth to meet without delay the grave events that shake and agitate us.

ROME. *L'Osservatore Romano*, December 9, 1941.

The tension, more or less concealed, that existed in the Pacific between the Anglo-Saxon powers on one side and the Japanese on the other, surprisingly exploded in open hostility, after a period of ups and downs that, within these last months, had again brought back the problems of the Pacific to first importance on the stage of international interest.

Of the naval conflict that exploded between Japan, the United States and England, one must examine the remote motives and the motives of the future. . . .

. . . in the spring of last year negotiations opened between the governments of Tokyo and of Washington for adding an agreement on all the existing problems between the two nations. The negotiations were suspended the first time following the secession of the strategic bases in Indochina, but then were revived and, with brief interruptions, were carried on until Sunday. They assumed a particularly lively course after the constitution of the actual government by General Tojo who, on October 20th, succeeded the resigning Prince Konoye. The new government decided to send to Washington, to specially advise Ambassador Nomura, ex-ambassador to Berlin, Kurusu, who in the name of his government had signed the Triple Alliance pact in Berlin. The negotiations continued with optimistic and pessimistic variants, and in general it can be affirmed that the pessimism of the press contrasted with the optimism of the official negotiators. Again last Friday the official voice of the Japanese government declared that the negotiations displayed, in a spirit of great sincerity, a determined attempt to solve the disputes in the Pacific. With equal optimism, Ambassadors Nomura and Kurusu expressed themselves . . . never dismissing the hope of obtaining an agreement without having to resort to war . . . .

. . . Last November 26th, the United States Secretary of State, Cordell Hull, in a note delivered to Ambassador Nomura and to Kurusu, proposed as essential conditions for the reestablishment of good Japanese-American relations the recognition of Chiang Kai-shek's China in its boundaries of July 7, 1937, and specifically, the withdrawal of Japanese troops . . . the response to Cordell Hull's note was delivered to the American ambassador in Tokyo only yesterday morning, when the hostilities were already underway.

. . . the conflagration of the war, in these last hours, extended itself to all the continents and on all the seas. The war certainly assumes the course and the name of worldwide more so than the other; the first world war was surely more definite and distinct than this.

LONDON. *The Times*, **December 8, 1941.**

Japan has struck. Faithful to what is now the well-established rule in Axis warfare and to the precedents followed by HITLER when he marched on Russia last June, she has attacked the United States without warning. While MR. KURUSU and ADMIRAL NOMURA were actually in the State Department continuing their talks with MR. CORDELL HULL, large forces of Japanese aeroplanes, apparently from naval aircraft carriers, bombed Pearl Harbor, the big American base in the Hawaiian Islands, and Manila, the capital of the Philippines. An American army transport carrying lumber has been torpedoed and sunk 1,300 miles west of San Francisco, though this may possibly have been the work not of a Japanese but of a German submarine. PRESIDENT ROOSEVELT, in his capacity as commander-in-chief of all the armed forces of the Republic, has ordered the American Army and Navy to take the action which had been arranged for such an emergency. A naval engagement is apparently in progress off Honolulu and it is reported that a Japanese aircraft carrier has been sunk. The war in the Pacific has in fact begun. The Japanese attacked without warning, but a declaration that a state of war exists between Japan and the United States and Great Britain "in the western Pacific" has since been issued not by the Japanese Government, but by the Japanese High Command. An American declaration of war must await the decision of Congress, but there can be no doubt of the decision when Congress assembles today. Both Houses of Parliament meet this afternoon, and MR.

CHURCHILL'S pledge that in case of war with Japan Britain will be at America's side within the hour is certain to be honored.

While portents of some impending action had been accumulating, few people expected this sudden attack on American bases in the Pacific. An invasion of Thailand seemed far more likely. Indeed it was this apprehension which apparently prompted MR. ROOSEVELT'S message to the EMPEROR. In his message the PRESIDENT, stirred by the reports received of Japanese troop concentrations and movements in and about French Indochina, declared that it was impossible to go on living "on a keg of dynamite." American opinion has been restive under the suspicion that, on the Japanese side, the talks in Washington were being used merely to gain time, without any real endeavor to reach a settlement. These suspicions were increased by reports that Japan was pouring troops into Indochina while MR. KURUSU and ADMIRAL NOMURA were holding MR. CORDELL HULL in long conversations which seemed to lead nowhere, while the Japanese Government showed no eagerness to reply to the United States' note of over ten days ago laying down the essential principles for any understanding between the two nations, and while Japanese Ministers, to say nothing of the Japanese press, indulged in language which appeared to make a breach inevitable. A few days ago, the American Government, feeling that it was useless to continue conversations in this atmosphere, sent an explicit request to Tokyo for an explanation of movements which appeared to foreshadow further Japanese aggression by an attack upon Thailand. The evasive reply increased American doubts of Japanese good faith.

Later reports made this evasiveness seem the more suspicious. They gave information of big concentrations of troops and of the movements of large and heavily escorted convoys. In these circumstances MR. ROOSEVELT, despairing of any straightforward dealing from the militarists now controlling Japan, decided to make a personal appeal to the EMPEROR in a final attempt to preserve peace. The movements of Japanese troops, the utterances of Japanese statesmen, and the bellicose attitude of the Japanese press had aroused serious alarm. Reports from Singapore, from Australia, from the Netherlands East Indies, as well as from Thailand, had shown how intensively preparations were being made to meet the crisis. In an attempt to lull these anxieties, a Japanese official spokesman at the end of the week declared that the Washington talks would continue in the hope of finding a common formula to ease the situation in the Pacific. At the same time the Japanese press, under rigid Government control, was exhausting its vocabulary in abuse of the American attitude, and a reply to MR. CORDELL HULL'S statement of principles was on the way. This reply MR. HULL described to the JAPANESE AMBASSADOR yesterday as "crowded with infamous falsehoods and distortions."

The issue has all along been very simple. MR. CORDELL HULL stated it with complete frankness at his Press conference a week ago. Japan, he said, had followed a policy depending upon force, upon conquest, and upon the oppression of subjugated peoples. She represented in the Far East what HITLER represented in Europe. Any settlement, he made it plain, must be based upon very different principles, which he defined in his recent Note to Tokyo. Japan has given her reply, not in words but in armed action. The United States and the Powers acting in concert with her will take up the challange. Japan has decided upon war and she now finds herself faced with forces which in the long run she will be powerless to resist. The presence in Malayan waters of the Prince of Wales and her consorts is proof that MR. CHURCHILL'S recent pledge to the United States was no empty assurance, and Australia, New Zealand, and the Netherlands East Indies, whose united forces make a formidable total, have shown plainly enough where they stand.

Topic 26

THE ATOMIC BOMB

1945

On July 16, 1945, an atomic bomb was successfully detonated at Alamogordo, New Mexico. On August 6, a second one exploded over the city of Hiroshima with an explosive force equivalent to 20,000 tons of TNT. Three days later, a more powerful one exploded over Nagasaki, and on August 10, Japan called for an armistice with the provision that Emperor Hirohito retain his throne. General Douglas MacArthur accepted the formal Japanese surrender in Tokyo Bay on September 2.

TOKYO. *The Nippon Times,* **August 10, 1945.**

In the air attack on Hiroshima Monday morning, the enemy used a new type of bomb of unprecedented power. Not only has the greater part of the city been wiped out, but an extraordinary proportion of the inhabitants have been either killed or injured. The use of a weapon of such terrifying destructiveness not only commands attention as a matter of a new technique in the conduct of war. More fundamentally and vitally it opens up a most grave and profound moral problem in which the very future of humanity is put at stake.

Whether the enemy fully realizes the moral implications of the use of such an instrument of destruction or not, he cannot escape the awful responsibility for his action. For there is no doubt that he has carried out this deed with cold-hearted calculation. This was no mere excess committed in the heat of battle. It was an act of premeditated wholesale murder, the deliberate snuffing out of the lives of tens of thousands of innocent civilians who had no chance of protecting themselves in the slightest degree. How deliberate and callous the enemy is in his unprincipled action is proved by the infamous threat of President Truman to use this diabolic weapon on an increasing scale.

How utterly unjustifiable is the resort to such an inhumane method of warfare needs no arguing. It goes without saying that such action flagrantly contravenes the basic principle of international law as expressed in Article XXII of The Hague Convention in Regard to the Laws of War which definitely proclaims that belligerent nations can have no claim to a right to exercise unlimited power. For, what is it but a presumptuous abuse of unlimited and unprincipled power when the United States resorts to the use of such a weapon as this bomb which spreads indiscriminate and wanton destruction upon an extensive civilian population?

But it is not primarily a matter of legal justifiability or even of the principles of international conduct. It is a matter which goes to the very heart of the fundamental concept of human morality. How can a human being with any claim to a sense of moral responsibility deliberately let loose an instrument of destruction which can at one stroke annihilate an appalling [sic] segment of mankind? This is not war; this is not even murder; this is pure nihilism. This is a crime against God and humanity which strikes at the very basis of moral existence. What meaning is there in any international law, in any rule of human conduct, in any concept of right and wrong, if the very foundations of morality are to be overthrown as the use of this instrument of total destruction threatens to do?

The crime of the Americans stands out in ghastly repulsiveness all the more for the ironic contradiction it affords to their lying pretensions. For in their noisy statements, they have always claimed to be the champions of fairness and humanitarianism. In the early days of the China Affair, the United States repeatedly protested against the bombing operations of the Japanese forces notwithstanding the fact that the Japanese operations were conducted on a limited scale against strictly military objectives. But where its own actions are concerned, the United States seems to see no inconsistency in committing on an unimaginably vast scale the very same crime it had falsely accused others of committing.

This hypocritical character of the Americans had already been amply demonstrated in the previous bombings of Japanese cities. Strewing explosives and fire bombs indiscriminately over an extensive area, hitting large cities and small towns without distinction, wiping out vast districts which could not be mistaken as being anything but strictly residential in character, burning or blasting to death countless thousands of helpless women and children, and machine-gunning fleeing refugees, the American raiders had already shown how completely they violate in their actual deeds the principles of humanity which they mouth in conspicuous pretense.

But now beside the latest technique of total destruction which the Americans have adopted, their earlier crimes pale into relative insignificance. What more barbarous atrocity can there be than to wipe out at one stroke the population of a whole city without distinction—men, women, and children; the aged, the weak, the infirm; those in positions of authority, and those with no power at all; all snuffed out without being given a chance of lifting even a finger in either defense or defiance!

The United States may claim, in a lame attempt to raise a pretext in justification of its latest action, that a policy of utter annihilation is necessitated by Japan's failure to heed the recent demand for unconditional surrender. But the question of surrendering or not surrendering certainly can have not the slightest relevance to the question of whether it is justifiable to use a method which under any circumstance is strictly condemned alike by the principles of international law and of morality. For this American outrage against the fundamental moral sense of mankind, Japan must proclaim to the world its protest against the United States which has made itself the archenemy of humanity.

LONDON. *The Times,* August 8, 1945.

An impenetrable cloud of dust and smoke, standing over the ruin of the great Japanese arsenal at Hiroshima, still veils the undoubtedly stupendous destruction wrought by the first impact in war of the atomic bomb. A mist no less impenetrable is likely for a long time to conceal the full significance in human affairs of the release of the vast and mysterious power hitherto locked within the infinitesimal units of which the material structure of the universe is built up. All that can be said with certainty is that the world stands in the presence of a revolution in earthly affairs at least as big with potentialities of good and evil as when the forces of steam or electricity were harnessed for the first time to the purposes of industry and war.

It has to be sorrowfully acknowledged that these epoch-making conquests of science are no sooner achieved than they are turned to the purposes of mutual destruction. Thus war battens on peace. This time, however, it is the pressure of war itself that has forced ahead a process which can be turned against war in the long run and at the same time promises a greater material enrichment of life than any single scientific discovery before it. Science itself is neutral, like the blind forces of nature that it studies and aspires to control. Nations fighting for their existence, however, seek to make science their ally by enlisting men of science in their service. As men of science they seek only truth, but as patriots in the hour of their country's danger they are legitimately called upon to deflect their researchers as policy and strategy require. The immense expenditure incurred in the quest of the atomic bomb— that is to say the immense share of the total manpower and material resources of the allied nations put at the disposal of the comparatively few scientists directing the quest—amounting as it has done to two thousand million dollars, is out of all proportion to anything that scientific research can command in time of peace. There is no need to interpret this fact cynically; these vast sums were risked—for the project was, as PRESIDENT TRUMAN says, "a gamble"—as a means to ensure the survival of a civilization in which the disinterested pursuit of knowledge might again be made secure . . . . the urgencies of war have but hastened—probably by many years—a discovery that the great physicists of the world have long foreseen, and towards which they have been moving by the patient processes of the laboratory for many years past.

Imagination shudders at the thought that this terrifying power might have fallen into the hands of the enemies of civilization instead of its protectors. It is known that Nazi Germany was seeking frantically after the secret; and many gallant British and Norwegian lives were spent in thwarting the design. The allies, however, have a right to feel that it is no accident which won them the momentous race. They have achieved an outstanding intellectual victory over the enemy, and it is a victory that comes to them by right. It is significant that two of the outstanding scientists named as collaborators in the Anglo-American programme experiment were German subjects exiled from their country on the ground of race. Preeminence in the pursuit of knowledge must belong to a social system in which men, whatever their origin, are free to follow "whithersoever the argument may lead"; in the intellectual sphere as on the battlefield, the discipline of free minds has its inalienable advantage.

Speculation can only peer a little way into the future that the new power opens for the world. The issue of the Japanese war, already certain, must be greatly hastened, whether the rulers of Tokyo acknowledge by surrender the demonstration that the allies hold them in the hollow of their hand, or insist on immolating their country before the irresistible power of the new weapon, which is amply acknowledged in their latest broadcasts. If they choose the second alternative, it seems likely that the allies may be able to accomplish, what RUNDSTEDT is said to have expected to achieve against Britain, the destruction of Japanese resistance in the home islands by air power alone, leaving to the army the role of occupation only. Beyond the Japanese war the consequences for strategy and grand tactics are vast but incalculable. Presumably all fortification, as it has been hitherto understood, becomes immediately obsolete, for nothing can resist the

new force. Schemes for world security founded on the maintenance of bases at the strategic points of the globe will call for
exhaustive reconsideration.

All strategic calculations, however, become insignificant before the evident challenge to the people of the world to rise to
the fateful occasion in such a degree as to make strategy itself
speedily irrelevant. Beyond all doubt, unless atomic power is
turned to serve the aims of peace, it can speedily make an end of
civilized life on earth. It will not serve those aims through the
mere dissemination of the knowledge that renewal of war now
means universal destruction and collapse. History, especially the
history of recent times in which the instruments of destruction
and torment have so rapidly multiplied, holds out no expectation
that men will ever be deterred from war by fear alone; and on
the whole that is to the credit of human nature. If the secular
curse is to be laid, it must be by the positive love of peace. Reason
will tell mankind that war is becoming with certainty suicidal.
But reason will no more avail than the appeal to fear. Humanity
must be able to call upon deeper convictions. All that can be
directly expected because of the existence of the new terrifying
power is a livelier sense among statesmen and the peoples to whom
they are answerable of the weight of the responsibility of choosing
between peace and war. . . .

CAPETOWN [SOUTH AFRICA]. *The Guardian*, August 9,
1945.

News of the most recent war weapon, the atomic bomb, with
a blasting power two thousand times greater than that of any other
bomb, will be used as a text for sermons on the horrors of war
and its immense dangers to the whole of humanity.

Other developments in the war against Japan could be used
to drive home the same lesson. As, for instance, the use of a
naval force some thousands of miles from any land base in order
to carry out devastating raids on the enemy.

No country, no matter how remote, can be held immune from

attack. South Africa today is as exposed to the dangers of war as any Balkan State.

But it is not the growth of the destructive weapons of warfare that will put an end to war. No matter how afraid we human beings may be of the consequences, we shall continue to be persuaded, bluffed and bullied into going to war if our rulers so desire.

In order to stop wars, we must put an end to the conditions that produce them. Not by atomic bombs, but by scrapping the system of imperialism, the search for markets and profits, will we stop war.

MEXICO CITY. *Excelsior*, December 9, 1945.

It is a presently known fact that universal science for some time has been studying, analyzing and writing about the explosive phenomenon of the atom and that in several countries like Germany, England and the United States, groups of scientists have absorbed themselves in the discovery of what someone has designated the philosopher's stone of the Middle Ages. It was a problem of life or death. Whoever produced the small bomb of terrifying effects not only would succeed in overpowering the enemy of the time and win that war but also could depend on that weapon [being] considered as definitive in the field of experimentation. First were the results on those deserted fields of New Mexico and it was seen how two men at a distance of eight kilometers were blown up. Secondly, a Japanese city of 300,000 inhabitants was erased from the map. Still, there is no definite data, only real observations and photographs to confirm the fact. The disintegrating power of that atomic force is of such a nature that the Japanese Cabinet of War convened convinced of the need to study the new conditions of attack; and the United Nations sent a new ultimatum to the Japanese Government assuring it that if it did not accept their conditions, the cities of its empire would fly into clouds converted into ashes. Once more the Latin phrase was confirmed: "If you want peace, prepare for war."

But this formidable scientific discovery, today in the power of the North American armies, has unusual repercussions. . . . Its possession concedes a world hegemony that can in certain circumstances be more dangerous than the anger of Nature. It suffices to think what would have become of us if the German scientists had handed over to Hitler the murderous bomb. That delirium of greatness of the Fuehrer would have been imposed on all the world and its diabolical power would have made the living of the five parts of world tremble. It can be nothing more than a system of destruction, we say. The chemical procedure can be carried out outside of the United States and, moreover, its power as a supreme recourse can be given over to a commission of nations, guardians of peace. The threat of the atomic bomb would suffice, perhaps, to keep within reason any abrupt rebellion of tomorrow. . . .

. . . As peace is hastened it ought to be credited in blood and money to the famous atomic bomb, and moreover, it should be expected that the morality of the conquering nations will permit use of it only as a heavy footstool of universal peace.

Topic 27

CONCLUDING THE KOREAN WAR

1953

A full-scale invasion of South Korea by North Korean armies on June 25, 1950, brought quick censure by the United Nations, and President Harry Truman ordered American military units to force back the invading armies north of the 38th parallel. Sixteen out of sixty United Nations members sent troops. Chinese troops joined North Korean forces in October 1950. Waging war for the limited objective of securing the 38th parallel, many Americans became frustrated. One of them, General Douglas MacArthur, was relieved of his command in 1951. A cease-fire agreement negotiated at Panmunjom on July 27, 1953, left Korea divided at the 38th parallel. At the time, the Korean conflict was America's third most costly war.

PEKING. *Jen-min Jih-pao,* **July 28, 1953.** *

Unflagging persistence by the Korean and Chinese people and tremendous efforts by peace lovers throughout the world have brought complete agreement in the 2-year-and-2-week-old

---

* From the *Survey of China Mainland Press.* Prepared by the U. S. Consulate in Hong Kong. Microfilm, Washington, D. C.

Korean armistice negotiations, after many twists and turns. The Korean armistice agreement to which the whole world has been eagerly looking forward was signed yesterday at Panmunjom. As Marshal Kim Il Sung and General Pang Teh-huai declared in the armistice orders: "The signing of the armistice agreement is the first step toward the settlement by peaceful means of the Korean question, and is therefore beneficial to the peace of the Far East and the world. It has received the fervent support of the Korean and Chinese people and has made all the peace-loving people of the world elated with joy." This victory won by the Korean and Chinese people in their great and just war against aggression and in their fight for the peaceful settlement of the Korean question has proved that the awakened Asian people are invincible in their just struggle to resist aggression and defend peace. It has proved that the world camp of peace headed by the Soviet Union is inviolable and that the forces of world peace and democracy are infinitely powerful.

Three years ago, the reactionary Syngman Rhee clique, working in collusion with the bellicose elements of the U. S., unleashed the Korean War which seriously jeopardised the peace and security of the Far East and the world. It represented a futile attempt by international adventurists to annex the whole of Korea, to invade China and to stir up a new world war. Even if they could not achieve this, they could at least build up world tension and amass great fortunes by utilizing war and the plans of war preparations to postpone the outbreak of economic crisis. But in deciding on these adventurist activities, they overestimated their own strength and underestimated the strength of the people of Asia and the world. They could not bear to see the profound changes taking place in Asia after the Second World War and especially after the victory of the Chinese revolution. But like all who refuse to recognize facts, they ran their heads into a brick wall. The heroic Korean and Chinese people dealt the aggressors smashing blows and held in check the most frantic aggressive actions carried out on the largest possible scale after the Second World War, in which the imperialist camp exhausted every effort. Thus the international adventurists have found themselves in a state of utter confusion, desperation and danger. Their timetable for unleashing a new world war was not accelerated but delayed. It became increasingly clear to the comparatively sane political leaders of the various countries that stood on the side of Syngman Rhee that to end the Korean War and settle the Korean question by peaceful means was the only way open to them.

Basically the Korean question is one of a number of international issues outstanding since the Second World War. As with other vital international problems, there was originally the necessary basis for settling this question by peaceful means. In the Three Foreign Ministers' Conference of the Soviet Union, the United States of America and Britain, held in Moscow in December, 1945, agreement was reached for the peaceful settlement of the Korean question. Had this agreement been respected and fulfilled, as the government of the U. S. S. R. scrupulously observed it, the Korean people could have achieved the unification and independence of their motherland and gone forward democratically. The Korean War could not have begun. However, the policy pursued by the U. S. Government after the war was to split Korea into South and North and to foster the reactionary Syngman Rhee clique. It finally unleashed the war of aggression against Korea in an attempt to unify Korea by armed force, to overthrow the Korean Democratic People's Republic and to set up in the whole of Korea reactionary despotic rule against the people. Not only so, but at the same time as it unleashed the war of aggression against Korea, the U. S. Government invaded China's Taiwan. And soon after, it ordered its invading forces to cross the 38th Parallel and push to the Yalu and Tumen Rivers on the borders of northeast China which created a serious menace to China's security. This adventurist policy pursued by the U. S. Government was not really abandoned even after it was compelled to accept the Korean truce negotiations as a result of failure in the war. This is the reason why the Korean armistice talks were dragged out for as long as two years.

In contrast to the diplomatic policy of the U. S., the Korean and Chinese people have consistently stood for a peaceful settlement of the Korean question. That we have had to wage war against aggression has also been for the sake of securing favorable conditions for settling the Korean question peacefully, on a fair and reasonable basis. Thus the Korean and Chinese people, throughout the intricate course of the negotiations in the last two years, have striven for an agreement on the armistice negotiations with extreme firmness and patience.

. . . Now though the Korean armistice agreement has already been signed, it is definitely not without obstacles that all its provisions will be fully observed and carried out. People all over the world still have to keep a most vigilant eye all the time on some of the bellicose elements of the American side, especially Syngman Rhee of South Korea, who is intensifying his clamor against the armistice. This puny American goldfish for whose ambition the youth or scores of nations in the world have already shed rivers of blood blindly, just because certain people in Washington need him, [*sic*] is threatening "to follow or go it alone" [as a] policy and to wreck the armistice. He knows the dilemma of United States' policy, and has therefore boldly taken up his gangsterlike stand, brewing obstacles on the road to the armistice and attempting to stop the wheel of peace in Korea. Therefore, the present problem depends entirely on whether the United States will continue to connive with the Syngman Rhee gang or is prepared to change its attitude. . . .

. . . It is worth noting that a number of influential personages in America have hitherto openly supported the sabotage activities of Syngman Rhee. Dulles, United States Secretary of State, even issued a statement on the 22nd encouraging Syngman Rhee's frantic cries about wrecking the Korean armistice, saying that he "is entitled to do so." In this statement, Dulles admitted that Syngman Rhee did not accept the armistice and "has reserved his government's position."

Syngman Rhee's so-called position, as indicated by Dulles, is the same as he has constantly been proclaiming, namely, that he would not obstruct an armistice only for 90 days; if America failed to serve his purpose of "uniting Korea" in 90 days, he would "resume hostilities." That Dulles can say Syngman Rhee "is entitled to do so," is an open encouragement to Syngman Rhee to "resume hostilities." However, it is universally known that the American negotiation delegate pledged to our side on July 13th that "there is no time limit on the effectiveness of the armistice agreement."

What we want to ask is whether the guarantee of the American negotiation delegate or the "statement" of Dulles is to count!

Three years ago, Dulles personally planned the unleashing of the war in Korea for Syngman Rhee in order to drown the country in blood. Now he has again given open encouragement to Syngman Rhee to obstruct the carrying out of the armistice terms. As a party to the Korean armistice, the U. S. Government has the responsibility of stopping and clarifying Dulles' absurd statement.

. . . to attain the further peaceful settlement of the whole Korean question, there must be consultation in the political conference of a higher level. In connection with this, the Korean-Chinese side has consistently advocated that all foreign troops, including the Chinese People's Volunteers, withdraw from Korea, and that the Korean question be settled by peaceful means, in the spirit of letting the Korean question be solved by the Korean people themselves, so as to facilitate the establishment of a united, democratic, peaceful and independent new Korea. This is the solemn mission of the political conference of a higher level. This political conference of a higher level is to be held within three months after the armistice agreement becomes effective, as recommended to the governments concerned by the commanders of both sides in the Korean War. The holding of this conference must be on the basis of equality in consultation. It is only thus that good results can be achieved. The Korean and the Chinese people and all peace-loving people throughout the world fervently hope that this political conference can proceed smoothly and will get the question settled. We will fight to the end for the peaceful settlement of the Korean question. If any bellicose elements dare to take advantage of the political conference to sabotage the armistice and wreck the conference, they are sure to meet with the strongest opposition from the Korean and the Chinese people and all the peace-loving people the world over and will invite still greater failure.

MOSCOW. *Pravda*, July 28, 1953.†

As a result of prolonged negotiations successfully concluded, a Korean truce agreement was signed in Panmunjom July 27. Hostilities have ceased. The cannonade which has continued more than three years is silent. The armed forces of the two warring sides are withdrawing along the whole front from the line of demarcation, leaving behind them a demilitarized zone. Preparation is beginning for a political conference which is to secure final settlement of the Korean question. . . .

. . . The peoples of the whole world view conclusion of a truce in Korea as the practical result of the long and stubborn struggle for peace which all progressive mankind has waged and is waging with growing vigor. The successful conclusion of truce negotiations in Korea inspired peace-loving peoples to fresh efforts in this great struggle.

The truce in Korea has shown graphically that in the present international situation the only correct and possible path to resolving disputed international issues is the path of negotiations among the interested parties and not the path of the notorious "policy of force." This most important event proves that the most complex international issues can be successfully settled by negotiations if there is the good will to settle them.

The initiators and executors of the "policy of force" have been convinced by their own experience that this policy yields no results when they try to use it against democratic countries where the peoples are masters of their own fate. The U. S. A. and the states dependent on it, which have sent their crack troops against the people of Korea, have been unable in three years of fierce fighting to break the heroic resistance of the Korean People's Democratic Republic and the Chinese people's volunteers who came to its aid.

U. S. Secretary of State Dulles, in his speech on the signing of the truce, permitted himself to boast cynically that during the

† Translation from *The Current Digest of the Soviet Press*, published weekly by The American Association for the Advancement of Slavic Studies at The Ohio State University. Copyright 1953; by permission.

course of hostilities in three years millions of Korean civilians were wiped out and the territory of North Korea "largely destroyed." Perhaps Dulles hoped to frighten somebody by this statement, but instead, the U. S. Secretary of State involuntarily stressed the true nature of American intervention, which was chiefly aimed at annihilating the peaceful population of Korea and destroying its national wealth.

The outcome of hostilities in Korea shows clearly that these methods of warfare have not helped the American command. Even American generals have had to admit that they were unable to win military victory in Korea. Former Secretary of Defense Marshall, who can hardly be suspected of harboring sympathy for Korea, once stated apropos of the progress of the war: "A myth is destroyed; we are not the mighty country we were supposed to be."

The fact is that consciousness of the justice of their struggle has imbued the Korean people and the Chinese volunteers who came to their aid with unconquerable strength and unheard-of steadfastness. The indisputable superiority of the people's democratic system, the unshakable unity of front and rear have set up conditions which enabled the Korean people, closely rallied around the Workers' Party and their government, to overcome all the difficulties of war. The People's Army, inspired by a great spirit of patriotism, has raised from its midst thousands of heroes whose exploits are immortal. As for the interventionists, the fighting spirit of their armies was low, for American soldiers realized the injustice of the cause for which they were forced to die.

That is why, though the very best divisions of the American army, experienced in the Second World War, as well as numerous air and naval units, were thrown into Korea, they were unable to win military success. After three years of war they were marking time on the same boundary from which they launched their aggression—the 38th parallel.

The American aggression against the peace-loving Korean people evoked unanimous protest throughout the world. A powerful movement against the interventionists developed in all countries.

All this led to the failure of the American ruling circles' calculations and forced them to take up truce negotiations. . . .

. . . What explains the fact that negotiations lasted so long—two years and 17 days? Only the fact that certain U. S. circles, interested in maintaining and expanding the center of war in the Far East, were making every effort to prolong and complicate if not finally to frustrate the signing of a truce. The failure of these intrigues testifies that the peoples' desire for peace has become a mighty force before which all the open and covert enemies of peace have had to withdraw.

Thus, the signing of a truce in Korea is a great victory for peace-loving forces. Lasting peace in Korea, however, will be only established when the Korean people are allowed to decide the question of their country's future for themselves, without foreign interference. Restoration of the national unity of the Korean state—a task which was at the center of all the Korean people's concern before the war—must play a definite role. Unification of Korea on a peace-loving, democratic basis is the vital concern of the Korean people themselves.

People of all countries will watch the further development of events in Korea with tremendous interest. They are showing the greatest concern that the truce agreement which was signed July 27 should not be violated by any aggressive forces. Therefore the broad public is vigilantly following the intrigues of the enemies of peace, who are trying to obstruct peaceful settlement of the Korean question.

In the U. S. A. many people are saying and writing that Syngman Rhee may "willfully" violate the truce one fine day. Everyone realizes that references to this puppet hardly relieve the United States of responsibility for observance of the agreement it signed. It goes without saying that the U. S. military command and government are responsible for carrying out the truce agreement signed by the U. S. A.

The truce in Korea has opened the way to peaceful settlement of the Korean question. Now, that the guns are silent the tasks of restoring the national unity of the Korean state, rebuilding damaged villages and towns and raising the national economy stand before the Korean people. In all this the Korean people are assured of the active help and support of the Soviet Union and other democratic countries.

The successful truce negotiations in Korea have proven convincingly that there are no unresolved international issues which cannot be settled by negotiation, by agreement among the interested parties. The consciousness of this gives peace-loving peoples new strength in the struggle to strengthen world peace.

TOKYO. *The Nippon Times,* July 28, 1953.

The effectivation [*sic*] of an armistice in Korea marks only the barest of beginnings toward the settlement of the multitude of problems facing the world which has been in in a state of constant tension as a result of the expansionist policies of the Communists. Representing the first "police action" ever taken by a worldwide organization, the Korean War and the truce which has been achieved have proven, however, that aggression does not pay. The Communist aggressors have suffered tremendous losses in lives, property and territory. And for all the Red propaganda claims of "a victory," the Communists failed in their original purpose to effect the military conquest of the Korean Peninsula.

But now that the Communists have signed an armistice agreement, it can be expected that the pressure will be on for the recognition of the Chinese Red regime and for the resumption of trade with the China continent. It will doubtlessly be argued that the Red Chinese are no longer aggressors since a truce has been arranged. A move may be launched in the United Nations to remove the "aggressor" label from the Peiping regime and to force its entry into the world body.

In Japan, the alarm will be raised that special procurement orders connected with the Korean War will come to an end, driving this nation into dire economic straits. The reopening of the China trade will be pressed as Japan's only salvation from economic disaster. The Communists and their agents may be expected to picture the Red Chinese dictatorship as peace lovers who would like nothing better than to open up the China markets for the "benefit" of the Japanese people.

This propaganda offensive must be expected. And it would be well for all of us to remind ourselves that an aggressor nation does not suddenly take on peaceful attributes just because it has signed a truce accord. Whatever may be the Communist reasons to agree to an armistice, it is certainly not founded on any real awakening to the evils of its ways. Nothing has changed fundamentally, except perhaps the Communist timetable for conquest. Red China today after the shooting war has ended is just as dangerous an enemy to freedom and peace as she was when she crossed the Yalu River and invaded Korean territory.

Peace is wonderful. But the price of that peace has been high, and it must be remembered that it is a peace with a foe that has yet to prove his sincerity. It would be dangerous for the Free Nations to let their guards down. And there must be no appeasement. International recognition of the Peiping regime, its entry into the United Nations and the resumption of trade with it must be predicated on more solid and concrete proof that it means henceforth to pursue peaceful ways than the signing alone of the cease-fire accord.

It will be well for the Allied nations to recall the events which followed the end of World War II when they blissfully went about the task of demobilizing their fighting units only to see the Communists retain their huge armies and to go steadily on with their program of conquest. It could happen again. The desire for a return to normalcy is strong. There will be pressure to have the soldiers get back to their homelands. There will be agreement that the crisis has passed. The feeling may arise, if the postwar political conference should hit a snag, that the recognition of Red China or the approval of her admission to the United Nations is not too high a price to pay, should the alternative be the resumption of the Korean War. But this is precisely what the Communists would like to see.

Now that the actual fighting is over, there was never greater need for vigilance, courage and determination. And there is an absolute necessity to maintain unity among the Free Nations. On too many of the issues which remain, the United States and Britain do not see eye-to-eye. Munich has become synonymous with degrading appeasement. History must not record Panmunjom in a similar light. Peace is still a long way off.

Topic 28

THE KENNEDY
TRANSITION

1961

*At the political conventions of 1960, Democrats selected Senators
John F. Kennedy and Lyndon B. Johnson as their candidates while
Republicans named Vice-President Richard M. Nixon and Henry
Cabot Lodge, American delegate to the United Nations. The campaign that followed focused on youth and moving the American
nation forward, concentrating on specific answers to domestic
issues such as unemployment, particularly in sections of New
England, West Virginia, and Pennsylvania. The candidates also
spoke about the American military position, particularly with regard to Russia, and as well, their own experience and ability for
dealing with Communist threats throughout the world. In addition
to carrying on the first televised debate of presidential contenders
before an estimated audience of 70,000,000 viewers, the candidates
campaigned with an energy and mobility never equaled in earlier
elections.*

*The election returns made Kennedy the youngest man ever
to become President; he won both the popular vote (34,227,096
to 34,107,646) and the electoral vote (303 to 219). The especially
festive Inauguration brought indications to the nation of a new
progressive spirit. Kennedy spoke eloquently of renewal, change,
and idealism, most memorably in his Inaugural Address with the
words: "Ask not what your country can do for you, but what you*

can do for your country." *Many Americans, especially young people
of all races and religions, believed that his Address promised a new
America, a better America.*

TOKYO. *The Japan Times,* January 21, 1961.

The Inauguration of Mr. John F. Kennedy as 35th President of
the United States took place in Washington yesterday in an atmosphere of excited anticipation, despite the wintry weather, for
it is widely felt that this change of President is of more than
ordinary significance, and that America, to use Mr. Kennedy's own
words, stands on the edge of a new frontier—a frontier of unknown opportunities and perils, a frontier of unfulfilled hopes and
threats.

The great expectations that center around the assumption of
office by Mr. Kennedy do not spring from dissatisfaction with anything Mr. Eisenhower has done, or failed to do, but from the
reason that a new man, whose circumstances are very different
from those of his predecessor, is bound to look at public affairs
in a new way.

This new way does not mean a break with anything that was
valuable in the past, and Mr. Kennedy, in his inaugural speech,
makes special mention of his Administration's intention to defend
liberty in the world at any price. And, as we know, liberty has
been the bedrock of all American political thinking since the days
when John Adams declared that the first necessary step to good
government was to depute power from the many to a few of the
most wise and good.

Much of Mr. Kennedy's address is devoted to the United
States' relations with the outside world, but the basis of his thinking throughout is the preservation of human rights in his own
country and the encouragement of the extension of such rights
throughout the world. "Let every nation know," he said, "whether
it wishes us well or ill, that we shall pay any price, bear any
burden, meet any hardship, support any friend or oppose any
foe in order to assure the survival and success of liberty."

To America's old allies, "whose cultural and spiritual origins
we share," Mr. Kennedy pledged the loyalty of faithful friends. He

was obviously thinking of the democratic nations of Europe, from whom much of American civilization derives and who have in turn learned much from America, and, indeed, since the last world war, have largely owed their preservation to America's generous help.

But Mr. Kennedy did not forget the newcomers to the comity of nations. "To those new states whom we now welcome to the ranks of the free," he said, "we pledge our word that one form of colonial control shall not have passed merely to be replaced by a far more iron tyranny." These are significant words, for, as we all know, the attempt has been made by those who hope to profit by the ending of the old type of colonialism to substitute their own domination over still weak peoples. Mr. Kennedy's words should be taken to heart not only by those who are seeking to build up national economies from small beginnings but by those who seek for their own ends to spread mischief among them. Mr. Kennedy's own graphic expression is a warning to remember that, in the past, those who foolishly sought to find power by riding on the tiger's back inevitably ended up inside.

. . . The United States, under the new regime, will not let down its defenses and if any think that Mr. Kennedy will be easier to take advantage of than Mr. Eisenhower, they are clearly doomed to disappointment. Mr. Kennedy puts it this way—"We dare not tempt them with weakness. For only when our arms are sufficient beyond doubt can we be certain beyond doubt that they will never be employed."

Nevertheless, he argues that no comfort can be taken from the present course of events, and he urges that an attempt should be made to begin anew. Whether this holding out of an olive branch will meet with any genuine response from Soviet Russia and the Communist bloc remains to be seen. It is at least something to congratulate America upon that the suggestion has been made. . . .

LONDON. *The Times,* January 21, 1961.

When PRESIDENT KENNEDY stood up yesterday to speak for the first time to the republic and the world he can scarcely have been without a thought of that other famous inauguration just a hundred years ago. He did not refer to the anniversary. But something of the cadence of ABRAHAM LINCOLN'S oratory can be heard in the sentences of his address, and underlying them LINCOLN'S sense of the spiritual mission of the great presidential office. PRESIDENT KENNEDY was voicing the American people's historic dedication to declared ideals and defined Christian standards—"the belief that the rights of man come not from the generosity of the State but from the hand of God"—and this is something which the American people of today will echo. Therewith goes the implication as clear to MR. KENNEDY as it was to LINCOLN, that in 1961 as in 1861 the great principles enshrined in the American political scriptures of the Founding Fathers stand in a crisis of history, full of menace but full of hope.

The PRESIDENT'S exalted hopes give warmth and colour to the whole speech, but over against them he sets the shadow, *corruptio optimi pessima,* man's expanding opportunity to master his environment as never before matched by his equal power to destroy it and himself. MR. KENNEDY held out the right hand of America's fellowship to all who would grasp it and cooperate, using the new scientific resources to release humanity from poverty and all other ancient ills. He reaffirmed his country's fidelity to "those old allies whose cultural and spiritual origins we share." He gave a welcome to the newly emancipated members of the international community. He pledged his country to the continued support of the pacific authority of the United Nations. And he made a new appeal or "request" to "those nations who would make themselves our adversary" to join with America in the search for peace before the forces of destruction can finally prevail.

MR. KENNEDY, however, made it very clear that the peace for which America will work, with all other nations of good will, can be only a peace of the strong. Giving a special pledge of economic help to "our sister republics south of the Border," he added a warning that they must not be allowed to become the prey of hostile Powers. The Monroe Doctrine, which has of late seemed to be called in question, was by implication reasserted: "This hemisphere intends to remain master of its own house." The emancipated nations must bear the responsibility of freedom, not allow themselves to succumb to new forms of tyranny. And, much as the PRESIDENT'S conscience revolts against that schism of the world in which both sides are "racing to alter that uncertain balance of terror that stays the hand of mankind's final war," sincerely as he proclaims his readiness to pursue by negotiation the development of the things that unite East and West instead of "belabouring" the things that divide, he yet declares in the plainest terms that while the arms race continues, there is no course for America and her friends but to remain so invincibly strong that their strength need never be deployed.

. . . There is little in the speech that bears upon domestic politics; no appeal to commercial self-interest; no promise of easier days; no reference to the unsettled conflicts of interest up and down the country which beset the election campaign. That does not convey any suggestion that MR. KENNEDY is unconscious of the practical urgencies or irresolute to grapple with them. Soon enough the new Administration will be required to descend into the mundane business of the marketplace. But it and the people it rules and serves will be the better equipped to meet their workaday cares for having taken an hour off to listen to noble words— generous, vigorous, leaderlike, resolute, and devout. Great ceremonial occasions have their indispensable place in the life of a nation, and it is right that they should be used to uplift hearts and call the people to service to the loftiest ideals. To such appeals to their native altruism Americans always respond. As what free people does not?

PARIS. *Le Monde,* **January 21, 1961.**

The youngest President ever elected in the United States today receives the powers handed over to him by a respectable man whose old age had helped to earn for him the confidence of his citizens and of his allies. In 1953 Mr. Eisenhower had constituted his government in the manner of a board of directors, giving all the key posts to businessmen, among whom happened to be a leading trade unionist, who resigned after a few weeks. Resuming the Democratic tradition, Mr. Kennedy has turned toward the "professors."

By age and by social background, the two teams are as different as the two men acclaimed today by the same crowd that, even in the change itself, wants to believe in the continuity of American policy. To the noble sentiments and the optimism of Mr. Eisenhower, Mr. Kennedy, in his speeches to the Senate as well as in his electoral campaign, gave a merciless critique of the Republican administration, sometimes even allowing himself to go so far as to blacken the picture. But the situation that he inherits from his predecessor is without any doubt closer to the severe analysis which he makes of it than to the idyllic description which the departing President leaves behind.

Often it was possible to blame Mr. Eisenhower for reigning without governing, for relying too much on Mr. Dulles for his foreign policy, for hesitating before deciding and for intervening too late in dealing with problems which he had allowed to fester. With regard to Mr. Kennedy, it is a different concern which appears in certain sectors of the United States and abroad: does he not risk, because of his dynamic temperament, reaching too rapidly decisions which he perhaps has not had the time to think through. Will he not want to do too many things himself, passing, if necessary, over the authority and the competence of the collaborators with whom he has managed to surround himself?

The fact remains that eight years of almost a "do-nothing" policy urgently calls for a change, an effort of imagination and invention, a powerful enthusiasm capable of drawing along a whole nation—and its allies—toward the solution of the problems which face them in domestic as well as in foreign affairs.

The themes and the tone of Mr. Kennedy's electoral speeches, like the personalities of several of his collaborators, have aroused impatient expectations for a great political change. But these expectations strongly risk being disappointed by the speech that Mr. Kennedy pronounces today on the occasion of his inauguration, as well as by the declarations that Mr. Chester Bowles made Thursday before the Committee on Foreign Relations of the Senate.

The problems which now face the government of the United States are in fact much more complex than those which greeted Roosevelt 28 years ago. The administrative machinery has grown large and unwieldy; its management is much more difficult. These are sufficient reasons for the Americans themselves to think it hardly likely that in the first weeks of Kennedy's administration, there will be an effervescence, an intellectual and political activity comparable to that which characterized the first hundred days of Roosevelt's presidency.

MOSCOW. *Pravda,* **February 5, 1961.***

[Although the Russian press reprinted President Kennedy's Inaugural Address, the first notable commentary on his administration appeared after his State of the Union Address.]

. . . How strange it is, after that, to find assertions in the State of the Union Message that "communist agents" have allegedly set up a base on Cuba! Everybody knows that on Cuban soil there is only one foreign base established against the will of the people of this country, an American base. The coordinates of this base are marked precisely on the map; it is located on Guantanamo Bay.

Kennedy repeats in his message the inventions about some kind of nonexistent "communist ambition for world domination" and speaks of some sort of "intrigues of communist agents" in Latin America. Why was it necessary to revive these dead myths? To repeat such fabrications means not to follow the road of common sense.

. . . The message does not reveal what specific steps the U. S. administration intends to undertake in the interests of peace. This is mentioned vaguely, as if in passing. The paragraphs on military preparations, on the other hand, are formulated with utmost precision. The message says that the President has taken prompt action toward "obtaining additional air transport mobility," to step up the Polaris submarine program and to accelerate the missile program of the U. S. A. These concrete actions run counter to the

---

* Translation from *The Current Digest of the Soviet Press,* published weekly by the American Association for the Advancement of Slavic Studies at The Ohio State University. Copyright 1961; by permission.

good intentions about strengthening peace. This is bound to put the peace-loving peoples on guard. The message itself generates doubts, and the American government alone can dispel them, not with words, but with specific actions in the interest of peace. It is doubtful that Mr. Kennedy himself can not see the contradiction in his views.

He tries to cover the obvious incongruity between some of his statements with the metaphor about the American eagle, who holds in his right talon the olive branch and in the left a bundle of arrows. "We intend to give equal attention to both," the President adds.

Military arrows with nuclear warheads are too heavy these days, and the eagle burdened with such a load will not rise very high and will not carry the olive branch of peace over the world. Either atomic and thermonuclear arrows or the olive branch, that is the choice before the world today.

It is pointed out in many international commentaries on Kennedy's message that the new administration of the U. S. A. now faces problems as acute and complex as those the administration of Franklin Delano Roosevelt faced 28 years ago. This analogy is by no means accidental. No matter how different the conditions of the 1930s may be from those of our time, there are nevertheless many similarities in the situation of the U. S. A. In both cases the governments assumed office under conditions when the people expressed the desire for a change in the country's policy.

Franklin Roosevelt had the courage and vision to steer the U. S. ship of state on a new course. For 16 years official America had refused to recognize the greatest fact of our time—the emergence of the first socialist state in the world. Roosevelt not only recognized this fact but, as his close collaborator S. Welles testifies, considered Soviet-American mutual understanding and cooperation "a necessary foundation for American foreign policy." . . .

Kennedy asserts in his message that he intends to explore promptly all possible areas of cooperation with the Soviet Union and other nations "to invoke the wonders of science instead of its terrors." There is no doubt, nor can there be, that any steps by the new American administration toward improving Soviet-American relations will meet with full support from the U. S. S. R. . . .

The new administration in Washington is taking its first steps.

The near future will show whether or not it is prepared to keep pace with life, which requires an abandonment of the outworn dogmas of the "cold war" and a new course in U. S. foreign policy —the only sane course, the course of peaceful coexistence with all countries and peoples for the sake of peace all over the world.

Topic 29

THE CUBAN
MISSILE CRISIS

1962

*During the summer of 1962 and unknown to the United States
public, Russian ships brought technicians and ballistic missiles to
Cuba. By mid-October an American reconnaissance plane, a U-2,
brought back photographs which proved that missile sites were
under construction. Subsequent photographs indicated the existence of short-range and medium-range missiles which could reach
as far north as Hudson Bay, and as far south as Peru. On October
18, Andrei Gromyko, the Russian foreign minister, assured President John F. Kennedy that the missile sites were "purely defensive."*

*On the evening of October 22, Kennedy revealed the missile
threat to American television audiences and described the selective
American blockade being placed around Cuba. He also warned the
Russian Premier, Nikita Khrushchev, that the United States would
not permit the existence of this threat to world peace. Khrushchev
replied that the missiles would be removed if Kennedy promised
not to invade Cuba. Kennedy agreed and the most critical confrontation (and, one might add, the most puzzling) between the
two major powers came to an end.*

LONDON. *The Times*, October 24, 1962.

In judging whether PRESIDENT KENNEDY is right in militarily blockading Cuba, almost everything depends on the accuracy of the evidence that the Russians are in fact building missile bases on the island. Past American mistakes in coping with Cuba, the violent emotions which possess so many Americans when FIDEL CASTRO and communism are mentioned, the wrong information which was served to the PRESIDENT before the invasion fiasco eighteen months ago, and even the PRESIDENT'S sudden display of toughness now during a mid-term election campaign in which he has been accused of softness—all these things were bound to make people in Britain extremely wary on first hearing the news. All that being said, the evidence appears to be hard.

Once the evidence is accepted as true, it has to be recognized that the PRESIDENT had urgently to face an ugly and disturbing change in Russian policy in Cuba. Until a short time ago it could be argued that the Russians had been drawn almost inevitably into support of the Castro regime. At first they were not too sure about CASTRO. The more, however, he cut himself off or was cut off from America, the more he leaned on Russia and China for all kinds of help. In the past twelve months the process became complete—CASTRO declared that he had been a Marxist-Leninist all along and the Russians, bypassing the Cuban Communist Party, sent in technicians to run many enterprises directly and promised to send heavier arms. PRESIDENT KENNEDY very properly contented himself with two most explicit warnings. On September 4 he said that there was still no evidence of a Soviet military base in Cuba or (he said specifically) "the presence of offensive ground-to-ground missiles." Were it otherwise, he added, "the gravest issues would arise." After the evidence about such missiles had come in eight days ago his own position within the United States would have foundered if he had not acted.

The Soviet Government may deny that the bases are there. Alternatively, it may say that the missiles are purely defensive and therefore within the terms of its assurances to the American

Government. By all accepted standards, however, the missiles are offensive. At the very least they are retaliatory or "offensive-defensive"—and in a more selective way than rockets from Russia could be. So long as they were kept secret, they could not even be called deterrent, for the essence of deterrence is public warning. Probably the Russians counted on catching America napping until the bases were complete and western hemispheric defence was indisputably breached. This is a development very different from moral, political, and defensive support of CASTRO and his revolution. PRESIDENT KENNEDY had to make some reply. There are many grounds for assuming that the Soviet Union does not seek war. She prefers to spread her doctrine, influence, and power through probing, sapping, propagandizing, and pressuring. Yet there is always the risk of her misjudging and going too far to recall if she meets no resistance. "The greatest danger of all would be to do nothing."

The dangers of acting are, of course, manifest. The speed with which PRESIDENT KENNEDY felt bound to act can mean that an American flotilla may meet Russian vessels before they have received instructions on how to act. With all the risks ahead MR. KENNEDY was wise to define his objectives in strictly limited terms, and it is of the utmost importance that they remain limited. They are not to topple CASTRO or defeat communism but to secure the elimination of the bases. Is even that within reasonable possibility? It is one thing to stop supplies coming in. It is another to secure the destruction or withdrawal of what has already been brought in. For that reason the struggle now engaged may be long; for that reason, too, a way forward should be sought apart from the confrontation of strength.

But how? There is no certainty at all that the United States will have the majority of the United Nations on her side. No doubt the PRESIDENT'S proposal that the United Nations observers may be sent to Cuba will be given some support. Cuba's reply, however, is all too likely to be an offended refusal, and many nations will join her in challenging the legality of such a blockade. The blunt terms in which MR. KENNEDY referred to Russian trickery may put off hopes that MR. KHRUSHCHEV may soon go to see him, and that in itself could mean that the prospect of worthwhile talks on Berlin will also be postponed.

Amid it all, the chief hope—slender at that—must arise after Russia has made the obvious riposte to the charge that a missile base so near to America is a threat to peace. What about American missile bases on Russia's frontier? In spite of all the differences between America's and Russia's records and motives—America's allies are well aware of them—there is just enough similarity in the siting of some of the bases to cause the question to be raised. While each side holds the supreme deterrent it is just possible, if the Cuban affair settles down to a kind of strong stalemate—admittedly a big if—that they may consider a bargain whereby each does away with a forward base or two. With a ban on nuclear testing added, the world's nerves could become steadier. Too much now depends on simply avoiding the more than usually explosive incident.

TOKYO. *The Japan Times,* **October 26, 1962.**

While there is a widespread opinion outside the Communist-ruled countries that the American President could not afford to have acted otherwise than he has done in the matter of preventing offensive weapons from reaching Cuba, Soviet Premier Khrushchev appears disposed to avoid a situation which might drift into a nuclear war on a scale which would involve the whole world. But whether the Soviet leader will consent to withdraw his missiles and rocket bases from Cuba, as the United States is demanding, is doubtful. It seems clear that, even from a Communist point of view, the Soviet Government made a mistake in going so far in Cuba as it has done, unless, of course, it had made up its mind to challenge the United States to a military showdown in the near future, which we do not believe.

But once having taken such strong measures in Cuba, it must be difficult for the Russians now to retract their policy.

That Moscow harbors a deliberate intention to subvert as soon as possible as many American countries to communism as can be conveniently approached has long been apparent, but communism, even if it is to be regarded as in the main an instrument of Russian imperialism, usually prefers nonmilitary methods to an open challenge to war.

The Communist program is consolidation in Eastern Europe, then expansion by subversion in Asia, Africa and the Americas; more or less in that order. From Moscow's point of view this program has not had quite the success looked for. The subjection of the Chinese mainland was no doubt a triumph for theoretical communism but the flouting of Russian leadership by the Peiping regime from time to time has been a bitter pill to swallow. Nor have Soviet ambitions in Africa been completely satisfied; many of the newly independent states have shown unmistakably that they do not intend to put themselves under Moscow's thumb as Dr. Fidel Castro—perhaps in a moment of emotional weakness—has now placed Cuba.

Soviet Russia is, then, engaged in an attempt to secure global domination and the case of Cuba is merely the latest, as well as the most flagrant, example of this policy. While this program of trying to dominate the world continues on the part of Moscow, it is idle to talk of peace, international harmony and disarmament.

Moreover, if Moscow's policy continues to be unchanged, there is no criterion, even if the Cuban crisis is smoothed over, that a similar situation will not develop elsewhere when the Soviet Government sees an opportunity to intervene.

Mr. Daniel Schweitzer, the Chilean representative at the Security Council debate on Wednesday, declared that Latin America was horrified that the cold war had exploded in the Caribbean. He might well be; but it is obvious that it may explode anywhere that Moscow sees fit unless international action is taken to see that this overall danger is prevented. "We have to note," said Mr. Schweitzer, "the sad fact that Cuba is a country that is being taken over by an extracontinental country and is being used as a pawn so that another country can use it for strategy in other parts of the world."

If Mr. Schweitzer is right, and there is good reason to think he is, we realize that although there is an immediate threat to the United States and the Latin American countries, there is a potential threat to the world as a whole.

The remarkable opportunity presented by the Cuban revolution to the Russians to secure a foothold in the Western Hemisphere was taken due advantage of, we believe, from the urge of the widest possible ambitions, and is regarded by the Kremlin as a significant step to the communization, or perhaps we ought to say, the Russification, of the world.

What then is the United Nations called upon to do? It must try to ease the present situation with regard to Cuba. But that is not enough. It must take full cognizance of Soviet Russia's interference in other countries and its determination to expand its influence throughout the world by using communism as an instrument. "What is now threatening the Western Hemisphere," Mr. Liu Chieh told the Security Council, "is not little Cuba but a Soviet armed base which is there to blackmail the entire hemisphere into submission."

While, then, we hope that the Security Council will be able to initiate measures to prevent the present situation in regard to Cuba drifting into a nuclear war, we want also to see the United Nations take energetic steps to end the "cold war." This must involve a change in Soviet policy, a change which the rest of the world, or so much of it as is sufficiently free, is entitled to demand.

PARIS. *Le Monde*, October 24, 1962.

Here we are again at the door of a grave international crisis. There was no warning. It seemed that . . . the American administration had decided to resist and take action against the presence of a Communist base a few hundred kilometers from Florida; the significance of which, at a time when intercontinental missiles put, at any rate, all countries in immediate line of attack, appeared more political than military.

Why did Mr. Kennedy brusquely decide to start action without recourse to the preamble of the United Nations or consulting his allies? One would like to be able to ascertain the exactness of the information on which he depends in announcing that the Soviets, contrary to their most solemn assurances, repeated Thursday again by Mr. Gromyko to the President himself, have installed offensive weapons in Cuba of a sufficient carrying power to reach the three Americas. But, unfortunately, experience proves that the American information services are sometimes mistaken.

At any rate, it is a right recognized until now by the sovereign states to choose their form of government, their allies, and their weapons. It is strange to declare that the Americans, who find it perfectly normal that a state such as Turkey, situated on the frontier of the Soviet Union, should shield missile sites which menace the whole basin of the Donetz, contest with the USSR the right to conclude with Cuba comparable agreements.

This refusal is certainly within the logic of a government which repeatedly has made known recently that "Communism in the Western Hemisphere is not an object of negotiation," in other words, that it would not bow before the *fait accompli* of the presence of a Marxist regime in the Caribbean. It is, however, contrary to simple common sense, as well as to the tacit rules which result from the division between the two camps with a practically equal capacity of destruction.

This being said, the concern of Mr. Kennedy to limit as much as possible the risk that he has decided to take is manifest. The "quarantine" that he instituted must only concern offensive weapons. If the Russians have not delivered any to Cuba or have no intention of doing so, they should voluntarily accept the control of the United Nations, as Washington suggests. And one can ask himself whether the President, in making such an uproar, did not want above all to convince the American voter of his resoluteness, thus neutralizing the increasing attacks of the opposition, rather than winning a decisive advantage over Moscow which the relationship of the forces in the world forbid him to hope for.

It would be better to propose to Mr. Khrushchev that negotiations be used to solve the basic and serious problems which menace international peace. The head of the Soviet government could well be inspired to follow that lead, rather than to try to raise the bid. Because if, on several occasions, the Western Powers appeared to back away from the Soviet show of strength, if last year Mr. Kennedy himself had not stopped in midstream in his first operation against Cuba, the Kremlin cannot ignore the fact that this time the young President of the United States cannot back away without losing all authority. One must therefore search for a compromise, one which could apply far beyond Cuba, rather than prepare clever thrusts which increase the risk of leading the powers to a general conflict: the interested powers would do well to work at this compromise in the hours ahead.

MOSCOW. *Izvestia,* October 31, 1962.*

The past few days have been a severe test for the cause of universal peace and a peaceful life for all peoples. Mankind found itself face to face with the threat of a thermonuclear war. Aggressively inclined circles in the United States did not conceal their intentions of kindling a military conflict in the Caribbean area, having undertaken an armed attack against the Cuban Republic. It is perfectly clear that had this happened, the conflict would not have been limited to this one area. From the very start of the aggravation of the Cuban situation, matters have been brought to the point of placing other countries of the Western Hemisphere under arms and creating a war scare in various parts of the globe, especially in countries belonging to the military blocs of NATO, CENTO, and SEATO.

Swift, decisive and effective measures were necessary in order to preserve universal peace, prevent a devastating thermonuclear conflict and ensure the security, independence and integrity of the heroic Island of Freedom—the Cuban Republic.

The threat to peace was created by hostile, adventurist schemes aimed at the very existence of the Cuban Republic. The Soviet Union could not disregard Cuba's predicament in the face of the imperialistic provocations. Our country, fulfilling its international duty, came to the fraternal assistance of the Cuban people, and in these troubled days of the provocational aggravation of conditions, it has stood, stands and will continue to stand firmly with Cuba.

The contemplated scheme of aggression against Cuba was

---

* Translation from *The Current Digest of the Soviet Press,* published weekly by The American Association for the Advancement of Slavic Studies at The Ohio State University. Copyright 1962; by permission.

built upon a very shaky foundation, but the danger with which Cuba was threatened was not thereby diminished. The pretext that was advanced in the U. S. A. for action against Cuba was the presence of Soviet weapons in Cuba that the United States termed "offensive." These weapons were depicted as representing a "threat" to America and the whole Western Hemisphere, although neither Cuba nor the Soviet Union was threatening the United States with its actions, while at the same time extremist, militant circles in the U. S. revealed in all their behavior a desire to end the independence of the Cuban Republic.

In that tense moment the Soviet government, which had displayed the utmost self-control, calm and firmness, took speedy and efficient action to prevent the outbreak of the imminent conflict and thereby preserve universal peace.

The progression of events showed that the farseeing, wise course of the Soviet government was the only correct one in the situation that had developed and led in a short time to the start of the normalization of the situation and the creation of conditions in which the interests of universal peace and of the independence and integrity of the Cuban Republic will be assured.

The decisive step of the Soviet Union—which foiled the aggressive plans of an attack on Cuba and deprived the authors of these plans of a reason and pretext for military action—was the indication that appropriate measures were being taken to stop the buildup in Cuba of objectives depicted by the United States as threatening American security, to dismantle these objectives and return them to the Soviet Union.

This step by the Soviet government was made possible as a result of the statement made by U. S. President Kennedy in his message of Oct. 27 to N. S. Khrushchev. The message states that there will be no attacks on Cuba, no invasion, not only on the part of the United States but on the part of the other countries of the Western Hemisphere as well, if the weapons termed "offensive" by the U. S. A. are shipped out of Cuba.

Thus reason and wisdom prevailed. At present all conditions exist for the total elimination of the conflict and for further efforts toward the strengthening of peace and security. All honest people, anxious over the fate of peace, render their due to our Communist Party, to the Soviet government and to Nikita Sergeyevich Khrushchev for the fact that the forces of aggression and war have been restrained and reason in international relations has prevailed over folly.

These days telegrams are being received in Moscow, in the Kremlin, from all corners of the globe. They express the impassioned voices of people of good will, conveying their support of the peace-loving position of the Soviet Union. Mrs. Biunen of New York, for example, in one such telegram says: "We thank you for your efforts to preserve peace at this most crucial moment for humanity. Let there be peace!"

Of course, much remains to be done. Negotiations on practical questions are only beginning. Storm clouds are still threatening the Caribbean basin, casting their shadow over the other parts of the globe as well. The Cuban counterrevolutionary bands and their U. S. patrons have not ceased their intrigues. It would be premature to exclude the possibility of new provocations against Cuba. As always, but especially at the present moment, the greatest vigilance is needed to foil each and every scheme of the forces of the aggressor.

The forces of peace have emerged from the severe test of the past few days even stronger and more tempered. Life demonstrates the efficacy of the method of the peaceful settlement of conflicts by means of negotiation rather than by arms or military strength.

That is why we should not allow an aggravation of conditions but should eliminate the sparks of dangerous situations, as well as take such other action as is dictated by the interests of the peace and security of all nations.

We have never been as powerful as we are now. The Soviet people are meeting the approaching 45th anniversary of the Great October Socialist Revolution in a new flowering of their creative forces. Our victories in the field of economic construction are at the same time victories in the great cause of peace. They inspire us to new achievements in the name of Peace, Labor, Freedom, Equality, Brotherhood and Happiness for all peoples!

MEXICO CITY. *Excelsior,* October 31, 1962.

Although a year has passed since Cuba lost her independence by joining the Soviet camp, the [Organization of] American States whose purpose is to insure the principles of self-determination still finds the Cuban situation a matter of serious discussion. This is not to say that the American States saw itself obligated to adjust or arrange the internal affairs of the island, since this would have meant interfering in the private matters of a third nation. It only wished to establish, and in this it was successful, that there was not enough conclusive evidence to pass judgment on the domestic situation of a nation of our hemisphere.

The protests which Fidel Castro set forth against the public[ly held] opinion that he had allied his country with an extra-continental power tended to make the opinion of the American States more credible. Denying any treaties with Soviet Russia, Castro's regime blamed first his political enemies, and later the so-called U. S. imperialism for lying about his country's loss of independence. Castro wished to appear as an immaculate leader who carried out the greatest social undertaking in history; and for this very reason he denies complicity or communist subordination.

Nevertheless, as his deception of 2,000,000,000 human beings could not last, Castro grasped the flag of Leninist-Marxism as if to palliate his situation, explaining, although superficially, the purpose of his dealings with Soviet imperialism. He asserted that these dealings were only of a technical and intellectual nature; but actually they were the adoption of a doctrine that was not established and sworn to by the states of our continent nor by the Inter-American System.

Castro's adoption of a communist government in the name of the Cuban Republic—without even the intention of consulting the Cuban people—brought about the meeting of the Ministers of Foreign Policy in Punta del Este whose declaration of the incompatibility of representative democracy with Leninist-Marxism was virtually a condemnation of the Castro regime; yet Castro and his leaders feigned ignorance and pretended to continue within a system which, like the Inter-American, is the antithesis of the Moscow-Havana political axis.

As it was known that the USSR was constructing platforms to launch nuclear weapons, this state of affairs could not continue. Nevertheless, Fidel Castro, believing himself able to play at soldiers and cannons and, like a mischievous boy, hide from the free world the treason he was committing against the American States—especially against Mexico, which so steadfastly defended Cuba's right to self-determination—continued to deny that nuclear emplacements were being constructed, hoping that by so doing the Russians would have time to finish the project, thereby being able to threaten the free world with atomic attacks from Cuban ground.

Neither Castro's lies nor his treason could last. With proof in hand, President Kennedy on October 23 [*sic*], revealed to the world the Russian-Castro plot. The preparations for nuclear war—war that President Dorticos emphatically condemned two weeks before in the General Assembly of the UN—were correctly and clearly revealed. The whole world was stunned, not so much by the existence of one more nuclear base, as by the vulgar and treacherous conduct of the USSR and Castro, since after the fact of Cuba, what guarantees of peace could there be? Will not Castroism be impudent enough to affirm, in reply, that President Kennedy's discourse makes a mockery of universal public opinion?

Now that the existence of nuclear projectiles in Cuba has been proved, the state of affairs within the suffering "island prison" has automatically changed.

Topic 30

THE GULF OF TONKIN INCIDENT

1964

After World War II, American involvement in Vietnam began when President Harry S Truman provided substantial assistance to French forces attempting to halt the expansionist efforts of certain Vietnamese nationalists led by Ho Chi Minh, a Communist leader in Hanoi. During the administrations of Dwight D. Eisenhower and John F. Kennedy, economic and military assistance to South Vietnam increased at a rapid rate. In addition, more than 15,000 American military advisers were training the South Vietnamese army in mid-1963. The overthrow of the Diem regime later that year lessened the country's stability and another 6,000 advisers were assigned in July 1964.

On August 2, in the Gulf of Tonkin, North Vietnamese torpedo boats attacked the Maddox, *an American destroyer, which the American government said was patrolling in international waters. Hanoi claimed the attack was a response to bombardment of North Vietnam by Saigon vessels being protected by the* Maddox. *On August 4, according to the Defense Department, the* Maddox *and another destroyer were attacked but suffered no casualties or damage. North Vietnam stated no attack had taken place. That same evening, President Lyndon B. Johnson reported on television that American air action against North Vietnamese gunboats and certain facilities was being undertaken. Three days later the House and the Senate overwhelmingly adopted the Tonkin Gulf*

Resolution declaring that Congress "approves and supports the determination of the President, as Commander in Chief, to take all necessary measures to repel any armed attack against the forces of the United States and to prevent further aggression." Moreover, the resolution would remain in effect until terminated by a concurrent resolution of Congress or until the President determined that the "peace and security of the area is reasonably assured."

PEKING. *Jen-min Jih-pao,* August 7, 1964.*

The Johnson administration of the United States has recklessly launched a surprise attack on the Democratic Republic of Vietnam, thus expanding its aggressive war in Indochina. This most nefarious action has completely laid bare the warlike features of the Johnson administration and has aroused the strong condemnation of all peace-loving peoples and countries of the world.

However, Johnson and his administration chiefs have vociferously declared, tongue in cheek, that U. S. naval vessels had been subjected to "unprovoked" and "deliberate" attack by the Democratic Republic of Vietnam and that U. S. armed aggression against the DRV was "defense" against "open aggression" and was "action in reply." They also alleged that such action on the part of the United States was "limited and fitting" and that the United States sought "no wider war." It is absolutely futile for Johnson and his ilk to try to resort to this "thief crying 'stop thief' " tactic to fool and deceive the peoples of the world.

Who, after all, was subjected to "unprovoked and deliberate" attack?

The Gulf of Tonkin is not an inland sea of the United States. But U. S. naval vessels have long been deployed there, threatening the security of the Democratic Republic of Vietnam. On August 1 and 2, a U. S. warship flagrantly intruded into the DRV territorial waters to conduct harassing activities. By giving a firm rebuff to

---

* From the *Survey of China Mainland Press.* Prepared by U. S. Consulate in Hong Kong. Microfilm, Washington, D. C.

the enemy that had intruded into the DRV territorial waters and carried out provocations, the naval units of the DRV were safeguarding State sovereignty. How can such a legitimate action be described as unprovoked attack? The U. S. is thousands of miles away from Vietnam. Why is it that the colossal U. S. 7th Fleet should go across the oceans to carry out provocations in the territorial waters of the Democratic Republic of Vietnam while the Vietnamese people should not fight in self-defense on the doorstep of their own homeland? The United States is a big country while Vietnam is a small one. Is there such a law that big countries can beat the smaller ones at will while the latter are not allowed to strike back? Certainly not. Nations, big and small, are equal. Since the United States is bent on making provocations, the Democratic Republic of Vietnam naturally has the right to strike back.

As to the second Tonkin Gulf incident, it was sheer fabrication on the part of the Johnson administration. On the night of August 4 there was not a single naval vessel of the Democratic Republic of Vietnam on the waters where the U. S. naval vessels were located. However, the U. S. authorities announced that U. S. warships had been subjected to attack and that several DRV naval vessels had been sunk or damaged. This is utter nonsense. Why did Johnson have to cook up such a ridiculous lie? It was only to create a pretext for his planned attack on the Democratic Republic of Vietnam.

The U. S. air raid on the DRV on August 5 was in every sense "unprovoked and deliberate" while the counterattack of the Vietnamese people in self-defense was absolutely just. On that day, U. S. planes wantonly bombed coastal towns of North Vietnam. The heroic Vietnam People's Army brought down eight of them and damaged three others. This indeed served the U. S. air pirates right. In defending their fatherland the army and people of Vietnam have dealt justified and well-aimed blows to the enemy. The 650 million Chinese people cheer and salute their heroic Vietnamese brothers.

The U. S. armed aggression against the DRV was long premeditated; since the beginning of this year, the military and administrative chiefs of the Johnson administration have been crying for the extension of the aggressive war from South Vietnam to the DRV, even at the cost of a total war. The U. S. propaganda machine has made no secret of the fact that the White House and the Pentagon have been actively working out various plans for extending the aggressive war in Indochina. UPI reported in last February that "discussions of raids in North Vietnam have been included in previous conferences" which U. S. Secretary of Defense McNamara "has held in the Pacific." It is an open secret that concrete plans for extending the war in Indochina were drawn up at the Honolulu Conference of U. S. Military and Administrative Chiefs held in early June. The appointment of Maxwell Taylor, former [chairman of the] U. S. Joint Chiefs of Staff, as U. S. Ambassador in Saigon indicated that the Johnson administration had put the plan for expanding the Indochina war on the agenda. True enough, in less than a month after Taylor's assumption of office, U. S. imperialism has gone over the "brink of war" and taken the first step in extending the war in Indochina.

After committing such heinous crimes, the Johnson administration had the cheek to declare that they merely took "limited and fitting" military actions. This is gangster logic, pure and simple. Can it be said that aggressive actions, so long as they are "limited and fitting" become legitimate? All acts of aggression are impermissible and must be severely condemned and punished. Moreover, all aggressors in the past started with limited aggressive actions. Beginning with the seizure of Czechoslovakia's Sudetenland, Hitler embarked on the road of launching the Second World War. U. S. imperialism has also expanded its aggressive activities in Indochina step by step. It has now extended its aggression in South Vietnam and Laos to intervention in Cambodia and armed aggression against the Democratic Republic of Vietnam.

Although the Johnson administration has extended its aggressive war in Indochina, it sanctimoniously declared that it knew "the risks of spreading conflict" and that "we seek no wider war." If the spreading of the war flames to the DRV is not extension of the war, how far must the Johnson administration spread the war flames to be called such? This only serves to show that U. S. imperialism has still more vicious steps in store in its plan to extend the war. . . .

LONDON. *The Times,* August 7, 1964.

The furious responses by China and North Vietnam to the American air raids are very much as could have been foretold. They throw every kind of charge—aggression, lying, madcap adventurism—against the United States, and declare that blood will have blood. What they carefully leave vague is the nature of their own military reply. Like the Americans yesterday, they issue no ultimatums or peremptory demands. China may indeed increase her help to North Vietnam: that is probable, but in the meantime North Vietnam has passed the crisis on to the signatories to the 1954 Geneva agreement, saying that those who set up the two Vietnams should curb the Americans. Elsewhere in the world the reactions have followed remarkably closely the predictable lines.

If PRESIDENT JOHNSON had announced that he was henceforth carrying the war by land, sea, and air into North Vietnam, or even was going on with air raids indefinitely, then many more of the allied peoples would have had qualms and doubts. It is true that some Americans would like to broaden the war in that way. Those who oppose this view have frankly to admit that no one has yet found an effective answer to the problem of the "privileged sanctuary" and the open frontier across which men, arms, and supplies can be sent to rebels in another country. North Vietnam, sending such help, claims the immunity of a sovereign, peace-loving state against any countermeasures. It is both galling and dangerous, yet the answer is not to let American or any other foreign servicemen invade or bomb North Vietnam indefinitely. Such an action, on China's doorstep, would almost certainly bring more havoc than profit. The best way of saving South Vietnam is to do better all the things that are already being done; building up the Vietnam forces and their foreign allies to the fifteen to one ratio which experience shows is necessary to cope with guerrillas; giving them the will to win; developing intelligence to watch and counter incoming supplies; and, the prime task, giving the people confidence that they have a worthwhile stake in the political and economic progress of their country. Without such an effort South Vietnam will surely be lost.

There is no reason to assume that PRESIDENT JOHNSON has altered this basic strategy. When ordering a special operation in response to a special attack, he took no strategic decision to fight the war in the north from now on. So far as he is concerned the operation is over. The chief danger would arise if the North Vietnamese and Chinese were bent on claiming the whole of the wide Gulf on Tonkin as a closed sea within their territorial waters. Such a claim would be unjustifiable. If it were pressed American and other warships might again have to reply. It is a matter on which the Security Council should give a ruling, before going on to see how the peace could be safeguarded in other ways.

MEXICO CITY. *Excelsior,* **August 13, 1964.**

Can we consider that the concentration of planes Communist China is making in North Vietnam, near Hanoi, announces the imminence of a war in Asia? According to reports made known yesterday by the United States Department of Defense, Communist Chinese jet planes are being sent to the explosive Asiatic region. Nevertheless, the characteristics of these planes, which are Mig 15s or 17s and therefore carrying antiquated motors, and likewise the scarce number of these planes that were or are being mobilized, show that the intentions of Mao do not pass beyond the limits that could imply the danger of a clash of these modest warlike forces with the great North American atomic fleet.

The element of surprise that in the first moments might have given spectacular success to the warlike action of Mao has now disappeared. On the other hand, one has to consider the spirit of decision which President Johnson maintains, such as in those dramatic moments of his reply to the acts of aggression by the Vietcong forces against the North American destroyer, "Maddox." Another circumstance that surely influences Mao so that he avoids precipitating a war that he would lose irremissibly, is the attitude of Soviet Russia, which has made it clear that it is not disposed to expose itself in a tragic war adventure in order to protect the government of Peking.

It is most probable that the concentration of planes in Hanoi tends more to console Ho Chi Minh and to reinforce the aerial defenses of the capital of North Vietnam than to constitute the preparatory phase of the launching of Red China into a warlike adventure without the slightest possibility of triumph on the part of the Communist government of Mao. China can consider that her human masses are more numerous than that of any other nation of the world, but the Chinese infantry has not been able to deter President Johnson, who knows that one hundred rockets or aerial bombardments can accomplish more than all the divisions that Mao can call together.

Nevertheless, Peking has not folded its arms. At the same time that Peking withdraws from meeting the North Americans in Southeast Asia, they attack in the very heart of North American territory, intending to make the twenty million black men that live in the American nation the base of a long and dangerous process of violence. It is thought, without a doubt, that the incitement of the Negroes of the United States will manacle the giant.

In the Negro problem of our neighboring country to the north, not only do they play with the just labors of those twenty million North American Negroes that aspire to civil equality with the North American whites, but also with the somber red plot that proposes to undermine the democracy and the peace of the United States and, if it is possible, involve the United States in a new civil war.

If Mao insists in converting the racial problem of the United States into a communist instrument of provocation against the government of Johnson, Harlem can become the stage for a new defeat of Chinese and Soviet communism. That is to say, Harlem can be a second Gulf of Tonkin for world communism.

Topic 31

THE ASSASSINATION OF MARTIN LUTHER KING, JR.

1968

On Thursday evening, April 4, 1968, in Memphis, Tennessee, violence in the shape of a rifle bullet ended the life of the Reverend Martin Luther King, Jr., who, as leader of the Southern Christian Leadership Conference, was himself an advocate of nonviolence in obtaining Negro civil rights.

Born on January 15, 1929, in Atlanta, Georgia, King received his bachelor's degree at Morehouse College in that city in 1948, and his Ph.D. from Boston University in 1955. In December of that year, he joined the boycott of segregated buses in Montgomery, Alabama, that lasted 382 days. Arrested for the first time on January 26, 1956, for going 30 miles per hour in a 25 miles per hour zone, King became the target of racial abuse and his home was bombed four days later. Nevertheless, he maintained his promise to avoid violence to attain equal rights. His speech, "I Have a Dream," delivered during the March on Washington in August 1963, his reception of the 1964 Nobel Peace Prize, together with other marches and jail sentences, gave impetus to his insistent demands for first-class citizenship for all Americans. When he came to Memphis to lead a march in support of garbage workers on strike, his pacifist campaign for justice, equality, and freedom ended on a second-floor motel balcony. The violence he abhorred broke out in the major urban areas of the United States.

PEKING. *North China News Agency,* **April 16, 1968.** *

[Statement of Mao Tse-tung, Chairman of the Central Committee of the Communist Party of China]

Some days ago, Martin Luther King, the Afro-American clergyman, was suddenly assassinated by the U. S. imperialists. Martin Luther King was an exponent of nonviolence. Nevertheless, the U. S. imperialists did not on that account show any tolerance toward him, but used counterrevolutionary violence and killed him in cold blood. This has taught the broad masses of the black people in the United States a profound lesson. It has touched off a new storm in their struggle against violent repression sweeping well over a hundred cities in the United States, a storm such as has never taken place before in the history of that country. It shows that an extremely powerful revolutionary force is latent in the more than 20 million black Americans.

The storm of Afro-American struggle taking place within the United States is a striking manifestation of the comprehensive political and economic crisis now gripping U. S. imperialism. It is dealing a telling blow to U. S. imperialism, which is beset with difficulties at home and abroad.

The Afro-American struggle is not only a struggle waged by the exploited and oppressed black people for freedom and emancipation; it is also a new clarion call to all the exploited and oppressed people of the United States to fight against the barbarous rule of the monopoly capitalist class. It is a tremendous aid and inspiration to the struggle of the people throughout the world against U. S. imperialism and to the struggle of the Vietnamese people against U. S. imperialism. On behalf of the Chinese people,

---

* From the *Survey of China Mainland Press.* Prepared by the U. S. Consulate in Hong Kong. Microfilm, Washington, D. C.

I hereby express resolute support for the just struggle of the black people in the U. S.

Racial discrimination in the U. S. is a product of the colonialist and imperialist system. The contradiction between the black masses in the U. S. and U. S. ruling circles is a class contradiction. Only by overthrowing the reactionary rule of the U. S. monopoly capitalist class and destroying the colonialist and imperialist system can the black people in the U. S. win complete emancipation. The black masses and the masses of white working people in the U. S. have common interests and common objectives to struggle for. Therefore, the Afro-American struggle is winning sympathy and support from increasing numbers of white working people and progressives in the U. S. The struggle of the black people in the U. S. is bound to merge with the American workers' movement and eventually end the criminal rule of the U. S. monopoly capitalist class.

In 1963, in the "Statement supporting the Afro-Americans in their just struggle against racial discrimination by U. S. imperialism" I said that "the evil system of colonialism and imperialism arose and throve with the enslavement of Negroes and the trade in Negroes, and it will surely come to its end with the complete emancipation of the black people." I still maintain this view.

At present, the world revolution has entered a great new era. The struggle of the black people in the U. S. for emancipation is a component part of the general struggle of all the people of the world against U. S. imperialism, a component part of the contemporary world revolution. I call on the workers, peasants and revolutionary intellectuals of all countries and all the people who are willing to fight against U. S. imperialism to take action and extend strong support to the struggle of the black people in the U. S.! People of the whole world, unite still more closely and launch a sustained and vigorous offensive against our common enemy, U. S. imperialism and its accomplices! It can be said with certainty that the complete collapse of colonialism, imperialism and all systems of exploitation, and the complete emancipation of all the oppressed peoples and nations of the world are not far off.

MEXICO CITY. *El Universal,* April 5, 1968.

While the bases for cessation of the bloody Vietnamese conflict, in which so many young North Americans have perished, have scarcely been outlined, one more political assassination presages black days which will shake the roots of the United States of America.

Luther King was a victim of gunfire in Memphis.

The consequences of this recent crime are unforeseeable, since the thirty million Negroes who in one form or another suffer the ignominies of racial segregation, continue to follow the teachings of Doctor King, who always condemned violence as a means to civil rights. By peaceful, although decided and forceful means, they have carried on a civic enterprise which has as its objectives the attainment of better living conditions, opportunities to work, free education, pleasant housing, equality before the law, and general access to the institutions of the American Union.

No doubt the terrorist organizations, which are spread throughout the nerve centers of the North American territory, will take advantage of this dramatic circumstance to lift the corpse of Dr. King as a flag to justify destruction and crime.

Recent days have witnessed an expansion of the ominous influence of the Black Muslims and the Blood Brothers, whose acts are inspired by hate and who have as their end the total extermination of the white race.

In Harlem, the vital center for this dark enterprise, Malcolm X, the black leader who spawned black terrorism, is still present, Malcolm X, who also died of a gunshot. Groups of his disciples increase and they see their power increase as they watch their organization solidify, more and more efficient in its mortal action. It calls itself to permanent war against the white race; their minds and hearts are indoctrinated with the thesis of the superiority of the black race over all other races of the earth, and they undergo a calculated training to make each militant a cold assassin, instructed in the art of Japanese combat, the use of fire arms, the Irish club and the Italian knife.

What will succeed the untiring labor of Doctor King?—an age

of malice overflowing into a lake of blood that could drown the substantial elements of the North American nation?

As a result of this tragedy which moved the world to its innermost feelings, the assassination of Luther King puts the United States under the scrutiny of all other nations.

The days to come will be decisive for the North American democracy. It will be up to everyone to define its future. If they close their souls and their eyes to reality, to the events which will inevitably come, there will be only shadows on the horizon; and one must consider that still today, there are five states of the Union that maintain the dehumanizing racism, exasperating to the most bitter degree: Texas, Maryland, Virginia, Alabama and Georgia. If on the other hand, their conscience moves according to the inspiration of Abraham Lincoln's thought, and the timeless wisdom of the Constitution, the free world will be able to signal with a white stone, after the fashion of the ancients, the moment in which human equality and fraternity became a fortunate fact.

For this to happen it is necessary that all those voices that have been shouting in the forums of the Country of Steel, of which Whitman sang, quiet down and listen.

In all those newspapers which constitute the harmony of the voices of all the nations, whichever they may be; in the Congress, the courts, and in the squares and gardens of the cities, large and small, the irrefutable thesis of human personality vibrates, one and alone.

Yet more than this, it is indispensable that the absurd interpretations of Christ's divine word cease.

In the states of the South there are Baptist churches which traditionally celebrate their services separately for blacks and whites and at different hours.

Upon asking some racists if attendance at the house of God should be free, there are some who hold that the Creator made the whites white and the blacks black for the purpose of differentiating them.

If God Himself wished to differentiate them, then what is supposed to be separate should not be mixed, they say. From this comes the prohibition of mixed attendance.

Doubtless the question lies deep in the hearts and marrow

of the North American people. It is painful to even think of it. But as a result of this very circumstance the entire world will toast the new nation with merriment when with a new body and spirit it will come forth as a stainless character, when the whites recognize the truth of their brotherhood with the blacks. There are already many of them who have arrived in this sense. There are influential groups such as the Congress for Racial Equality, CORE, whose officers are mainly of the white race; and the National Association for the Advancement of Colored People.

But nobility, generosity, and human solidarity have not taken root in everyone.

PARIS. *Le Monde*, **April 6, 1968.**

"We have behind us a past of crime, fire and blood," said Pastor Martin Luther King in evoking the tragic history of a people stolen from their native land, transplanted to a far away continent, forced to submit to a hard exploitation, to every violence, to injustice, to offenses difficult to forgive. However, the pastor, held fast to the right, to order, and to the hope for a more equitable society which may be born from the conscience of a white population rediscovering finally the demanding purity of the "American dream."

But this dream of equality and happiness for all has never excluded violence in social, union, racial, and political battles. A still young society, her development very rapid, has often thought to find in crime the means for correcting a questionable justice and a contestable order. For the majority of white Americans today, the blacks are the principal ones responsible for the bloody disorders which have not finished spreading the seeds of insecurity in the big cities. But the tradition of violence which marks the history of the United States is certainly not the monopoly of one race. If the blacks have assassinated, three years ago, Malcolm X in New York, the murderers of Dallas, as yesterday those of Memphis, were whites.

From John Fitzgerald Kennedy to Martin Luther King, a similar tragic bond unites in effect the men who feel overwhelmed by the same fight. Beyond all election calculations, Senator Robert

Kennedy has given evidence of the bond by sending at once a telegram to the widow. Already, in 1960 when his brother was campaigning for the White House, he suggested to him, at the risk of losing the Southern vote, that he telephone personally Mrs. King, whose husband had just been imprisoned again. But confrontation took on such magnitude that abstention was only false prudence and mistaken wisdom.

The paradox is that a man who, all his life, searched to find peaceful solutions was exposed thus to the murderous blows and that his death has already released violence. True to the principles which guided his action, his last deed, incompleted, was still another deed of peace. But peace was for him only a means in the service of a superior ideal, of which one can ask if it will ever be attained.

Martin Luther King, moreover, knew very well the limitations of his program and the fragility of his peaceful hopes. Everyday he saw the hatred and the passion disfiguring the face of a white America which wished to be respectable and could not prevent herself from being racist. He also saw the young blacks, attracted by his prestige and by his courage, exposed like him to the humiliations and brutalities, but who did not have the patience to support the outrages and the bludgeons which so quickly threw them into the extremism of despair. How many young blacks, like Carmichael, have discovered their vocation of militancy in the wake of the apostle of nonviolence and found themselves again, with a bitter enthusiasm, in the ranks of Black Power. The assassinated pastor knew also that violence unchains violence, and he did not hesitate to say that the massive use of force in Vietnam encouraged everywhere recourse to arguments which will never be settled by reason. For having sown peace, he has reaped the tempest.   ·

With the death of Martin Luther King, it is a hope again awaking which risks being extinguished.

TOKYO. *The Japan Times,* **April 6, 1968.**

. . . It is too early to try to assess the consequences of the crime—whether it will unduly inflame Negro opinion or whether it will lead to a greater realization that only a sensible give-and-take attitude can be the only reasonable path to more racial harmony. Dr. King consistently pleaded for nonviolence but it is obvious that some of his supposed followers did not accept his example and direction in this respect. Some Negroes, in fact, have behaved during demonstrations in such a way as to provoke ill feeling among those who were otherwise inclined to sympathize. Contrary to Dr. King's strictest instructions they took the occasion to indulge in arson, looting and pillage. It is because of these actions that the civil rights movement has encountered somewhat less support of late than it deserves.

Whether Dr. King was wise, in view of the past misconduct of this small minority of his people, to persist in leading further demonstrations is, of course, another question.

He evidently expected to be able to prevent violence on future occasions but perhaps showed overconfidence in his powers of leadership. If white men were involved in his murder, as at the time of writing seems probable, it is likely that they had the misguided notion that if the Negro leader was made away with, the overall situation would be eased. Such an idea, if it prevailed among them, in no way modifies the wickedness and stupidity of the act.

Whether the martyrdom of Dr. King will now provide a turning point for the civil rights movement remains to be seen. President Johnson himself stands foursquare for racial equality and he has the support in this matter of the majority of forward-looking Americans.

Of course, many people will ask what can now be done in the way of bringing about something more than legal racial equality. This is a difficult question to answer because large social difficulties, which can only be overcome gradually, appear to stand in the way. If, however, all concerned will keep clear of violence, as the President urges, we may well believe the result will be material advance.

If the cruel death of Dr. King should lead to widespread conviction that nonviolence is the only sensible road to reforms, he will not have died in vain.

LONDON. *The Times,* **April 6, 1968.**

All through history it has been common to assume that when a man is murdered for his principles his death may give new impetus to the spread of those principles. Yet the immediate result of the tragic murder of DR. MARTIN LUTHER KING has been a wave of the very violence he so abhorred. If he is to enjoy posthumous victory it must come either later or in the form of the new advances for the American Negro that may now be stimulated by shock, guilt, or fear.

Yet for DR. KING even genuine advances won by violence or the threat of violence would be a negation of what he stood for. He believed that means were as important as ends. The Negro's claim to equality must be justified by the methods used to pursue it. It was this that made him the object of such intense hatred, especially in the white south, for he proved his moral superiority over his enemies in a way that completely shattered the racial doctrines on which southern society was based.

The whole nation was able to see on television screens the contrast between the well-dressed Negro youths who sat in at the lunch counters of Greensboro in 1960 and the white louts who taunted and attacked them. The Civil Rights Act of 1964 might not have been passed in that form or at that time if the racist police of Birmingham, Alabama, had not set their dogs on DR. KING'S orderly marchers in full view of the television cameras the previous year.

In other words, DR. KING was not just using a convenient form of pressure to win concessions for the Negroes. He was consciously demonstrating the Negro's moral right to equality, and he was doing so by attempting to put into practice the Christian teachings to which white society paid lip service. This made his position almost unassailable in the south. It also infuriated and frightened his enemies.

His strength lay not only in his own personality but also in the special position of the church in the south. The slave owners who justified themselves by claiming they were bringing heathens to Christianity could hardly have realized that the Negroes would interpret Christianity in one of its purest and earliest forms as a revolutionary message to an oppressed people. It was DR. KING'S role to fuse this revolutionary message with that of love for one's enemies and then to add the practical teachings of MAHATMA GANDHI in nonviolent action. It was a combination exactly suited to his own temperament, to the needs of the south, and to the ambitions of his early followers.

It was less successful in the north for many reasons. The Negro church was much less organized. There was no conscious doctrine of white racial superiority against which the Negro could prove himself. Racial discrimination was not embodied in state laws that could be attacked in the federal courts. There was just indifference, confusion, hypocrisy, and mounting bitterness on all sides. But although the headlines and the younger militants were mostly stolen by the teachers of violence such as MR. STOKELY CARMICHAEL, DR. KING continued to do valuable work in quiet discussions and negotiations with politicians and civil leaders.

He leaves behind him a solid and historic achievement in the south which nothing can now destroy entirely. In the north he leaves a hope and question mark. His memory and his movement will remain a rallying point for those who still believe that there is an alternative to violence. Even if violence prevails for the time being, and even if many people can sympathize with the desperation that provokes it, the existence of an alternative remains vital. The time may well come when violence is merely breeding violence, and when this time comes there will be a need for responsible men whose hands are clean and whose principles are intact. Then the men trained and inspired by DR. KING could come into their own again. Meanwhile, his name will continue to rank high among those invoked to answer people who argue that the Negro is not fit or ready for equality. His death is a great loss to all Negroes, to the United States, and to a world that had come to love and respect him.

Topic 32

PRESIDENT NIXON'S INAUGURATION

1969

Richard M. Nixon, after a spirited election campaign, won 301 electoral votes, as compared with Hubert H. Humphrey's 191 and George C. Wallace's 46. President Nixon entered office at a time when anxiety over urban violence and military frustrations in Vietnam gripped the nation. Hopeful observers looked to the incoming Republican administration for major changes—particularly for improving the quality of urban life and for implementing a less costly foreign policy.

MOSCOW. *Izvestia*, **January 11, 1969.** *

Some two weeks before the presidential elections, Walter Lippmann, the patriarch of American political journalism, wrote in Newsweek [*sic*] magazine that the chief difficulty of the next President's position will be that the problems confronting him cannot be solved in the period of his presidency—if they can be solved at all.

---

* Translation from *The Current Digest of the Soviet Press,* published weekly by The American Association for the Advancement of Slavic Studies at The Ohio State University. Copyright 1969; by permission.

Of course, people may say that a great many serious problems practically always confront any large country. This is especially true of a country such as the U. S. A., whose problems are engendered not only by its size but also by its "involvement," to put it mildly, in almost all the conflicts and Gordian knots of world politics, by the traditional tension in social and racial relations and by the contradictions of the world's largest and most complex economic mechanism. It is obvious that the pressure of these problems becomes especially perceptible and rises to the surface in national election years, when competing groups, sometimes even to the detriment of the collective interest of solidarity of the ruling class, themselves help to uncover many realities that at other times are carefully masked.

But of course W. Lippmann had in mind not these ordinary features of American political life, but something quite different—the fact that the United States today is experiencing an accumulation of acute problems such as it has not faced for decades, at least not since the beginning of the 1930s, the time of the "great crisis" that shook the whole capitalist world.

It is no longer only Marxists who are reaching such conclusions. People in the West have become accustomed to suspecting Marxists of tendentiousness and one-sidedness, of an inclination to perceive any economic hitch as an economic crisis and a commonplace strike as a portent of imminent revolutionary battles. No, this time we see that quite respectable bourgeois authorities—people who, it is said, are received in the "best homes" in Boston, Philadelphia, New York and Washington—are saying the same thing at the top of their voices.

. . . Of course all these problems did not appear yesterday. The majority of them involve the chronic sores of American society, which can justifiably be regarded as logical results of the social system and way of life prevailing in the country. It may be asked: If this is the situation, cannot America go on, as it has for decades, living with these problems while continuing to squander fabulous sums on the arms race and foreign-policy adventures?

. . . It cannot because the events of recent years and months have shown to what extent the present situation is fraught with serious social upheavals and explosions. This is precisely why even many of the old, truly "traditional" problems have today become quite different from what they were some 10 or 15 years ago.

. . . But one reason often pointed out in the American press is undoubtedly that even such a rich capitalist country as the U. S. A. is unable to give the people "both guns and butter" at the same time. In this connection many people talk about the very logic of the arms race and about the appearance, in the era of the new scientific and technical revolution, of weapons systems whose unrestrained production (on which many spokesmen for the U. S. military leadership insist) might bring the U. S. A. to utter ruin. Of course, one cannot fail to agree with this.

But in our opinion the problem of "guns and butter" has taken on another aspect in America today. People have begun to demand "butter," and to demand it so insistently that to continue denying it to society becomes increasingly dangerous. A great many suggestions are now being made about why this has happened. Some people blame economic progress itself, for against the background of this progress much that people used to accept submissively is now becoming intolerable. Others blame television, which has brought the realities of political life closer to the masses. We too could add something to this and to the many other explanations. Has not a role been played, for example, by the circumstance that American public opinion has ceased to believe the fables regarding the nation's vital interests, which allegedly require guns, and increasingly more expensive ones in ever greater quantities at that? One can also recall the simple everyday truth that all patience eventually comes to an end, and after many years of waiting Americans are beginning to demand more and more resolutely what was promised to them long ago in the talk about the "Great Society" and "the society of universal prosperity." And the point here is not only that the organizers of such ideological campaigns must always seek to avoid a boomerang effect. In an era of struggle between the two social systems the enlightenment of the masses and the growth of their awareness progress especially rapidly despite the streams of misinformation that bourgeois propaganda pours down on people.

But in this case I daresay the fact itself is more important than explanations. And the fact is that the present course of U. S. foreign policy, a policy that has led to the ruinous and bloody Vietnam war, a policy that continuously reproduces the arms race and, on an ever great scale, has become one of the major sources of this country's weakness, a factor that exacerbates domestic problems and acts as a real fuse for serious domestic explosions. . . .

LONDON. *The Times*, January 20, 1969.

Whether Mr. Nixon does well or badly he will be exposed to some captious criticism from Britain, as indeed he has been in the past. British public opinion is a good deal more liberal in American politics than in our own; it is only a year or two since people who have become Mr. Powell's admirers were complacently deploring the failure of the United States to deal with the race issue. Britain also owes a great deal to two American Presidents, Woodrow Wilson and Franklin Roosevelt, in two world wars. They both happen to be Democrats, and it is only reasonable that this should have left a lasting feeling of gratitude.

However, there is nothing more unwise than being partisan in somebody else's party politics. The Americans in Britain who equate the Labour Party with the Democrats, and Mr. Wilson with Mr. Humphrey, are as irritating to us as British visitors who think that Abraham Lincoln must have been a Democrat because the Democrats are the party of liberally minded men. President Nixon deserves to be regarded on his own merits, as well as on the not inconsiderable merits of the modern Republican party.

His inauguration does, however, provide an opportunity and a reason for looking again at Anglo-American relations. The truth is that Britain has never been less regarded as a factor of power in Washington, and has perhaps never been more accepted as a cultural partner. Washington, particularly since the professors arrived, is a city where power is measured by the milligram. The power of a senator is measured by the committee appointments he holds, by his seniority, by the state he represents, by his personality and prospects. Nations are measured in the same way as senators, though on somewhat different grounds.

Judged in these terms Britain is a useful second-class power, generally friendly, economically weak, reluctant to maintain her present levels of responsibility, with some particular liabilities and some particular assets. This is a very respectable international position, but it is not a special position. So long as it is accepted for what it is, Britain is well placed, but we look absurd if we turn up dressed as the head of the Commonwealth or the hero of Dunkirk.

The cultural and social relationship is, however, still there. Britain, more than any other country, is part of the cultural history of every educated American, and is also accessible to the culture of all Americans and partly shares in it. After all, the classical literature of the English language is English literature, and the early history of the United States is English history.

All this was true before, yet in the past Americans were inhibited by a certain resentment of Britain. Nineteenth-century Americans resented British power; twentieth-century Americans regarded the declining British Empire as illiberal and against their principles. Liberal Americans disliked Britain's class structure for the same reasons which made rich Americans marry into our aristocracy. All these rancours have gone; the resentment of British power has vanished with the power that provoked it.

This leaves a relationship which works remarkably well, perhaps better than before, provided it is not stretched too far. In President Johnson's Washington the British have not been in a position to bargain, but they have been in a position to be accepted. The relationship can perhaps be compared with that of Canada, which the United States can hardly remember is a foreign country at all. Britain is not as close as that, but the facts of British good will and of the identity of British and American interests are accepted as something completely normal in a way that did not used to be the case.

This sensible, familiar, low-keyed relationship is what we should expect and try to maintain with President Nixon. No doubt from time to time we shall have to ask him for support for British interests. Perhaps the best start would be to consider what support Britain can offer for legitimate American interests, for the United States has never been more heavily laden with the responsibilities of defending the Western alliance. To paraphrase another President, do not ask what the United States can do for us, but ask what we can do for the United States.

TOKYO. *The Japan Times,* January 22, 1969.

. . . It is heartening to note that the new President promised to keep his "lines of communications" open to all nations. In these difficult times when many parts of the world are wracked by wars and dissensions, it is of the utmost importance that the greatest democracy in the international community maintain an open stance in its dealings with all other countries. In what might be a reference to Communist China, the President said, "We seek . . . a world in which no people, great or small, will live in angry isolation."

The hope is held that Mr. Nixon's search for peace will extend as well to the Middle East where the prospects of settlement remain dim.

In Japan, the new American President's emphasis on a policy of peace should find a warm response. Mr. Nixon should find the great majority of the Japanese people in full accord with the kind of peace that he seeks—which is healing and compassionate toward sufferers, which shows understanding toward opponents and which gives the opportunity for all peoples to choose their own destiny.

The relations between Japan and the United States have been warm and cordial. There is no reason to believe they will be otherwise with an America under the Nixon leadership. The U. S. policy on the reversion of Okinawa was evolved during the Eisenhower Administration in which Mr. Nixon served as Vice-President.

Japanese concern over future American trade policies rests on the President's ability to deal with a possibly protection-minded Congress under Democratic party control. Mr. Nixon states in his inaugural address that he seeks an "open world" which is "open to the exchange of goods and people."

It is apparent the new U. S. Chief Executive has taken great pains to dissolve any preconceived image that he is a militant "hawk." He is obviously keeping an open mind toward all countries—in the broad sense all of us earthlings are brothers with a common destiny.

The eyes of the world will be upon Mr. Nixon as he takes up his heavy responsibilities. We hope that his quest for unity at home and peace among all nations will succeed. We wish him well.

MEXICO CITY. *El Universal,* **January 21, 1969.**

. . . Contrary to what one might expect, Nixon reduced the brief and inspired concepts of his message to a central theme of peace; peace in the interior of nations as a result of a consciousness of understanding and unity; similarly in the exterior, as a product of conciliatory arrangements to bring about an understanding and agreement throughout all the nations of the earth, suggesting that negotiations constitute the only means to achieve this peace.

In the first case he spoke with mystical elegance of the equality of men before God, it being obvious to consider all human beings of similar rights, endeavoring with this ideal in mind to concentrate the powers of his politics on the solution of the many social problems among which the racial problem is dominant.

More than just words, referring to concrete material issues, his address is made up of a series of general outlines and suggestions as to the behavior of men, based on freedom, love, decency, and kindness.

With reference to the states, he declared that in his politics there is only room for peace which must come with compassion and understanding for the conquered, helping them in their suffering and their rehabilitation. No doubt he is thinking of Vietnam, where so much damage has been done, apart from sacrificed lives, in the destruction of material goods.

One must hope that both attitudes have a pacific effect, causing to disappear from this world of agitation the anguish and suffering of the last years, confiding in a diplomatic agreement from the talks which are taking place in Paris between the opponents of this bloody and sterile Vietnamese war, which can benefit neither of them.

. . . The President asserted strongly that this country must achieve an equal treatment of blacks and whites thereby guarding the United States against the subversive threats which can cause so much material and moral evil.

In speaking of the common progress he maintained that where an error is found it must be corrected; this makes us think of the good light in which the North American executive will see our serious and sharp problem, that is, the crisis provoked by the prohibition on our exports of certain vegetable products to the United States.

One must not forget that President Nixon's address ascends to a level which in its interpretation does not permit us to find well-defined orientations as to the development of his politics as much in the domestic as well as international arena. It is a peaceful discourse, a superior one, humanitarian in its deep sensibilities.

To achieve such noble purposes he will have to overcome many obstacles. It will be necessary for him to maintain these ideals vigorously, with constant energy and with a conciliatory spirit and an understanding of all the aspects of his government— toward his fellow citizens, as well as in the relations which he maintains with the other States.

His emotional inspiration brings him to evoke once again the latest and extraordinary feat of his country's astronauts, affirming that the fundamental problems are found in the world which we inhabit, for whose harmonious and human progress we should concentrate our total effort.

PEKING. *Jen-min Jih-pao*, January 30, 1969.†

The string of despondent wailings uttered by Richard Nixon, new chieftain of U. S. imperialism, in his "inaugural address" is an obvious sign of the fast decline of U. S. imperialism.

It may be recalled that soon after World War Two the U. S. imperialists arrogantly called the 20th century the "American Century" alleging that the United States had assumed "the spiritual

---

† From the *Survey of China Mainland Press*. Prepared by U. S. Consulate in Hong Kong. Microfilm, Washington, D. C.

leadership of all countries in the world." The first postwar U. S. president Harry S Truman in his "State of the Union Message" dated December 1945 bragged unblushingly that the United States shouldered the permanent responsibility of leading the world. He even said: the responsibility that had lain upon Genghis Khan, Caesar Augustus, Napoleon Bonaparte, Louis the Fourteenth or any other great leader could not be compared with that upon the U. S. president. What insolence! What swaggering.

But now Richard Nixon came out with an inaugural speech that sounded as flat as a punctured balloon. . . .

U. S. imperialism raked in fabulous ill-gained fortunes in the two world wars, thus speedily swelling its economic strength. In the postwar period, holding the dollar in one hand and the atom bomb in the other, U. S. imperialism ran amuck like a mad dog, in a vain attempt to build a big empire unprecedented in history and dominate the whole world. However, the fate of U. S. imperialism is worse than that of the big, once all-mighty empires in the past. The British Empire, where it was claimed "the sun never sets," had maintained its "prosperity" for more than 200 years, but has declined in the end. U. S. imperialism which climbed up to the pinnacle of "power" just after the second world war is speedily rolling down from it only after 20-odd years.

. . . in the early days of the postwar period, when U. S. imperialism was baring its claws and behaving most arrogantly, our great leader Chairman Mao pointed out: "Speaking of U. S. imperialism, people seem to feel that it is terrifically strong. Chinese reactionaries are using the 'strength' of the United States to frighten the Chinese people. But it will be proved that the U. S. reactionaries, like all the reactionaries in history, do not have much strength." The historical development of U. S. imperialism which has been steadily declining in the past 20 years and more has fully borne out the correctness of this brilliant thesis of Chairman Mao's.

U. S. imperialism has always been a paper tiger. The brittle nature of this paper tiger has become more and more obvious as it goes further and further downhill daily. Nixon, who has just come to power, can only use ambiguous and empty words to cover up his innermost fear and hopelessness. This precisely shows that

U. S. imperialism has landed itself in the hopeless situation of being beset with difficulties and finding no way out both at home and abroad.

But, all reactionary forces will never step down from the stage of history of their own accord. Though the new chieftain of U. S. imperalism, Nixon, realized his own predicament and gloomy future, he raved that he would "sustain" [sic], crying hysterically that the United States "will be as strong as we need to be for as long as we need to be." In other words, Nixon still wants to keep up the hollow posture of U. S. imperialism and continue to make trouble. However, the deathbed kicks of the U. S. reactionaries can only speed up their own doom.

Topic 33

THE MOON LANDING

1969

At 10:56 P.M., eastern daylight time, on Sunday, July 20, 1969, Neil A. Armstrong said as he stepped on the moon's surface, "That's one small step for a man, one giant leap for mankind." The space voyage by Armstrong, Edwin E. Aldrin, Jr., and Michael Collins climaxed a costly and fantastically complex technological adventure.

When the Russians launched the first space satellite, Sputnik I, in October 1957, the contest for space supremacy by Russia and the United States assumed a new urgency and political orientation. In May 1961, President John F. Kennedy announced to the Congress that "landing a man on the moon and returning him safely to earth" came under the heading, "Urgent National Needs." Annual American appropriations for space exploration soon exceeded $5 billion. Moreover, a commitment was made to land a man on the moon before the 1960s ended: the last July in that decade witnessed the fulfillment. Aldrin summed it up in his address in September to a joint session of Congress: "It is with a great sense of pride as an American and with humility as a human being that I say to you what no men have been privileged to say before: We walked on the moon. . . . And, since we came in peace for all mankind, those footprints belong to all the people of the world."

MEXICO CITY. *El Universal,* July 21, 1969.

THE SUPREME ACHIEVEMENT

The dream nourished by man for centuries or perhaps milleniums finally has been fulfilled: that is, to put his foot on a celestial body other than the Earth.

At last, the feat of transporting oneself to the natural satellite of our planet has been accomplished and the descent from the ship was conducted successfully in a voyage that until a few years ago would have seemed impossible, and only the most brash thinkers or the most imaginative novelists would have dared to conceive of it.

. . . The North American citizens, aboard the ship "Apollo," have arrived at Selene as a result of the enormous technical and economic effort, which for more than a decade the United States has been sustaining in its plan for the conquest of space, paralleling other advanced programs of surprising scientific development.

It is natural, consequently, to salute this effort and the triumph in which it has ended with all the jubilation that it warrants, with the recognition and the gratitude which humanity owes to those lucky ones who are contributing notably to the development of civilization, whose benefits will reach in the long run all the peoples of the Earth.

Yet one cannot forget the notable attainments that the Soviet Union achieved in the same scientific speciality, that it has among its assets the placement of the first artificial satellite in earth orbit, the first manned circumnavigation, the sending of the first missile to the Moon and the first investigative probe to the planet Venus.

Finding themselves, or so it seemed, at first disadvantaged with regard to the USSR, the North Americans set upon recuperating themselves and setting themselves on an upward course with the spectacular feat that all the world now celebrates with jubilation, although the Soviets had almost simultaneously sent another airship that, it was assumed, would surpass the head start of the U. S. "Apollo."

Until now they are the only countries that are participating in the so called "space race" or rather they are the ones extending their efforts to continue their progress in space navigation; they possess between themselves an advantageous posture both technical and economical that gives them a monopoly in this class of enterprise, although it is not a remote possibility that in the near future other nations in the technological vanguard can exhibit the same effort and secure important achievements.

Though at the moment there does not exist the perspective of what a third power can do to overtake the two contenders, the possibility is not to be definitely dismissed.

What is interesting to point out in any case is [that] the spectacular triumphs achieved by the North Americans and the Soviets constitute the culmination of a long trajectory of feats that numerous countries have supported with all the generosity with which culture is always produced, with the mystique that the completion of a mission carries with it for the men of science, who for centuries have labored in many sectors in order to make possible the interesting advances that have been produced since the beginning of civilization, until the advances culminate in the notable feat on which we are commenting, that which by no means represents an insurmountable limit, but rather is one more stage in the interminable chain of triumphs that the genius of man uninterruptedly produces.

Thus considered, the conquest of the moon is a victory for all of humanity. And one ought to understand that precisely in order to put out whatever embers of rivalry could exist between such highly developed powers: one must remain open to the perspective of mutual collaboration that is going to be needed in order to carry onward the outlined programs—like the arrival at the neighboring planets of the earth, and transportation to the most remote regions of space—which will demand much greater efforts than those expended to achieve the arrival at Selene.

On the other hand, the resources of science are by no means exhausted in the exploits of space navigation; they include other important opportunities that will permit the conquering of lamentable deficiencies that afflict man on the face of the Earth.

It has been insistently repeated that so much vigilance and money should not be dedicated to a program of lunar conquest when there still exist miseries with which man profoundly sympathizes.

Without yielding completely to this theory, to the point of condemning the investigations and the work that culminated in the landing of man on the moon, it is important that this triumph, like those of all humanity, ought to be translated into a consciousness of mutual solidarity, into a wider sense of responsibility for that which signifies the fact of being man and of inhabitating a planet that has gone beyond its first cosmic demarcation. Moreover, mankind has not overcome even its most elemental deficiencies, nor avoided the absurd rivalries in which, unfortunately, it is still bogged down.

We hope, then, that the triumph of mankind, consists not only in the conquest of the moon, but also and primordially in the conquest of himself, which means the elevation of morality and the further development that will put all human beings in the harmony of peace, unity and progress.

PARIS. *Le Monde*, July 23, 1969.

The silence jealously guarded by Peking sufficed to show the vigor of the nationalist sentiment which surrounds the most extraordinary scientific accomplishments. Neither the press nor the Chinese radio has announced the launching of Apollo 11, and North Korea like North Vietnam have observed the same discretion. The successes of the adversary are hidden under the bushel. But for how long? It is perhaps less surprising that the Arab countries have given to the crisis of the Middle East a clear priority over the conquest of the moon, thus recalling that no exploit could know how to eclipse the dramas and the miseries of daily life. Cuba, on her part, has systematically jammed the broadcasts of the Voice of America, but how can one suppose that the latter, obtained by underground everywhere else in Latin America, could make people forget the sombre balance sheet of the recent visit of Mr. Nelson Rockefeller? As to the Soviets, if they have refrained from minimizing the American success, they do not appear thus far resolved to engage in scientific cooperation from which all humanity would benefit.

It was this direction that the international space treaty wished to open when it was begun with vigor in 1967. This text proclaimed that the exploration and utilization of space are the "lot of all humanity." The terrain had been prepared in 1963 by a resolution of the General Assembly of the UN affirming that in no manner should outer space and the heavenly bodies become the object of a national appropriation. But the sole means of translating such principles into acts should have been to organize methodically a cooperation which, without of course eliminating all rivalry, would not have permitted the exacerbation of rivalries, sources of waste and of the loss of energy.

The only domains in which Americans and Soviets have [been] engaged [in] a certain collaboration concerns meteorology, the study of the magnetic field of the earth and communications by satellites. An accord concerning biology and space medicine practically remained a dead letter.

Justification for a common effort by the two major powers is not lacking: help to the cosmonauts in difficulty, ground watch of the spaceships, exchange of information, experiments worked out together, exploration of other planets, and so forth. To each proposition from Washington, Moscow has either kept silent or answered that the proposition could not be accepted "in today's circumstances." On September 20, 1963, before the UN General Assembly, President Kennedy suggested that the USSR and the United States work together for the exploration of the moon. Moscow did not even deign to react, although President Johnson again pursued this idea.

How can one be surprised, under these conditions, that the United States seems to have lost all hope of reaching any cooperation whatsoever? Would the technological and scientific difference between the two great powers be too vast? The Americans don't seem to think so and rather attribute the attitude of Moscow to political considerations. At the time of the signing of the international space treaty, the ambassador of the USSR, Mr. Dobrynin declared: "Let us hope that we will not have to wait long for the solution of earthly problems . . ." The solution, despite all the "planning together," is not much more advanced. The explored limits of the universe can move back, but the provincialisms and the chauvinisms remain stronger than the aspirations toward a

332 From the Foreign Press

truly universal vision. The Congress of the United States itself has refused to have the flag of the UN placed on the moon. Only the starry flag is, in its eyes, a symbol worthy of the exploit accomplished.

TOKYO. *The Japan Times,* July 22, 1969.

Mankind made a successful rendezvous with history on Monday, July 21. The dream of the ages has been fulfilled—man has set his footprints on the surface of the moon, a terrain not of the planet Earth. Indeed, a historic landmark in man's adventure into space has now been dedicated.

. . . Reading from the plaque which will be left on the moon, astronaut Armstrong said in a steady voice, "Here man first set foot on the moon, July 1969. We came in peace for all mankind." In these words of peace are entrusted the hopes and aspirations of all humanity and its civilization which made this unparalleled feat of the Apollo 11 possible.

. . . The fantastic thing about the whole performance was that it was being followed by millions of earthlings by television and radio. Everyone had the thrill of participating in the making of history. Never before had so many people watched a single event. Everywhere there was unbounded joy in the success achieved, and prayers that the astronauts' journey back would be as successful.

There is no question of the dangers involved. It was only that the astronauts made it look so easy. But behind them were their strenuous training and the superior technology making the project possible. And there was also, as pointed out by Prime Minister Eisaku Sato in hailing this magnificent achievement, the courage, confidence and energetic devotion of the spacemen and the many thousands of people involved.

As the American astronauts opened up a new frontier in space in the presence, as it were, of millions of earthbound people, the contrast has surely been noted with the secrecy in which the Soviet Union has conducted its unmanned moon probe with the Luna 15. A cloud of mystery still surrounds the mission of this

Soviet spaceship, which was launched toward the moon a few days prior to Apollo 11 and which latest reports say was placed in an orbit bringing it within 16 kilometers of the lunar surface. It may well be the Russian way of making known that the Soviet Union is still very much in the space race. That, of course, brings us back to reality—the fact of a "competition" between the two superpowers. This need not remain so. In fact, we hope that as the barriers to man's confinement on Earth are broken so will the artificial obstacles to the cooperative activities of mankind be torn asunder.

The conquest of the moon is only the beginning. Man's quest for knowledge is limitless just as his curiosity is boundless. What was proved Monday was that whatever man's mind can conceive —even as science fiction—he can achieve. But as man moves further outward toward the stars, he must buttress his determination to put his own Earth in order. . . .

LONDON. *The Times,* July 21, 1969.

Most of the world was able to share the drama of the moon landing, a drama which obviously could have ended in disaster, and indeed there are still more hazards to come. As the television clock showed the last twenty minutes ticking away, second by second, and we heard the matter-of-fact voices of the American astronauts, any family with a television set was present at one of the most exciting moments of man's history. July 20, 1969, will be remembered when little children who were brought down half asleep are grandparents. It is the first event of such historic significance to be shared so widely and known so immediately.

Yet what does it mean? Obviously it is an epic of human bravery, similar to the conquest of Everest or the great voyages of discovery. Obviously it is a great feat of scientific and professional skill, of particular appeal to so professional an age. Obviously, also, it is a reproach; the nation which personifies this and other advances is unable to solve social problems which should perhaps be simpler but are more difficult. Obviously, also, it is a symbolic act, man reaching out of his previous confines, an astonishing demonstration of the capacity of the most ridiculous of animals.

This celebrated event is also most mysterious in its consequences. It may be little more than a brilliantly lit blind alley, a successful act of scientific curiosity, but also an intrusion into an atmosphere so alien that it will remain of as little use to man as the much more convenient explorations of the polar regions. It could therefore be a step that leads little further than itself or it could lead to a whole series of further explorations, to a new way of life for man and not merely to the satisfaction of his curiosity or the extension of his psychological boundaries.

For the present we have the fact itself and the fact is so remarkable that it is enough. The American astronauts have landed on the moon and we have heard their conversation from the moon and seen their progress. Their achievement will always be one of the wonders of the world.

Topic 34

THE ATTACK ON SANCTUARIES IN CAMBODIA

1970

On April 30, 1970, President Richard M. Nixon reported in a major television address that American and South Vietnamese forces were attacking Communist areas in Cambodia in order "to clear out major enemy sanctuaries on the Cambodian-Vietnamese border." Moreover, he said that after the enemy's military supplies were destroyed and enemy forces were driven out, the attacking forces would withdraw. This action was being taken, he stated, in order to end the war in Vietnam and secure a just peace. Some Americans viewed President Nixon's decision as an extension of the war and nationwide protests, particularly on college campuses, shook American society.

TOKYO. *The Japan Times,* **May 2, 1970.**

. . . In going before the American people with this new development in Indochina, U. S. President Richard M. Nixon stated, "This is not an invasion of Cambodia. The areas in which these attacks will be launched are completely occupied and controlled by North Vietnamese forces." He went on to say that the purpose is not to occupy the region. And once the Communists are driven out of their sanctuary, the allied forces will withdraw. Mr. Nixon expects this action to take from six weeks to two months.

It is certainly to be hoped that the military action which has now been undertaken will work out as the American President has stated in his broadcast from the White House Thursday. But in view of the past record of the American involvement in South Vietnam, the plans for a quick military decision and a speedy withdrawal may not turn out to be that simple. The North Vietnamese troops, for one thing, may prove to be as elusive on Cambodian soil as they are in South Vietnam. At the same time, Hanoi can be expected to do all it can to keep the allied forces from pulling out, especially in view of the propaganda value of having U. S. soldiers in Cambodia. The Communists are, of course, aware of the effects this action will have upon the American people, ignoring the fact they have been there for years.

President Nixon himself has taken this move with full cognizance of the reaction from his nation. As to be expected there have been comments both praising and castigating the presidential action. Those in favor have pointed out it takes true statesmanship to make such a difficult decision. They agree with him that this is the only way to save American lives, to end the war and to bring the troops home.

There have also been strong criticisms voiced against Mr. Nixon's move. These critics claim it will only expand the war and cause more bloodshed. They feel that it was "ghastly" and "deplorable."

It is apparent that President Nixon has at least the courage of his conviction—and in this case, it involved directly the weighing of the facts whether the risk of doing nothing at this time was greater than the risk of taking limited action. Aside from this military consideration, it dealt with the political question of how his party would fare at the coming midterm elections in November and of how his [own] chances of reelection . . . would be affected.

The President answered this by saying, "Whether my party gains in November is nothing compared to the lives of 400,000 brave Americans fighting for our country and for the cause of peace and freedom in Vietnam. Whether I may be a one-term President is insignificant compared to whether by our failure to act in this crisis the United States proves itself to be unworthy to lead the forces of freedom in this critical period."

The Communists appear to be set upon turning the Vietnam war into an all-out ideological battle between the forces of democracy and communism. There is evidence that the Communist Chinese are now organizing an alliance among the Communist forces fighting in Indochina—the North Vietnamese, the Viet Cong, the Laotian Pathet Lao and the Cambodian Rouge Khmer. These were the forces brought together in support of ousted Cambodian Head of State Prince Norodom Sihanouk in a meeting somewhere in South China with the attendance of no less a personage than Premier Chou En-lai.

The Soviet Union, not to be outdone by Communist China, has also voiced its backing for the Prince's attempts to organize a "united front" among Indochinese Reds.

It remains our hope, however, that these efforts which obviously are looking for military solutions to the conflict on the Indochina peninsula will be replaced by sincere endeavors to find the ways and means of achieving a political and negotiated settlement.

TOKYO. *Asahi Shimbun**

Contrary to previous expectations that U. S. actions in Cambodia would be limited ones, within the bounds of the Nixon Doctrine, President Nixon Thursday ordered U. S. ground combat troops into Cambodia as well as raids by B52s. The U. S. seems to have stepped out of the Nixon Doctrine which calls for less U. S. military involvement in Asia. It is rather extending the war in Vietnam into Cambodia. Considering the particular terrain where Cambodian, Vietnamese and Laotian borders converge,

---

* As reprinted in *The Japan Times,* May 2, 1970.

the Communists will probably resort to a prolonged guerrilla war. This will make it difficult for the U. S. to achieve its military objectives in Cambodia and withdraw its troops quickly. The Vietnamese Communists are also supported by the Soviet Union and Communist China. We oppose the U. S. intervention in Cambodia. It will escalate the war in Indochina and pit Asians against Asians. The U. S. action seems hardly justified both under its own domestic as well as international laws.

PARIS. *Le Monde,* **May 6, 1970.**

While the leaders of the Kremlin wanted to give the impression that they were reacting vigorously to the entry of American troops in Cambodia, they also tried to avoid a direct confrontation with the United States. Such is the impression that one gathers from Mr. Kosygin's press conference. He categorically condemned President Nixon's policy, and stated that his government would draw from the recent events the "appropriate conclusions." Which ones? The head of the Soviet government left his listeners wondering.

The prudence of Moscow contrasts with the much more militant attitude of Peking, which promises its complete support to the people of Indochina, without, however, specifying what form this would take. It is true that the USSR has no reason to take any major risks in order to defend Prince Sihanouk when she never threw all the weight of her power to help the Vietnamese. Until proof appears to the contrary, she keeps to her policy of coexistence with the United States. But in order to pursue this policy, she finds herself obviously in a very uncomfortable situation. It is not easy to entertain normal relations with the government of Washington, while taking up the cudgels for those who are fighting against "Yankee imperialism."

Not long ago, the Soviets had attached some importance to the Paris talks. They can no longer entertain many illusions about them. Are they then going to accept a new negotiating procedure and facilitate, for example, as Paris and London have suggested, the convening of a conference to which all parties interested in the settlement of the Indochinese problems would be invited? Mr. Kosygin brushes aside this proposal: "Now is the time for action, not for conferences. As far as we are concerned, we must deal energetically with aggression." These militant words would have been more widely acclaimed if the head of the Soviet government had given a hint of what he wanted, and of what he was able to do in order to procure the evacuation of the American troops "in Vietnam as well as in Cambodia."

Mr. Kosygin limited himself to giving a lesson in law and in ethics. He tried to refute the arguments that Mr. Nixon had used in order to justify the intervention of American troops. He said that enlarging the theater of operations could not possibly hasten the end of the war. He made himself the defender "of the sovereignty of states and of the inviolability of their territories." He extolled the right of peoples to decide for themselves, and condemned "the arbitrariness that exists so strikingly in international affairs." He asked who had authorized the United States to play the role of "policeman of the world." Finally he reproached Mr. Nixon for carrying out a policy contrary to his declarations.

Who would not subscribe to such remarks? While listening to Mr. Kosygin's declarations or reading the report of them, many people, however, must have thought that the lesson would have been more effective if the USSR brought her own actions in harmony with her doctrine. The United States attributes to herself the role of "policeman of the world"; the Soviet Union does not hesitate, when she considers it necessary, to act the policeman in her own camp. Is it possible to denounce the invasion of Indochinese territories when one has justified the "fraternal aid" that the Russian soldiers have imposed on the Czechoslovakians? Mr. Kosygin speaks admirably when he condemns the claims implied in President Nixon's most recent speech. He would be more convincing if he also rejected a certain Brezhnev doctrine on the limited sovereignty of the socialist states, and if he respected everywhere in the world the will of peoples, great or small, to decide for themselves as they wish.

LONDON. *The Times,* May 6, 1970.

. . . There is however the more important question whether the United States can be held to a course which does not promise further withdrawals from Vietnam. The state of feeling in American universities is an extremely serious problem for the President. Before the latest developments in Vietnam it was already doubtful whether the universities were not going to have their worst summer so far. The university strikes and the Ohio shootings are only a foretaste of what could happen.

Vietnam is the great issue which divides radical youth in the United States from its elders. It is even more important to the white majority of university students than the question of colour, let alone university democracy or pollution. The feeling of helplessness before the power of the Washington machine, and the feeling also that the Washington machine is controlled by a man they neither like nor trust, has thrown many students into a posture of aggressive despair.

They feel that they cannot do anything but demonstrate but they will certainly demonstrate to the limit. In fact this strong and violent expression of student opinion is bound to have an influence on the policy of the American Government and will strengthen the forces who want to be sure that the intrusion into Cambodia is a temporary measure to help the Americans to get out and not a permanent measure designed to allow them to stay in.

The extension of the war into Cambodia and the further demonstration at Kent State University of the vicious incompetence of some sections of the American National Guard have also caused a great shock in Europe. This shock is both real and reasonable. There is a conviction that President Nixon is pushing inexorably ahead down a road which leads to disaster, probably to disaster in war and certainly to disaster at home.

Yet the European view, including the British view, seems a pointless piece of wisdom when one contrasts it with the failure of all European countries to take responsibility for their proper share of their own defence. Europe is infinitely willing to criticize the American defence effort and infinitely reluctant to cease to rely on it. In Britain it has for a decade been held to be axiomatic that conscription is politically impossible. As a result we have a defence policy which consists of hoping that the Americans will agree to fire off nuclear weapons in the first days of any general European war. The fact that this policy is immoral, unrealistic and suicidal does not stop a government of left wing views clinging to it because they have no other. Nor does it stop an opposition of right wing views from giving only a somewhat less enthusiastic assent.

Obviously the present course of the war in Vietnam makes it still more unreasonable for Europe to rely on American defence. The criticisms that come from Europe cannot add to American enthusiasm for spending their resources when we do not spend enough of ours. The burden of the Vietnam war must in any case reduce America's capacity to support her present European defence effort. The transatlantic difference of view over Vietnam is prying open the alliance, and Vietnam necessarily concentrates American attention on Asia. . . .

Topic 35

THE SUPREME COURT DECISION ON THE "PENTAGON PAPERS"

1971

On June 13, 1971, The New York Times *began publication of top secret selections and documents from a forty-seven volume study entitled, "History of U. S. Decision-Making Process on Vietnam Policy." Commissioned by Defense Secretary Robert McNamara in 1967 and prepared by the Defense Department, the study traced the increasing involvement of the United States in Vietnam during and after World War II. Additional parts were published on June 14 and 15 before the federal government designated the publication harmful to the national security and ordered it stopped. The government next prohibited the* Washington Post *from publishing the series for the same reason. On June 30, 1971, the Supreme Court, in a 6 to 3 decision, ruled against the government's prohibition, saying the government had failed to justify the necessity for the enforcement of prior restraint of expression in these two cases. The ruling of the Court was interpreted as an historic victory for freedom of the press guaranteed by the First Amendment to the Constitution.*

LONDON. *The Times*, July 2, 1971.

By voting 6 to 3 to allow publication of the Pentagon's hitherto secret study of the Vietnam war the United States Supreme Court has erected another important milestone in the constitutional history of the United States. The ill-defined balance of power between the press and the executive has been sharply altered in favour of the press. From now on the "top secret" stamp will have much less meaning. It will remain an administrative convenience defining the area in which a document may circulate inside the bureaucracy, but once such a document reaches a newspaper the only restraints on publication will be the judgment of the editor and a fairly narrow definition of the immediate defence interests of the United States.

The Administration's case was that the publication of the documents would not merely expose recent history but would harm the future conduct of policy in areas such as the Vietnam war, the negotiations for the return of American prisoners, and the SALT talks with the Soviet Union. It invoked the constitutional power of the President over the conduct of foreign affairs, and his authority as commander-in-chief of the armed forces.

Rejecting the case, the court split roughly three ways. The dissenting minority complained that the indecent haste with which the case had been dealt with had prevented proper consideration of the evidence. The majority was made up of two camps. One invoked the absolute validity of the First Amendment, which states that "Congress shall make no law . . . abridging the freedom of speech or of the press." Thus Justice William Douglas said that there was "no room for governmental restraint on the press," and Justice Hugo Black said that if publication of news could sometimes be stopped it would "make a shambles of the First Amendment."

This absolutist doctrine was not shared by the third group. Justice Byron White could not say that in no circumstances would the First Amendment permit an injunction against publishing information about government plans. Nor did he deny that the Vietnam documents would damage public interests. But he felt that the Administration had not satisfied the "heavy burden which it must meet to warrant an injunction against publication in these cases."

This middle position seems the one that is likely to prevail. All governments must be able to protect some secrets, particularly those concerned with immediate defence or tactical plans. The only valid question is where to draw a line that will permit proper public control of the government without making the conduct of policy impossible. In the United States the line has always permitted a very wide role for the press as an important public check on the executive. If this role is now being widened still further it is partly a response to the widening powers of the executive and to the immediate shock of discovering just how much policy-making in the Vietnam war had been kept secret.

The ball is now clearly with Congress. If it feels that government security is insufficiently protected it can attempt to amend the Constitution or pass laws defining more clearly the meaning of security. It is, however, unlikely to do either, so that what remains is a situation in which the onus is on the Administration to prove that in any future case the constitutional authority of the President is being infringed. This will not be easy, but there will be relatively few mourners. In most countries, including Britain, the national interest is too easily invoked to conceal incompetence or dishonesty. The Supreme Court has set a better example than the Administration.

MOSCOW. *Izvestia*, July 2, 1971.*

The court ban, by means of which the Administration attempted to avert further publication in the American press of the secret documents of the Pentagon, has been declared unconstitutional by the Supreme Court of the U. S. A. In practice this means that *The New York Times,* the *Washington Post,* and other organs of the American press can continue to publish materials based on secret government papers concerning the American aggression in Vietnam. The *Washington Post* at once published three articles

_____

* Translation made especially for *As Others See Us.*—Ed.

which bring light to bear on Kennedy's Vietnam policy, and on that of the first years of the Johnson Administration. This newspaper discloses new facts which until now were hidden from the American public. In particular, the role of the CIA in preparing the palace revolution in Saigon is openly described for the first time. Thus, the dike of secrecy with which the Administration had tried to protect itself in order to prevent further disclosures of the dirty intrigues of the U. S. military clique in Vietnam has finally been broken. The next few days will enable millions of Americans to look once more into the private studies of Pentagon and other strategists, and to find out how they planned their military adventures.

This decision of the Supreme Court was reached, in particular, in opposition to the stand of the Chief Justice W. Burger—one more proof of the serious differences of opinion that exist in ruling circles of the U. S. A.

BOMBAY. *The Times of India,* July 1, 1971.

Now that the U. S. government has decided to lift the veil of secrecy from the "Pentagon Papers," scooped by *The New York Times,* is it too much to expect that wielders of classified stamps in New Delhi will draw the appropriate lessons from the episode which is both agonizing and amusing?

Those secrets which must be kept, in the interest of national security, will be better maintained if official documents are not marked "top secret" indiscriminately. There have been instances in this country of copies of ministerial tour programs being classified and passed around in envelopes crushed under the weight of official seals. Indeed, in this matter, the Indian record has in some ways been worse than that of the U. S. A. and most other democracies. . . .

LONDON. *The Observer,* July 4, 1971.

The United States Supreme Court's decision to reject the American Government's plea that the newspapers should be forbidden to publish the secret "Pentagon Papers" about the Vietnam war strikes a blow for the freedom of the press. It also shows the markedly different approach taken in the U. S. and in Britain towards the protection of State secrets.

The principle underlying the British Official Secrets Act is that every piece of Government information, however trivial, must be kept secret unless the Government authorizes its publication. In the U. S., the First Amendment to the Constitution guaranteeing the freedom of the press puts the onus the other way: everything must be open to public view unless its nature is such that, in the interests of the *security of the State,* secrecy must be maintained.

Naturally, this can make things difficult for government. Negotiations may be prejudiced unless they are kept confidential—at least until agreement is reached. Even then, disclosures may embarrass relationships with foreign Powers. President Woodrow Wilson's call for "open agreements openly arrived at" was a counsel of perfection.

It is a Government's duty to keep its real secrets. The duty of the press is to disclose what is going on for the benefit of the public who are "entitled to know." The necessary conflict between these two duties should be a source of fruitful tension between two equally important roles.

If anything, the U. S. errs on the side of freedom, Britain on the side of authority. . . .

JERUSALEM. *The Jerusalem Post,* July 4, 1971.

The United States celebrates today the 195th anniversary of its independence—an occasion of moment for all the world. When the representatives of the 13 colonies met at Philadelphia, little could they know how great a Power was to emerge from their deliberations, and even less that that Power was to derive its essential greatness from the principles they laid down in their Declaration that summer day.

The concept there set forth that "governments are instituted among men, deriving their just powers from the consent of the governed" was profoundly revolutionary. It was the first formal assertion by a whole people of their right to a government of their own choice. Whether he realizes it or not, every contemporary advocate of the self-determination of peoples is following the path marked out by Thomas Jefferson and his friends. (As Jefferson himself was to write prophetically in his old age, "the flames kindled on the Fourth of July, 1776, have spread over too much of the globe to be extinguished by the feeble engines of despotism.")

(The basic ideas of the Founding Fathers, enshrined 11 years later in the Constitution which has stood like a rock ever since, have never been called into question by the American people as a whole. But many Americans do wonder today how well they are being applied to current problems.)

The United States, having attained unexampled heights of prosperity and power, is in our day experiencing a period of intense self-criticism and doubt. It is indeed faced with problems, on the domestic and external fronts, which might totally have shattered any society less firmly built on principle and freedom. But Americans meet their problems openly, with lively public discussion and participation, sometimes with violence. There is no aspect, for example, of the Vietnam war or of race relations that is not debated with a liberty such as exists in scarcely any other society, and there is always the Supreme Court, as a very recent ruling has once again shown, to stand up for fundamental rights.

The United States is going through the excruciatingly painful process of adjustment to the social and economic change made necessary by the scientific and technological advance of modern times. (It is mainly because of this active grappling with some of the deepest questions of human life that there is turmoil in the United States today.) The fact that the achievements of modern science and technology are largely the fruit of the genius and dynamism of the Americans themselves does not make the process any easier. (It has come to the United States first, and the rest of the world will go through it in its turn, learning from this bitter American experience as it has learnt from America so much else. It is not without reason that a French thinker has recently suggested that the true world revolution of our day is taking place in the United States, making the "revolutions" of self-styled revolutionary societies look pale and old-fashioned by comparison.) . . .

Topic 36

COLLAPSE IN SOUTH VIETNAM

1975

Saigon's surrender finally marked the end of American military involvement in South Vietnam. After decades of costly military assistance, the United States withdrew from that beleaguered nation. The rapid and powerful emergence of a Communist-controlled Vietnam embarassed Americans. The defeat also precipitated speculations about a new foreign policy concensus which would attract the support of the Executive, Congress, and public opinion. While Communist nations rejoiced over the victory, American allies anxiously evaluated future prospects for a balance of power throughout Asia, and indeed, the world.

PEKING. *North China News Agency,* **May 20, 1975.**

The victory of the national liberation war in Indochina and the defeat of the U.S. aggressor is eloquent proof of the truth that "a just cause enjoys abundant support while an unjust cause finds little support. A weak nation can defeat a strong, a small nation can defeat a big" and that by "strengthening their unity, supporting each other and persevering in a protracted people's war, the three Indochinese peoples will certainly overcome all difficulties and win complete victory."

After the Second World War, the United States, basing itself on the military and economic strength it has rapidly accumulated in war time, stretched out its hands in all directions to grab everything it wanted all over the globe as if it would like to swallow up the whole world at one gulp. Moving against the current of history, it spread out its claws to suppress the national independence and national liberation movements in all parts of the world. An unjust cause, however, finds little support. The history of events in the post-war years is characterized by the fact that imperialism, the U.S. imperialism in particular, carried out repeated intervention and aggression abroad only to be repeatedly and thoroughly defeated. Historical developments have turned out to be the complete opposite of what U.S. imperialism intended. The defeat of the United States as a reputed world power and superpower by the people of the small and weak nations of Indochina is another striking manifestation of the law of history.

The bankruptcy of the U.S. policy of aggression in Indochina makes it clear once again that in war the decisive factor is people, not things, the nature of the war and the feelings of the people, not modern weapons nor a "position of strength". The people of Cambodia and Viet Nam were bound to win because they fought against U.S. aggression in defence of national independence and for national liberation. U.S. imperialism was bound to lose because it fought unjust wars of aggression in far-away places, trying to shore up puppet regimes and thus represented the reactionary, decadent and declining forces.

As an imperialist superpower, the United States is indeed militarily and economically powerful. At the height of its war of aggression in Viet Nam, it threw in a force of no less than 550,000 troops, it mobilized 75 per cent of its infantrymen and paratroops, 68 per cent of its marines, more than 50 per cent of its tactical air force, 40 per cent of its aircraft carriers, and 52 per cent of its cruisers, it spent more than 200,000 million dollars, dropped nearly 8 million tons of bombs—more than the total dropped during the Second World War—and used all kinds of modern weapons excepting nuclear arms. Nevertheless, facts demonstrate that the U.S. military superiority was a transient factor which could play only a temporary role; on the other hand, the just nature of the struggle·of the people of Viet Nam and Cambodia and the unjust nature of the U.S. war of aggression, and the feelings of the people towards the war were factors that played a constant role. As the Indochinese peoples persisted in their struggle, the military position of the United States was gradually changed from one of superiority to one of inferiority, with the result that all the U.S. operational programmes ended in the most resounding defeats in two centuries.

U.S. intervention and aggression in Indochina in the past two decades and more has deeply sharpened the contradictions inherent in the U.S. imperialist system, plunging the foremost capitalist country into a complex of crises. Internationally, it stands opposed and condemned by all peoples of the world, and also by its major allies who left it in the lurch and thereby placed it in unprecedented isolation. By launching the war of aggression in Indochina, the U.S. government unwittingly tempered the American people and taught them the lesson that its imperialist policy of aggression caused suffering not only to the Indochinese peoples but also to the Americans themselves. With this new awareness, the students and other sections of the people in the United States waged impressive protest actions. They staunchly proclaimed their aim to carry on, in the "heart" of the United States, a struggle against the U.S. war of aggression abroad. Their struggle opened up a new front in the fight against U.S. imperialist policy, affording a powerful support to the Indochinese people. Speaking of the U.S. aggression, the western press noted that the U.S. "got in a mess abroad", and "Viet Nam convulsed every aspect of American life." The war "undermined the American economy" and touched off a severe inflationary spiral, bringing about what the western press called the saddest chapter in a century.

Failing to win the war of aggression with its own troops, the United States turned to its usual practice, that is, signing with a handful of traitors treaties whose terms called for the United States to supply the money and guns, in this way abetting others to serve the U.S. schemes of aggression. However, the history of the Indochinese war proves that those supported by the United States were out-and-out traitors who had been spurned by the people and were only capable of harming the country and ruining the people. Therefore, the more the United States bolstered up these traitor regimes, the more it lost popular sympathy; the more it was "faithful" to this handful of "old friends", the more it met with strong popular opposition; and the more it wanted to abide by its "commitments to the treaties concluded with its allies", the more accelerated and thoroughgoing its defeats. This is another major factor in the doom meted out to the U.S. in Indochina.

Contrary to the situation of the United States, which won little support for its unjust cause, the people's armed forces of the three Indochinese countries, equipped as they were with inadequate weapons, won the full support of the people of their own countries and broad sympathy and support of the people in the rest of the world. This was because they were carrying out a sacred war of national liberation and a noble cause for national independence. The Indochinese peoples dared to take their destinies into their own hands by taking up arms to engage in protracted fighting. They turned the enemy's temporary military advantage into disadvantage, gaining total victory. The recent complete liberation of Cambodia and South Viet Nam in quick succession marks the victorious results of a protracted people's war waged by the heroic Cambodian and Vietnamese peoples. Under extremely difficult conditions, the Cambodian armymen and civilians persisted in their just war of national liberation for over five years; the South Vietnamese armymen and civilians persisted in their just war against U.S. aggression and for national salvation for over 10 years. In the course of fighting, each founded a people's army and established vast liberated rural base areas. In accordance with the particular conditions in their respective countries, they launched a people's war, with the revolutionary spirit of defying brute force, having no fear of sacrifice, working hard, persevering, and relying on their own efforts. As they fought, the Cambodian and Vietnamese peoples in consequence became stronger and more valiant and won greater and greater victories.

The United States has been dealt a crushing defeat and been duly punished in its war of aggression against Indochina. Under the signboard of "supporting the national liberation movement", another superpower which has been fiercely contending for hegemony with the United States, engaged in the dirty trick of betraying the Indochinese peoples to facilitate its own expansion. Recently, it slandered the victory of the Cambodian war of national liberation by referring to it as "the ending of the fratricidal war"; it cast a slur on Indochina's heroic resistance to the imperialist aggression by calling the region a "hotbed of war". This once again strips the renegade of its mask.

Nevertheless, the law of history is irresistible. In spite of obstruction and sabotage by one or the other superpower, the historical torrent of the desire of countries for independence, of nations for liberation and people for revolution is bound to triumphantly surge ahead, sweeping away all dregs and obstacles.

LONDON. *The Times,* **May 1, 1975.**

The American armed forces were not militarily defeated in Vietnam, any more than the French armed forces were militarily defeated in Algeria. But America has undoubtedly suffered a political defeat as France did: both countries were obliged to accept a political result which they had been trying to prevent, because they found the military cost of preventing it was higher than they were prepared to pay. Once this had happened, most people in both countries concluded that it had been a mistake to let their armed forces become involved in the first place.

Americans are naturally anxious to avoid making the same mistake again somewhere else. This has led them to take a much more critical view of all kinds of foreign aid and foreign commitment, and this has naturally provoked further anxiety, in varying degrees, among the foreigners who receive American aid or depend on American commitments. Not many of them were seriously worried—indeed most of them were on the whole relieved—when America withdrew her armed forces from Vietnam. But what has been at issue for the past two years, and especially in the past few months, was not any suggestion that American forces might be sent back there, but the question whether America should continue giving material aid to the South Vietnamese Government, which was trying to carry on the struggle with its own armed forces.

It was obvious that Congress was not satisfied by the withdrawal of American troops. It was increasingly reluctant to sanction the use of American weapons or the spending of American money in Vietnam, even by a government which had been given every encouragement to look to America for aid in the recent past. The withdrawal of one sort of commitment had led, almost imperceptibly, to the withdrawal of another and quite different sort. Many Americans believe (and Dr. Kissinger is perhaps one of them) that the Administration's original mistake was thus compounded by a second, Congressional mistake, and that South Vietnam could have been saved without American troops, but with a more generous allowance of American weapons and money.

The majority in Congress would presumably reject this reasoning. They would argue that there was no prospect of South Vietnam winning the war, but only of its being endlessly and pointlessly prolonged. They are probably right in this particular case. But this particular case should not be allowed to obscure the general truth that different levels of commitment are possible, and that even where a higher level (eg, American troops in a combat role) is inappropriate, a lower level (eg, the supply of weapons and material aid) may still be fully justified and desirable.

Obviously the highest level of commitment is the "nuclear umbrella"—an undertaking to use American nuclear weapons in defence of an ally. This is the level of commitment which Western Europe at present enjoys. But it involves so high a degree of American self-sacrifice (since it implies readiness to provoke nuclear retaliation against the United States itself) that its credibility is open to serious question.

Next comes the commitment of American conventional forces. This too is enjoyed by Western Europe, and most of us would not wish to see it removed. On the other hand, most of us would probably find it difficult to define exactly the circumstances in which we would wish to see it used. Without the "nuclear umbrella", conventional forces in Europe would not be strong enough to hold back a full-scale attack by those of the Warsaw Pact, which greatly outnumber them. But against anything less than a full-scale attack, should we not be able to defend ourselves? Certainly most West European governments would hesitate to ask for American military intervention if confronted by any threat of an internal character, and any government which did ask for it would now find itself closely scrutinized by Congress for resemblances to the regime of former President Thieu. Indeed Congress is probably now very close to believing that any government which needs actual American troops to save it is a government not worth saving.

But Congress has not yet reached the same conclusion—and would certainly be wrong to do so—about governments which ask for American weapons and financial aid. It appears to be groping its way towards a set of criteria by which candidates for this type of commitment can be judged. Various questions can be asked. Is the area one of vital strategic importance to the United States? (A difficult yardstick to use, since almost every area of the globe has been so described by spokesmen of different American administrations at different times in the recent past.) Is the country in question able to make a contribution in return to the security or the economy of the United States? (Dangerous because such a question is easily interpreted as evidence of "imperialist" objectives.) Will the aid be put to good use, or will the recipient prove to be "a barrel with a hole in the bottom?" (Again, difficult to be sure, especially when the recipient is involved in an arms race such as that between Israel and the Arabs.) Will the recipient not embarrass the United States by its conduct of local or regional conflicts? (A question explicitly addressed to Turkey by Congress, but also implicitly to Israel by the Administration.)

Finally, but perhaps most important, are the government and people of the country united in wishing to defend themselves with American help? This was the criterion too often neglected in the past, but which Congress lately applied with increasing scepticism to South Vietnam, and is now beginning to apply also to South Korea. If a country fails this test, passing the others is unlikely in the long run to help it.

TOKYO. *The Japan Times,* **May 2, 1975.**

The surrender of Saigon was accompanied by yet another spectacle of hurriedly departing Americans and their friends and of a non-Communist leadership that fell flat once the U.S. prop was withdrawn. To foreign observers who could not be aloof to the tragic conflict in Indochina, it aroused the whole gamut of feelings ranging from a sad resignation to delight in one's redeemed ideology or point of view. But the relief felt by all in the unconditional surrender by the Saigon Government was that the hapless millions of Vietnamese trapped in the doomed capital had been spared further bloodshed and destruction.

For General Duong Van Minh, put in power only two days ago to negotiate peace with the Provisional Revolutionary Government for South Vietnam (PRG), the capitulation he ordered on Wednesday was the sole option open to him. While masses of the PRG and allied North Vietnamese forces pressed on Saigon, any hope of organized resistance had long been gone.

And all the time, the PRG's demands were escalating—from expulsion of the entire "Thieu clique" and American withdrawal at first and then to a refusal to deal with the Saigon Government altogether. They no longer talk of a tripartite coalition to settle the political future of South Vietnam, a provision of the 1973 peace agreements consistently defied by former President Nguyen Van Thieu. It is their turn now to ignore it.

Concern continues to be felt about the plight of those millions of Vietnamese who voted for a non-Communist way of life by their exodus from North Vietnam in the 1950s and their more recent flight from Communist-held areas within South Vietnam. Except the 50,000 or so of their more favored brethren who had the benefit of means and facilities to flee the country, those accustomed to freedom, even a curtailed one at that, face an uncertain future.

Initial PRG policy statements, intended to calm the South Vietnamese populace and announced over the radio by its spokesman in Paris and Foreign Minister Mme. Nguyen Thi Binh, are encouraging. They offered to replace hatred and division with national unity and reconciliation. Even a measure of ideological and religious freedom were held out as people do not obstruct "the revolution." Those in the outside world uneasily looking for hints of the new Communist rulers' posture in external relations can take some heart in the PRG's professed intention to pursue a nonaligned policy and make themselves open to "political and economic assistance from any country."

But these early, ameliorating aspects of the Communist takeover of South Vietnam does not alter reality. The reality is that the geopolitical face of Indochina has been transformed, probably for good, in a matter of months. Particularly because it involved an ignominious American retreat, the Communist conquests of Cambodia and South Vietnam are bound to have a profound effect on countries in Southeast and Northeast Asia.

While crucial elements of U.S. strategic power and defense commitments to priority allies—Japan, South Korea, Australia and New Zealand, among others—are likely to remain unaffected, the Indochina setback damaged confidence in the American ability to sustain the status quo in the Asia-Pacific region. Successive U.S. administrations from President Harry S. Truman to Lyndon B.

Johnson invested so much American prestige, human lives and wealth in Indochina that the current debacle must send reverberations far and wide.

The Nixon-Kissinger diplomacy certainly succeeded in taking out the sting of bipolar confrontation over Indochina and reduced it to a localized dimension with the 1972-1973 "openings" to the Soviet Union and China. By disclaiming a hegemonial role for the U.S. in Asia and the Pacific in dialogues with Moscow and Peking rulers and through painstaking negotiations backed with the use of force in dealing with the PRG-Hanoi alliance, the Nixon-Kissinger team was able to extricate American forces out of Vietnam under the 1973 Paris agreements.

In question now is not a tactical retreat but the cumulative constraints on America's world role resulting from division and skepticism at home, the limited powers of the presidency and the continuing strain on U.S. economic resources. On a different plane of impact, the Vietnam fiasco spreads disbelief in the American ability to enforce vital agreements and bring quarreling parties together, whether the arena is the Middle East or the questions of oil supply and prices.

U.S. President Gerald Ford is eager to call an end to a chapter in American experience and have the U.S. look to the future. But neither can he evade the central problems of realigning U.S. world policy nor escape the ramified consequences of the loss of Indochina, though not a trouble of his own making, merely by so wishing. For one thing, he and Dr. Henry Kissinger must reexamine the traditional U.S. approach to developing countries, all of them undergoing as much social and political revolution as those in Indochina.

The emergence of a Communist-controlled Indochina, in itself, should not be the cause for panic or complacence. Whether non-Communist countries in the rest of Southeast Asia can continue to stand on their own depends on the quality of leadership and national cohesion. It is important that their leaders will work to make life better for all instead of the privileged few, and that nations in the area choose cooperation and not conflicts among themselves.

Rebuilding a firm domestic base in the U.S. for its Asian policy and robust efforts toward self-help in countries of the region are requisite steps if we are to bring about a new stable order, embracing the "liberated Indochina" as an element, in the Asia-Pacific region. We could, then, wish to put the Vietnam episode in perspective and regard it as a delayed fulfillment of independence by the Vietnamese in the post-Second World War period, though the inevitable process was tragically deformed by the spillover from the Cold War.

Topic 37

THE BICENTENNIAL CELEBRATION

1976

The nation's 200th birthday was celebrated in an atmosphere somewhat somber and uncertain. Her world leadership damaged badly by political defeat in South Vietnam, the United States set aside the harsh memories of the events which precipitated the resignations of Vice President Spiro Agnew and President Richard Nixon. Foreign press evaluations recognized the nation's strength despite the prevailing mood of disillusionment.

TOKYO. *The Japan Times,* **July 4, 1976.**

The United States of America today marks the bicentenary of its emergence as a free, independent nation, dedicated to the proposition that "all men are created equal" and that "life, liberty and pursuit of happiness" are among their inalienable rights."

These principles and others stated in the American Declaration of Independence laid the basic foundations for an experiment in democracy which has not only endured to this day but has also inspired people around the world.

Over the years, the American nation and the tenets on which it was founded have passed through numerous tests and challenges. The War of American Revolution itself did not run its course until 1783. The Civil War between the North and the South was one of the most tragic and bitterest of the trials.

In more recent years, the American nation was wrenched by the deadly quicksand of the Vietnam war and the debilitating trauma of the Watergate scandal.

But the wounds from these nightmarish experiences have been rapidly healed and have left the nation wiser and more determined to maintain its democratic ways. And today on its bicentennial anniversary, the United States can look forward to a new beginning and a fresh start toward an even brighter and more promising future. The Bicentennial coincides with the year for presidential election. And it should serve the American people as an opportunity for taking stock of their nation's present role and status as the world's most powerful democracy and the leader of the free nations. They must not forget that the United States today represents above all the indestructibility of democratic principles.

It was thus most propitious that Prime Minister Takeo Miki was able to convey personally the warm greetings of the Japanese people to President Gerald Ford at the White House. In the words of our Prime Minister, "The people of Japan greet the American people on the occasion of their Bicentennial with respect, affection and full confidence in the future of democracy."

Although Japanese-American relations go back only 120 years, they have been marked by much goodwill and cordiality, despite the unfortunate interlude of World War II. While it was the U.S. which brought Japan back into the stream of world affairs and contributed much to its modernization, one exceptional fact that must not be allowed to pass without notice is the tremendous impact of the Declaration of Independence, the American Constitution and the Bill of Rights on the young Japanese leaders of the Meiji Restoration.

American independence thus has a significance for Japan dating back to the early days of its development into a modern nation.

We join happily the host of nations which will be congratulating the United States today on its 200th anniversary. As America begins its third century, we will look forward to its providing continual inspiration to peoples and nations seeking equality, freedom and peace in a troubled world.

LONDON. *The Times,* **July 5, 1976.**

Those with a taste for the romantic in politics will no doubt regret that the United States did not celebrate its bicentennial when President Kennedy was proclaiming his countrymen's readiness to "pay any price, bear any burden, meet any hardship, support any friend, oppose any foe, in order to secure the survival and success of liberty". That was the apogee of American idealism and of their perception of their power. Much has changed since then. The price of global responsibility has become higher and there is no longer the old confidence that American involvement guarantees either the survival or success of liberty. At home the United States has been rent by assassination, racial conflict and corruption. The dominant mood of the moment is of anti-Washington sentiment, which represents the disillusionment of the American people with both their institutions and their political processes.

But it is when things are going badly that one can best assess the enduring strength of a nation. One should never underestimate either the speed with which attitudes can change in the United States or the differing facets of American life. It was only a few years before Kennedy was capturing the imagination with his rhetoric that the country was going through the era of McCarthyism.

There were two factors of particular interest throughout the years of American travail. The first was that there were many Americans who were as disgusted as anybody by the activities of their own Government. Whatever politicians and officials may have been doing, the voice of protest was never stilled. That is the first test of the political health of a country. It is the evident dissatisfaction of Americans with sordid government that offers the best hope of political renewal now. Mr. Jimmy Carter's meteoric rise can largely be attributed to his perception of this yearning for decency in high places. That is the context within which American politicans of all parties are now having to operate, even if they are not all likely to undergo a spiritual conversion overnight.

The second factor was that, bitterly though the United States was criticized by international opinion for its role in Vietnam, the worst fear of many countries was that in reaction there might be a new phase of American isolationism. The point was never reached where the withdrawal of America from an active part in international affairs would have been regarded as a blessing. American authority and moral standing were sadly diminished, but nobody else was able or willing to take on the task of creative international leadership.

That is still the American role today. But it does not follow that with an appropriate pause for breath the United States will shortly be able to resume the position it held in Kennedy's day. The world, as well as the United States, has changed since then. Power has become more fragmented. Neither the Nato nor the Warsaw Pact countries are such cohesive groupings as they were. China has become more active in international affairs. With the greater importance of commodity prices in international economics the third world has acquired a potential bargaining strength it did not possess before. Less tangibly, but no less significantly, there has been a change in the international atmosphere which imposes restraints on whoever may wield power, whether economic or military.

This means that American power can be exercised effectively only with the approval of other countries, which depends in turn partly upon the United States being a source of creative ideas and partly upon that spark that touches the imagination. That is needed now abroad as well as at home because the active involvement of the United States is as necessary as it ever was. Most obviously, it is essential to preserving the military balance with the Soviet Union, without which the whole international order would be transformed. Secondly, while one of the most constructive acts of statemanship in the past thirty years has been the positive American encouragement to the establishment of the EEC, international economic and political stability still requires active cooperation across the Atlantic. Then the chances of achieving a better understanding with the primary producers would be much poorer without vigorous American participation in the search for a solution. As the United States celebrates its bicentennial it should know that other countries are looking not just to its romantic past but also to the role of international leadership it still has to play. The context of that leadership has changed, but without it the world would be a yet more dangerous and uncertain place.

BOMBAY. *The Times of India,* July 7, 1976.

The United States has entered the third century of its existence as an independent nation full of doubts regarding its own future. And yet no other country is as vigorous, innovative, productive and well placed to influence the course of events in coming years and decades. Indeed, it will not be much of an exaggeration to say that peace and stability in our era and the well-being of the rest of mankind are to no small extent dependent on the strength and prosperity of the United States.

The second point is so obvious that it is hardly necessary to belabour it. Even so it may be useful to recall that governments of almost all leading industrialized countries have over the past one year been urging Washington to reinflate its economy and stimulate demand so that they can step up their exports to it and thereby revive their own growth. And this interest in the revival of the U.S. economy has not been limited to its West European and Japanese allies. The Soviet Union, East European socialist states and several developing countries like India have been equally keen to increase their exports to America in order to be able to pay for the imports they need from it. In other words, they, too, have a stake in the continued strength of the U.S. economy, whatever criticism they may otherwise make of it.

The United States, of course, no longer dominates the international economic scene as it did in the 'fifties and early 'sixties when it produced nearly one-half of the world's wealth. Also the dollar is no longer the coveted currency it was till the mid-'sixties. But America is still the world's largest and most dynamic economy and it cannot be ruled out at all that it will continue to enjoy and even increase its technological lead over its nearest rivals in critical areas for years and decades. Above all, America's agricultural surpluses and the capacity to increase food output at will give it considerable leverage in dealing with friends and foes alike.

The point about peace and stability is not equally self-evident. In fact, many countries have seen the United States as a disturber rather than as a promoter of stability and peace—a point of view which cannot be dismissed out of hand in view of the American performance in Viet Nam, its role in the overthrow of President Allende and its extraordinary inept attitude towards China till the late 'sixties.

But peace in the larger sense of the absence of a world-wide conflagration has in our era been the product broadly of something like an overall power balance between the United States and the Soviet Union and of the willingness of Washington to act with a measure of restraint in the immediate post-war period when Moscow did not possess the nuclear bomb and, indeed, even much later when it could not match the U.S. nuclear armoury.

More pertinently, a dramatic decline in America's military power in the foreseeable future can destabilise the entire world scene to a dangerous extent with possible consequences which are too dreadful to contemplate. Not to speak of countries which are dependent on the United States for their security one way or another, even its principal rival, the Soviet Union cannot wish its power to decline seriously. For it, too, cannot view with equanimity the prospects of West Germany and Japan going in for nuclear weapons.

To return to America's self-doubts, these are clearly the result largely of Vietnam, the Watergate scandal, aggravating distrust of the once widely respected office of the president, the disclosures regarding the activities of the CIA, the decline of the relative value of the dollar, the strange combination of inflation and stagnation, the sharp increase in dependence on the natural resources of other countries, specially oil, the growing awareness that the earth's non-renewable resources are finite and cannot support an unlimited growth, the impact of the chemical revolution on the human habitat and the simultaneous and dramatic growth in the Soviet Union's military prowess.

In absolute terms the Soviet Union's military power would have grown even if the other developments destructive of America's self-confidence had not taken place. For, as Mr. Kissinger put it in his Boston address on March 11, 1976, "nothing we could have done would have halted this evolution (of the Soviet Union as a super power) after the impetus two generations of industrial and technological advance have given to Soviet military and economic growth." But relative power is a different proposition. Indeed, it is difficult to believe that Washington would have failed to take note of the Soviet advance and to step up its own efforts in that field if for five long and critical years its political leadership was not almost wholly preoccupied with the war in Viet Nam.

Similarly, while it is obvious that the discovery of the limitation of the earth's non-renewable resources and of the pollution of the atmosphere, lakes, rivers and the oceans by automobiles and the chemical industries has nothing to do with the Viet Nam war, the American people's response to them would almost certainly have been very different if they were not already suffering from a loss of self-confidence as a result of that most divisive external involvement in their history. And there cannot be any question that the war fed inflation and aggravated, if it did not create, other economic difficulties. It certainly accounted for the devaluation of the dollar, thrice in barely 18 months in 1971 and 1972. Also it created an atmosphere in which both the Watergate episode and the disclosures regarding it became possible.

Thus one cannot escape the conclusion that involvement in the Viet Nam war accounts to a large extent for most of America's difficulties which have made the bicentenary celebrations a rather low-key affair. It, of course, does not follow that the recovery of America's self-confidence is assured as the country overcomes both the trauma of the failure in Viet Nam and other debilitating consequences of that foolish investment of human and material resources on a colossal scale. But the process of recovery is on, as is evident from the remarkable come-back the United States has staged in West Asia and, in a peculiar way, even from the recent investigations into the activities of the CIA.

These investigations are doubtless partly an expression of the puritanical spirit which promotes self-flagellation from time to time but these were also an expression, however faulted, of the American people's confidence that even in these complicated days, it is possible for them to live by the simple and noble principles which inspired the founding fathers. Which other country can think of turning the floodlight on the activities of its intelligence agency even in less troubled times and circumstances?

But it is ironical that just as the United States unthinkingly slipped into the fatal Viet Nam war at the height of power and influence in the wake of the Cuban crisis, the current recovery of the economy and self-confidence is accompanied by the feeling of what one may call spiritual isolation.

Mr. Daniel Patrick Moynihan is doubtless the most articulate exponent of this feeling. As he puts it: "Liberal democracy on the American model increasingly tends to the condition of monarchy in the 19th century: a holdover form of government, one which persists in isolated or peculiar places here and there, and may even serve well enough for special circumstances, but which has simply no relevance to the future. It is where the world was, not where it is going." But Mr.

Moynihan is not alone in taking this pessimistic view. The "danger of a philosophical isolation without precedent in American history" is, for example, the theme of an article by another distinguished American academician, Mr. Brzezinski, in the summer issue of *Foreign Policy*, New York. The little "America in a hostile world" is by itself revealing of the theme.

There are doubtless American intellectuals like Mr. William Bundy, editor of the *Foreign Affairs* quarterly, who believe that "there are bound to be ebbs and flows to the tide of democracy, as there surely were in the years from 1715 to 1867—from Magna Carta to the second Reform Bill—in the Anglo-Saxon history" and that if the situation regarding the future of democracy appears discouraging "it is surely not so much so as in the 1930's." There are also other Americans who are alive to the fact that the urge for greater quality has not been able to extinguish the demand for individual freedom either in the communist or the third world.

But right now the voice of the pessimists is dominant in the United States perhaps because it accords better with the popular mood. This will doubtless change if the process of recovery, economic and psychological, continues. America's may not be institutions towards which, to quote Lord Bryce in the *American Commonwealth*, as if by law of fate, the rest of civilized mankind are forced to move. But they will continue to inspire and influence man in his endless journey towards freedom.   —Girilal Jain

Topic 38

RECOGNITION OF THE PEOPLE'S REPUBLIC OF CHINA

1978

On December 15, President Jimmy Carter announced that the People's Republic of China would be recognized as the sole legitimate government of China. Formal diplomatic relations with Taiwan would be severed on January 1, 1979. Carter explained that the recognition of the People's Republic, a nation which contains about one-fourth of the world's population, would enhance the stability of Asia and expand trade and cultural relations. These crucial decisions opened an intriguing era in international relations for the United States as a new balance of power became evident.

TAIPEI [Taiwan]. *Central Daily News,* **December 17, 1978.**

The Carter administration of the United States decided to recognize the regime of Communist Bandits (Mainland China) January 1, 1979, and at the same time, to denounce the diplomatic relationship with the Republic of China. This historical mistake is not only a big setback to our nation, it is a severe blow to the free and democratic system of mankind. And it is also the most shameful event in American history. The Carter administration mistakenly uses "Bandits" (Mainland China) to restrain Russia. This can only sharpen the world crisis, strengthen China's ability for aggression and therefore push international peace and security out of reach.

After being informed about the U.S. decision by Ambassador Unger, President Chiang made a strong protest to the United States government and declared that the decision to abrogate the security

367

treaty with the Republic of China will not only severely damage the governmental and human rights of the Republic of China but will also have a tremendous adverse impact upon the entire free world. The government of the United States alone should bear full responsibility.

Since the visit of Nixon to mainland China and the declaration of Shanghai Communique, the relationship between the United States and the Republic of China has not been smooth. We have repeatedly and clearly expressed our viewpoints to the U.S. for the last six years about the fact of our common interests, which means that we will benefit by staying together and suffer by separation. In the United States, we still have great support from the Congress, the majority of the American people, as well as all the people in the free world. Therefore, this is the turning point, and also the milestone, of the struggle between democracy and communism, between freedom and totalitarianism.

The most pitiful thing is that the Carter administration uses the banner of human rights while establishing a diplomatic relationship with a regime known for its horror, dictatorship, cruelty and inhumanity. The United States, lured by Communist Bandits (Mainland China), has destroyed its own integrity, and has denied the hundreds of millions of enslaved peoples in the Chinese mainland their hope for an early restoration of freedom. The crime that Carter committed is much more serious than what Prime Minister Chamberlain did with Hitler on the eve of World War II. The consequence of compromise would surely be a thousand times more severe than that of the shameful Munich Agreement.

Our nation has faced many difficult situations, one after another. At the time when we decided to withdraw from the United Nations, our late President Chiang taught us to strengthen ourselves with great solemnity, and not to be alarmed by the changes, but to think, plan and judge carefully. For the time being, the United Nations is dominated by evil groups and is at the edge of collapsing. Yet the Republic of China is stronger than ever. Yesterday, President Chiang emphasized that no matter how the international affairs develop, the sovereignty of our nation remains. We are proud of our tradition. We will unite ourselves and do our best to improve social, economic and political affairs. As long as we work faithfully toward our national goal, we have great confidence in the future of our nation. During this time of change, this is the direction of our collective efforts.

We would like to sincerely inform our fellow countrymen all over the world that we have been aware for years of the possible adversary development of the relationship between the United States and the Republic of China. Our government has long been prepared for this event. Yesterday, President Chiang, in accordance with laws, issued urgent orders to reinforce our military force, to secure our society and stabilize our economy, and to suspend the partial election temporarily. Of course, we do not underestimate the difficulties and pressures imposed on us due to the normalization of relations between the United States and the Communist Bandits (Mainland China). However, we have a glorious revolutionary tradition: the more setbacks we had, the more courageously we fought. We have a leader with perseverance, bravery, diligence and love toward his people. Furthermore, at this difficult moment, everyone has the determination of self-discipline, of self-sacrifice, of sincere unity, and of anti-Communism. We are sure that the spirit of self-support and mutual destiny will be flourishing and we will overcome any difficulties.

President Chiang addressed our entire fellow countrymen yesterday on television and said that we must have the determination of relying on ourselves and, for the sake of freedom and survival, we will always be antiCommunist. Our strength comes from the unity of millions of people. There is determination, there is strength. A glorious Chinese should be able to break through all kinds of obstacles.

From Taiwan, Que-Moi, . . . to the entire world, every fellow countryman who loves his own country and freedom feels indignant at the United States-China (Bandit) tie. This is the time that everybody shows his great self-awareness and self-confidence. This is also the time to testify to the patriotism of every Chinese.

We must unite ourselves, under the leadership of President Chiang, stick to our national policy, rely and support our government and smash and destroy the enemy's plot.

We want to rely on our determination and strength. The Republic of China is a nation that will fight for freedom. The Chinese is a race that will fight for integrity. The bigger turmoil we are in, the tighter we unite ourselves. The more difficult situation we face, the stronger we are. Only sincere unity and self-discipline can save our country.

SEOUL. *The Korea Times,* December 17, 1978.

President Jimmy Carter's announcement of the opening of U.S.-China diplomatic relations, even though long anticipated, was surprising because of its suddenness and because of its probably deep implications for political developments in the Far East.

... The establishment of relations between the United States and China has been long foreseen but Carter's announcement yesterday was sudden, for the United States and China had long maintained that formal relations between the two countries were being delayed because of the Taiwan question, and that question seemed to remain unresolved in some senses.

Chinese Premier Hua Kuo-feng said in a press conference after the announcement that there were still differences of opinion between the United States and China over American sale of weapons to Taiwan.

He said that the United States wanted to continue to sell weapons to Taiwan but that China was opposed to it. He indicated that the difference of opinion still remained unsolved.

The question concerning U.S. sale of weapons to Taiwan may seem trivial in the face of the opening of U.S.-China diplomatic relations.

But that same question can mean death or survival for the Nationalist Chinese government of Taiwan in accordance with the development of the issue.

The Nationalist Chinese government on the island has mainly relied on the United States for weapons for its survival.

Now that China has made its position on the continued U.S. sale of weapons clear, it is evident that the Peking government will intensify its pressure on Washington to suspend arms supply to that country. And it is no less evident that the United States will concede to the Peking demand sooner or later.

The American magnanimity in conceding to others, especially to Communists, is well known. It was shown in the Korean War and in Paris during the Vietnamese war.

The United States may have needed formal relations with China more than China did in spite of the general belief to the contrary.

It has been the general consensus of Western politicians and political scholars that China needs the United States for its development and its confrontation with the Soviet Union and Vietnam more than the United States needs China for its containment of the Soviet Union.

The Sino-American ties formally put the two countries in a loosely-knit triangular alliance against their common enemy, Russia.

This development of the situation can bring about a remarkable change in the political climate on the Korean peninsula, on the Korean question in the long run.

China has maintained and still maintains a position lopsidedly supporting north Korea, and it is not categorically unlikely that it will revise its stand on the Korean question as its contacts with the United States, Japan and other Western countries deepen.

On the other hand, it is very likely that the Soviet Union will further strengthen its support of north Korea and Vietnam in its intensified efforts to surround and isolate China in Asia.

It all depends on the future development of the situation whether the U.S.-China relations will have favorable effects on the solution of the Korean question.

But the key to the solution of the Korean question is in the hands of south and north Korea themselves, and the best thing for us to do is to develop our national strength so that we may play a determing role in the solution of our question.

WINNIPEG [Canada]. *Winnipeg Free Press,* **December 20, 1978.**

For the United States to resume diplomatic relations with what is the most populous nation on earth is a momentous undertaking. Historically, it is a step as precedent-shattering as once was the recognition of the Soviet Union, for years shunned by the world's major powers; moreover, it is a valid confirmation of the dictum that diplomatic ties put no seal of approval on any regime.

What, however, sticks in the craw is the fact that what should have been a major diplomatic feat was degraded to an unworthy gimmick. The secretive and precipitious action of severing diplomatic relations with Taiwan as of January 1, and the unilateral abrogation of the U.S. defence treaty with Taiwan (without consulting the U.S. Senate) will send shivers down the spine of every American ally. The excuse put forward by the Carter administration, that Taiwan was a unique case, is specious: every alliance is unique and each has its weak points that can be used when needed.

Originally, the United States had insisted that any treaty with China specifically oblige the Peking government to undertake not to use force or threat of force against Taiwan. The Peking government balked at this stipulation, and the United States now has acquiesced by signing an agreement that includes no obligation on the part of China to abstain from any warlike adventure against the ten million highly prosperous people who want no part of any Communist regime, of whatever stripe.

The abject surrender to Peking's demands and the brusque dismissal of the Taiwanese, good allies since 1949, as if they were a bunch of thieving servants, is wholly incomprehensible other than in the wider context of President Carter's domestic needs. The Camp David accords have collapsed, largely because of the relentless hostility to President Sadat's initiative on the part of Saudi Arabia, which has become a deciding factor in Washington's foreign policy; the chaos in Iran is spreading and the West may well lose all influence in the oil-rich Persian Gulf; in the Horn of Africa the Russians and the Cubans are now firmly established ("Who among us had ever heard of the Horn of Africa six months ago?" Arthur M. Schlesinger, the liberal Democratic historian, confessed in an aside reminiscent of Chamberlain's quip about Czechoslovakia); Afghanistan is a soviet satellite; Pakistan is in isolation. With Christmas approaching, the world scene as viewed from Washington does not look at all festive. Indeed, its aspect is wholly black. Something then had to be done to retrieve President Carter's fortunes, and his court magician, Zbigniew Brzezinski, was allowed to play the China card.

However, a nation of almost a billion people is no card, and anybody who believes that he can "play" China is in for a bitter disappointment. The second point is that the abandoning of Taiwan was unnecessary. At the moment, China needs Western help far more than the United States needs the problematic help and the equally problematic markets of China. This year, Taiwan will register an economic growth of seven percent and it is quite possible that also in the future Taiwan's free-enterprise market of ten million people will prove more profitable than the primitive and regimented markets of China. But the worst part of the deal is the harsh reversal of alliances.

As Senator S.I. Hayakawa of California remarked, "Israel and Japan ought to be nervous as hell right now. We are telling the world that we cannot be trusted." Every ally, from Norway to Belgium, from France to Turkey and, of course, South Korea, will have second thoughts about the value of the American alliance, and the worth of the U.S. nuclear umbrella.

If the situation unravels as can be reasonably expected, Mr. Brzezinski's week-end surprise package might have tragic repercussions. The president of Taiwan is Chiang Ching-kuo, the eldest son of the late Generalissimo Chiang Kai-shek. Mr. Chiang was educated at the Sun Yat-sen University of Moscow and at the Soviet military academy, as well as in Soviet higher political insitutions. He spent many years in Moscow, and for a long time was suspected of harboring Soviet sympathies. Will President Chiang, abandoned by Washington, now play the Moscow card? A mutual defence pact with Moscow would render Taiwan quite secure. It might also provide naval bases for the Soviet Union that would checkmate China and terrify Japan out of the U.S. alliance. It could yet turn the Pacific into a Soviet lake. Does nobody in Washington look any farther into the future than the day after tomorrow?

MOSCOW. *Pravda*, **December 25, 1978.**

In the press of the western countries, more and more communications are being published alerting people who are vitally concerned about the fate of the world. The matter concerns the dangerous game with Peking, which certain powers in the NATO countries, suffering from political short-sightedness, are beginning to play.

As is well known the rulers of China endeavor in every way to stress their enmity towards the Soviet Union and the other socialistic countries. Not for the last time this has been called forth by the desire of Peking to gain access to the war arsenal of NATO in order to realize her imperialist aims. Unfortunately certain circles in the West "take" this bait of Peking...

The attention of the world is drawn in particular to the news of the impending sale to Peking of the English war plane, "Harrier," with vertical takeoff ability. Somebody is trying to pass this airplane, which is part of the equipment of NATO, as a defensive weapon. But this trick deceives no one. Even the English newspaper, *The Financial Times*, admits the Harrier planes will give China an offensive potential. Therefore this trick is a deliberate attempt to mislead the people. . .

While encouraging its allies to supply arms to China, Washington itself constantly sends atomic specialists to Peking. Let us remind the reader only of the reception given in China to the former chief of the Pentagon, J. Schlesinger, now U.S. secretary for energy. Huo Kuofeng, greeting the American visitor, called him "our old friend", and the latter in reply, explained that the "might of China" is of vital importance to the U.S.

In its turn Peking, seeking armament markets, keeps sending new delegations to France, Japan, West Germany, Italy, and other countries. They say that in France the Peking envoys are asking about the possibilities of buying anti-aircraft missiles, artillery guns, missile-carrying ships, torpedo boats, and other armaments. Emissaries of the Chinese militarists are also quietly approaching the Italian armament market. Information has also reached the foreign press that "Peking and Tokyo intend conjointly to build tanks."

Attention is drawn to the sale of powerful atomic reactors to Peking. Such an agreement, as the Associated Press reported, was signed between France and China this month in the Chinese capitol. . . Of course it is possible to say in this case that a series of conditions has been set up concerning the use of the atomic equipment only for peaceful aims. But who will guarantee that the used rods of the reactors will not be used in the future by China for warlike purposes. Indeed, as was pointed out in the western press, there is in China an installation for deriving plutonium from used atomic fuel, utilized in nuclear reactors—that plutonium which they use in making atomic arms.

What does this transaction lead to? The question is far from being superfluous. Among the corporations of the U.S. and of other leading capitalistic powers a sharp struggle for Chinese markets is growing, and they undoubtedly make use of Peking for the purpose of strengthening their military-economic bases.

The flirting with Peking is inspired in the West by the most reactionary imperialist circles, who are averse to a slackening of tension, who are ready to scrap the Helsinki agreement, and all other agreements which aim at ameliorating international conditions. The forces trying to impose on the West a policy of encouraging expansion of the Maoists are not so very big, but they have at their disposal several possibilities, among which are those of propaganda. Those in the West who count on playing the "Chinese card," assume that they will succeed in directing the blade of Chinese expansionism in only one direction—against the USSR. Meanwhile the arming of China is dangerous for peace in all the world, and for the future of relaxation of tensions. "The friendship of China towards the West," the *Washington Post* remarks, "represents a tactical maneuver with the aim of injuring Soviet-American relations and in the final account, provoking a confrontation between the U.S. and U.S.S.R....As a result much greater harm will be done to American interests."

Chinese expansionism is a threat for many nations. Peking's ambitions for hegemony in South-Eastern Asia are well known. Already more than ten countries have shown themselves to be the object of the so-called "cartographic aggression" of the present Chinese rulers (i.e. of territorial pretensions shown on maps published in Peking).

It is not by chance that the news of the intention of Western countries to furnish Peking with arms arouses growing concern in India, Indonesia, and other Asiatic countries. And, we shall speak frankly, there is ground for such concern.

...Recent events bear witness to the fact that Peking is seeking also "keys" to the countries of the Arabian East and the Persian Gulf, rich in oil, and its maneuvers with regard to the countries participating in the movements of non-alignment are clearly dictated by the effort to establish its hegemony in this movement, and at the same time to move in on the large resources of developing countries in order to realize the plans of "modernization", the heart of which is formed by the growth of China's armed forces.

The policy of encouraging the expansionism of the Maoists is clearly not popular among the vast majority of Americans. As clear evidence of this are the results of the public opinion poll conducted by the Washington organization, "Potomac Associates." Seventy per cent of those questioned were opposed to granting American armaments to Peking. Seventy-five per cent of the Americans favor an understanding with the USSR on SALT II...

Of the danger of an alliance with Peking, warning is given by an analyst like H. Morgenthau, whom it is difficult to suspect of sympathy towards the Soviet Union. He writes: "If playing the Chinese card were something like a drawing-room game at an institution of learning or at staff drills, it would be possible to dismiss this as an innocent pastime. It is another matter when they try to make this the official policy of the United States. "Evidently," remarks H. Morgenthau, "the interests of China are not identical with the interests of the United States. At the same time that the United States imagines that it is playing the Chinese card, China intends playing the American card against the Soviet Union. . . Consequently, playing the Chinese card for the U.S. is pregnant with great danger."

The results of the policy of favoring the expansionism of Peking are no less obvious for Europe. The English journal, *New Statesman*, warns with reason that purchases by China of armaments from the West may bring with it a general increase in tension in the world. The *Welt der Arbeit* published in Cologne adds: "We must not forget that the Chinese have always been masters at two-faced diplomacy. . ."

The course of the present Peking leaders is fraught with several dangers for peace and socialism. However, as the weekly *Horizon*, published in East Germany remarks, "The aspiration of Peking's leaders to world supremacy will shatter on reality. The nations have not thrown off and are not throwing off the yoke of imperialistic exploitation merely in order to be enslaved in the Maoist 'Reich.'" The world wide revolutionary process is leading mankind away from the last bastion of exploitation towards socialism and communism. There is no room for the hegemony of Peking.

Vitalij Korionov

INDEX

Index